CARMELITE STUDIES

JOHN OF THE CROSS:
Conferences and Essays
by Members of
THE INSTITUTE OF CARMELITE STUDIES
and Others

Steven Payne, OCD
Editor

ICS Publications
Institute of Carmelite Studies
Washington, D.C.
1992

ICS Publications
2131 Lincoln Road NE
Washington, DC 20002-1199

Typeset and produced in the United States of America

ACKNOWLEDGMENT

An earlier version of the article, "The Influence of John of the Cross in the United States: A Preliminary Study," appeared in *Teresianum* 42 (1991): 123-152. We are grateful to the editors for their permission to print a slightly revised version here.

Library of Congress Cataloging-in-Publication Data

John of the Cross: conferences and essays by members of the
   Institute of Carmelite Studies and others / Steven Payne, editor.
      p.   cm. — (Carmelite studies: 6)
   Includes bibliographical references.
   ISBN: 0-935216-18-9
   1. John of the Cross, Saint, 1542-1591.   2. Spiritual life—Christianity—
History of doctrines—Modern period, 1500-
I. Payne, Steven, 1950-   . II. Institute of Carmelite Studies (Washington,
D.C.). III. Series.
BX4700.J7J575   1992
271'.7302—dc20   92-20477
                                                          CIP

TABLE OF CONTENTS

v

ABBREVIATIONS

Unless otherwise noted, all quotations from John of the Cross are taken from *The Collected Works of St. John of the Cross*, trans. Kieran Kavanaugh and Otilio Rodriguez, rev. ed. (Washington, DC: ICS Publications, 1991). For his major works, the following abbreviations are used:

ST. JOHN OF THE CROSS

A = Ascent of Mount Carmel   (In A and N the first number
N = Dark Night   indicates the book)
C = Spiritual Canticle
F = Living Flame of Love

Also, references to John's Letters and Sayings are based on the numbering in this revised Kavanaugh/Rodriguez translation, which sometimes differs from the numbering in other editions.

Similarly, unless otherwise noted, all quotations from Teresa of Jesus are taken from *The Collected Works of St. Teresa of Avila*, trans. Kieran Kavanaugh and Otilio Rodriguez, 3 vols. (Washington, DC: ICS Publications, 1976-1985). For her major works, the following abbreviations are used:

ST. TERESA OF JESUS

L = Book of Her Life
W = Way of Perfection
C = Interior Castle   (In C the first number indicates the Dwelling)
F = Book of Foundations

Finally, throughout this volume there are extensive references to Federico Ruiz, et al., *God Speaks in the Night: The Life, Times and Teaching of St. John of the Cross*, trans. Kieran Kavanaugh (Washington, DC: ICS Publications, 1991).

INTRODUCTION

In 1965, with a shared interest in Carmelite scholarship, a few friars of the Washington Province of Discalced Carmelites joined together to found the Institute of Carmelite Studies (ICS). Its first steps were modest enough, but aspirations were high. Among other activities, the group met occasionally to encourage each other in their work and share the fruits of their research; some of the results made their way into the pages of the province's quarterly, *Spiritual Life*.

Events took a new turn in 1973, however, when the Institute sponsored a republication Doubleday & Co.'s 1964 edition of *The Collected Works of St. John of the Cross*, translated by Kieran Kavanaugh and Otilio Rodriguez. Suddenly the Institute found itself increasingly involved in the publications ministry; sales grew, providing resources for each new book that followed, including including now classic translations of the works of Saints Teresa of Avila and Thérèse of Lisieux, the writings of Blesseds Elizabeth of the Trinity and Edith Stein, and this series as well.

Since 1991 marked both the twenty-fifth anniversary of ICS and the world-wide celebration of the fourth centenary of the death of St. John of the Cross, the members of the Institute wanted to honor the occasion with a tribute to the Mystical Doctor with whom our fortunes are so closely tied. During the centenary year, with the organizational help of Fr. Kevin Culligan, O.C.D., various members of ICS offered free public conferences on the life and teachings of John of the Cross, through the local communities of the Washington Province.

These talks met with an enthusiastic response, and have been gathered here to make them available to a wider audience. Other contributions arrived later, and were added to round out this volume. This accounts for the variation in tone from article to article; wherever possible, we have retained the original oral style in which the talks were delivered, while adding appropriate notes for sources.

The essays by Michael Dodd, Daniel Chowning, Kevin Culligan, Denis Read, Regis Jordan, Emmanuel Sullivan and Steven Payne were part of the original lecture series. ICS members John Sullivan and Kieran Kavanaugh contributed material delivered at other centenary celebrations honoring the Mystical Doctor. Finally, we added articles from other authors whose essays, some originally intended for *Spiritual Life*, seemed especially suited to this volume.

This editor's main regret is that the present volume thus ended up including only male contributors. Certainly this was not by design (except insofar as the ICS members are all Discalced Carmelite friars). Women have been among the most perceptive commentators on John's doctrine, and among his closest friends, beginning with St. Teresa herself down to Bl. Edith Stein and St. Thérèse of Lisieux in modern times; contemporary women are writing some of the best articles and books on the Mystical Doctor today, as we hope future volumes from ICS Publications will show. But this volume especially represents an opportunity for the Discalced Carmelite *friars* to express their gratitude to the one we call "our Holy Father," and to explore his timely message, not just for ourselves, but for the whole contemporary church and world.

Yet at the same time, our contributors are well aware of John's words in "Stanzas concerning an ecstasy experienced in high contemplation":

Este saber no sabiendo	This knowledge in unknowing
es de tan alto poder,	is so overwhelming
que los sabios arguyendo	that wise men disputing
jamás le pueden vencer;	can never overthrow it,
que no llega su saber	for their knowledge does not reach
a no entender entendiendo,	to the understanding of not understanding,
todo ciencia trascendiendo.	*transcending all knowledge.*

These essays, then, make no claim to fully explain or capture the inexhaustible riches of John's doctrine, or the experience of God he describes. Our hope is, rather, that they may provide readers with some guidance in understanding John, and some nourishment for their own journey into the infinite mystery of the divine.

On a final note, 1990-1991 brought other important changes. Fr. John Sullivan, O.C.D., long-time chair of ICS and editor of this series, was elected first to a position of provincial leadership, and then to the General Definitory of the Discalced Carmelite Order in Rome. I have thus inherited his many editorial responsibilities, just at the moment when ICS Publications is expanding its scope. This volume, then, is also special tribute to Fr. John, in the hope that we may continue and even increase (though perhaps with fewer gifts and certainly with more limited energies!) the great work he has begun.

Steven Payne, O.C.D.
Editor

"HOW IS IT GOD LOVES US?":
A HOMILY FOR ST. JOHN OF THE CROSS

John Sullivan, O.C.D.

John Sullivan is a former chair of the Institute of Carmelite Studies, and past provincial of the Washington Province of Discalced Carmelites. He currently serves as second definitor of the Order at the Generalate in Rome, and has written widely on Carmelite themes.

During this past year's commemoration of the 400th anniversary of St. John of the Cross's death the Carmelites have been doing much to mark the occasion, publishing magazine articles and books,[1] for example, and organizing prayer services (like this beautiful eucharist here in the Cathedral)[2] and study days all over the world. I had the opportunity to attend a study symposium on the Mystical Doctor in Avila last October. At it a respected third-world theologian (the non-Carmelite, Fr. Gustavo Gutiérrez) paid tribute to St. John of the Cross. He told us he felt at ease relying on St. John whenever he had to give his people in Peru an answer to one of their most pressing questions: "How is it God loves us in spite of what we are going through, in spite of all we are suffering?"[3] His words were—and still are—very haunting for me as a priest, because whether we live in the first or third world, we frequently find ourselves asking the corresponding questions: "How do I tell people, *reassure* them, that God loves them? How do I show the people of my time and place, with all their problems, tics and defects, that God really does care for them, that God is not indifferent to their plight, the passion and the problems of daily living?"

Happily, there is much in St. John of the Cross's message to provide a constructive answer to these questions. Furthermore, today's readings in his honor fit well with the assurances the Mystical Doctor gives us.[4] In fact, we can find in both a threefold answer to the Peruvian priest's haunting question about the realness of God's love for us. Formulated in brief phrases, the reply might sound like this: 1) God made us loveable; 2) God has linked himself to us in lasting love; and 3) Love alone is the solution.

GOD HAS MADE US LOVEABLE

The prophet Isaiah, in our first reading, couldn't have put it more clearly, as he has the Lord God say, "You are precious in my eyes, you are honored and I love you" (Is 43:4). The solid basis for knowing that God truly loves us, right now, "wrinkles and all," is the root-love God shows by creating us in the first place. We need to remind ourselves of this constantly: *God's plan for us is always a plan of love.* Still, we often let wanderings and deviations on our part affect that divine plan for our lives, and doubts then set in. Doubt can lead to feelings of unworthiness, and then we somehow feel distant from our loving Lord. Another more contemporary word for that feeling of distance is "alienation." Many are its sources and its manifestations: people feel disconnected from each other and from events all around them. While visiting my cousins from Streatham several years ago I heard them worrying over measures being taken by the government to curb drug addiction here in central London. Since then, I doubt if the drug problem has gone away, though I would hope some progress has occurred. But drugs are just one form that alienation takes: we could add to the list such problems as racial intolerance, domestic violence, neglect of the elderly and so on. These are due, at least in part, to the distance or "alienation" we allow to take shape in the external realm, and oftentimes this tends to influence our sense of closeness to God.

Still, we believe God made the world good, and we believe the words of the prophet found in the first reading :"You are very precious in my eyes." A few words from the cofounder of the Discalced Carmelites, St. John of the Cross, will reinforce this belief. He too was convinced that God created the world good and has always looked at the people in it with eyes of love, despite all we have done to mess it up. He very frequently depicts God's concern for his creation in terms of a lover looking after his beloved. In a long lyric poem that describes the coming and birth of Christ into our world, John of the Cross writes (with God the Father speaking to the Son):

My Son, I wish to give you
A bride who will love you.
Because of you she will deserve
To share our company,
And eat bread at our table
the same bread I eat.[5]

There is no distance between God and God's creation in this vision
of things. God is attracted to the bride because she is brought into God's
shared company by the Son. *We* are the "bride," and *God loves us*. Christ,
the Son, came not to condemn us, but to give us fullness of life. One
ought to ponder this mystery at length; we have the right to, and it's well
worth the time spent. For now, let us recall just one more passage from
St. John of the Cross confirming this same vision:

> In this elevation of all things through the incarnation of his Son and
> through the glory of his resurrection according to the flesh, the
> Father did not merely beautify creatures partially, but rather, can we
> say, clothed them wholly in beauty and dignity. (C, 5, 4)

GOD HAS LINKED HIMSELF TO US IN LASTING LOVE

Someone might still object, all the same, that the warm manifesta-
tion of Christ's kindliness for the people he met, and the tenderness of
his personal affection for them, was a one-time thing; now he is off, back
in his eternal glory, while we are left in misery. Again, we feel the nag-
ging doubt about that distance. We fear that the grandeur of God allows
no room for the messiness of what we usually serve up in our shabby
existence.

But nothing could be further from the truth. The second reading
from Scripture for the feast of St. John assures us that: "we are heirs as
well...co-heirs with Christ...[and] we know that God cooperates with
those who love him, by turning everything to their good" (Rom 8:17,
28). Paul weaves into the words of this passage the acknowledgment that
"we suffer in this life," so he means to tell us not to lose hope in God regardless of the darkness. We are called to bear up under it all, and we
can, because he who suffered, Jesus, has made us sharers in his destiny.
Otherwise, why call us "co-heirs"? Or do we suppose Jesus could forget
the very ones he made his sisters and brothers before the Father?

John of the Cross never allows such doubts about our sublime calling. Quite the opposite! St. John assures us that even the heartbreak of human existence, which Jesus once knew first-hand, is still cherished by the Savior. At the very end of the poem just quoted, where John describes the birth of Christ—that touching event we prepare to celebrate during this Advent season—he writes:

> Mother [Mary] gazed in sheer wonder
> On such an exchange:
> In God, man's weeping,
> And in man, gladness.
> To the one and the other
> Things usually so strange.[6]

What a consoling thought! Our weeping now lies in God, since Jesus bears it with him. He came to bring us gladness, but he did not disregard our sadness and is willing to include it in the reality he bears even now in heaven. God's love is not just for those who have "made the grade" and rest in the peace of his eternal embrace. The little friar from Castile who was willing to be known as John of the Cross and who shared in the demands of bearing the cross, willingly embraced the pain and suffering of this life because he knew that God's love never fails, that it is tenacious and really capable of "turning everything to our good."

LOVE ALONE IS THE SOLUTION

In the end, we still have misgivings about love's power to transform our lives, because—in spite of what we've learned from the first two readings and St. John's poem—we all too often fail to see love at work around us; we have to go on believing and hoping against hope that it will triumph. What other law did Christ give us, after all? "Love never wrongs the neighbor, hence love is the fulfillment of the law," said one apostle (Rom 13:10); another tells us "anyone who has no love for the person he has seen cannot love the God he has not seen"(1 Jn 4:20).

Today's Gospel text shows us how we disciples here need to imitate our Master, who says: "I have loved them as much as you loved me." Just as Jesus trusted in his mission to show how intently active is God's love at work in the world, so we need to overcome the obstacles to showing our world that same love, and showing that this love counts. It is often hard to pay such good service to love, when we see old hostilities breaking out again into open warfare, not just at the other end of the world, but now in Europe, in Yugoslavia and elsewhere; when we notice the selfishness and greed ruling people's lives (as in the case of so many once respected financial organizations and so-called tycoons); when wandering, homeless children (on the same continent where that Peruvian priest-theologian lives) are slaughtered by death squads; when indifference marks the attitudes of so many respectable citizens as they're faced with poor, unemployed people around them. One asks, "Why bother to try, anyway? What difference will it make?"

St. John of the Cross gives us a forceful answer. He himself was born into poverty, struggled through economic hardship as he grew (having to accept assistance from others to gain an education), suffered much mistreatment at the hands of the religious of the order he was trying to renew along with St. Teresa, and yet did not distance himself from reality or give in to feelings of defeat. Quite aware of how adversity can erode one's willingness to be kind to others, he still was able to write the following piece of advice to a religious, a scant five months before he died four centuries ago: "Think nothing else but that God ordains all, and where there is no love, put love, and there you will draw out love."[7] Here one has a reliable recipe for happiness: Instead of waiting for love to happen, put it to work and you will then harvest its fruits.

Jean Guitton, a philosopher friend of Pope Paul VI, once said the great saints have the ability to say deep, deep things in the span of just a few concise words. Their sayings prove their spiritual genius.[8] "Where there is no love, put love and you will draw out love," surely qualifies John of the Cross as such a Christian spiritual genius. He was author of many others,[9] but he forged pure gold when he penned these wise lines. They bespeak a certain positive-minded serenity that is very appealing. Just as they hold out the promise that investing in love builds up the reserves of love in the world, so too they invite us to tell others with conviction that, indeed, *God does love us.* Along with Fr. Gutiérrez, who welcomes St. John of the Cross's message, I can say that: God loves us because he has created us lovable; he still welcomes us with all our problems into the realm of his bliss, right here and now; and he works along with us in bringing love to birth where it's missing. Thanks to the witness and advice of St. John of the Cross we can rest assured of the power of God's love and the power of its presence in our lives.

NOTES

1. The most beautiful yet informative volume is *God Speaks in the Night: The Life, Times and Teaching of St. John of the Cross*, trans. Kieran Kavanaugh (Washington, DC: ICS Publications, 1991), with over 800 color photos and maps.

2. This homily was delivered in Westminster Cathedral, London, on December 14, 1991, the feast of St. John of the Cross.

3. Gutiérrez's talk, entitled "Relectura de San Juan de la Cruz desde un pueblo y circunstancias nuevos," was given in Avila on September 26, 1991; an English translation appears in the Winter, 1992 issue of the journal *Spiritual Life*.

4. The liturgical readings for the eucharist on the Solemnity of St. John of the Cross are: First Reading, Is 43:1-3a, 4-5; Second Reading, Rm 8:14-18, 28-30; and Gospel, Jn 17:11, 17-26.

5. From "Romances" 2, "On the communication among the Three Persons" (in *Collected Works*, rev. ed., 61-62); this entire sequence of poems is sometimes called "Romance on the Gospel text: *In principio erat Verbum*," the title of its first section.

6. From "Romances" 9, "The birth," (in *Collected Works*, rev. ed., 67-68).

7. Letter 26, to Madre María de la Encarnación, Segovia, July 6, 1591 (in *Collected Works*, rev. ed., 760).

8. See Jean Guitton, "The Spiritual Genius of St Thérèse," *Spiritual Life* 20 (1974), 163-78.

9. Recall, for example, the famous saying from the *Spiritual Canticle*: "Nothing is obtained from God except by love" (C, 1, 13).

JOHN OF THE CROSS:
THE PERSON, HIS TIMES, HIS WRITINGS

Michael Dodd, O.C.D.

Michael Dodd is a member of the Institute of Carmelite Studies, and has served as director of postulants and novices for the Washington Province of Discalced Carmelites. He is currently superior of the Discalced Carmelite community at Holy Hill, WI, which cares for the Shrine of Mary, Help of Christians.

To begin this series of lectures on St. John of the Cross, I want us to reflect on spontaneous images or associations we have for saints. St. Francis: gentle figure surrounded by birds entranced by his preaching. St. Thérèse: childlike tenderness scattering roses. St. Teresa of Jesus, Teresa of Avila: laughing and vital, dancing before her nuns with castanets. And St. John of the Cross? What image do you have? A friar on Christmas Day picking up a statue of the Christ child and dancing around the room? A small friar composing songs and singing to entertain his companions on a hot and dusty journey? A careful administrator, giving advice on how to deal with unscrupulous landowners over the purchase of a convent? An artist drawing sketches to give to the sisters whose confessions he hears, or designing the cloister of a monastery or supervising the construction of an aqueduct? A manual laborer working in the garden, picking chickpeas and threshing them? A religious superior surrounded by political intrigue who concerns himself first with making sure the sick are fed, even preparing and serving them the food himself? The poet, the lover of nature, the beloved brother? What is your image?

PAST IMAGES OF THE SAINT

My guess is that none of these is the first that comes to mind, although they are all easily shown to be John of the Cross. Instead we think of the mystic, eyes gazing abstractedly into the distance, hands clutching a cross, a whip or other instrument of penance. This is the man, "dry-eyed and bleeding," called by some the butcher saint for his harsh demands and rigors. This is the saint of the dark night of the soul, the saint of the naked ascent of the Mount of Carmel. This is the saint of the *nada*—nothing, nothing, nothing. This is the saint whose motto, reproduced on holy cards and paintings, is "To suffer and be despised for you, Lord." If the province of Avila is the land of *santos y cantos,* saints and stones, in John of the Cross it seems to have produced the saint of stone. Or so it can appear.

Yet when he died, crowds of the poor flocked to view his body, to kiss hands and feet. In spite of the efforts of friars to prevent it, visitors tore pieces from his habit to remember him by. The cities of Ubeda, where he died, and Segovia, to which his body was transferred secretly two years after his death, fought over possession of the remains, petitioning all the way to the Holy See for resolution. The common people venerated him so much that it actually delayed his beatification, because the reverence shown went beyond that permitted by the Church until after serious and official inquiry has pronounced on the virtues of one with a reputation for holiness. For a while the place where he was buried had to be concealed to prevent people from leaving flowers or candles there. When visiting Ubeda some years ago, I was told that the city, long before John's beatification, had gone so far as to proclaim him co-patron along with the archangel Michael. Do people respond thus to a saint of stone?

Some may be inclined to say that it does not matter what image you have of John of the Cross, since it is primarily his writings that interest us today. Yet people will also say that they find John of the Cross difficult to read or to believe or to accept. It is a commonplace to say that John of the Cross's writings should not be given to beginners in the spiritual journey or that no one should read them without the guidance of a knowledgeable director. Yet he did not write his works for specialists in human development or those with doctorates in spiritual theology. He wrote for nuns and friars, novices and laywomen, for any who love God and desire God with passion. These people received his writings with joy and understanding. For them the writings were a precious gift, not an incomprehensible mystery. They were light, not obscurity. On their lips we could place the words of Jessica Powers about John's books, written two years before she entered Carmel as Miriam of the Holy Spirit:

> Out of what door that came ajar in heaven
> drifted this starry manna down to me,
> to the dilated mouth both hunger given
> and all satiety?
>
> Who bore at midnight to my very dwelling
> the gift of this imperishable food?
> my famished spirit with its fragrance filling,
> its savor certitude.
>
> The mind and heart ask, and the soul replies
> what store is heaped on these bare shelves of mine?
> The crumbs of the immortal delicacies
> fall with precise design.
>
> Mercy grows tall with the least heart enlightened,
> and I, so long a fosterling of night,
> here feast upon immeasurably sweetened
> wafers of light.[1]

Why this difference? I believe that it was at least in part because they knew the hands from which they received the writings that John's first disciples found them to be "immeasurably sweetened/wafers of light." It is at least partly because other readers do not know him that his teaching seems dry and cold. In order for us to experience them as light, we need to know the hands that wrote the words: hands that cared for the sick, hands that sketched and drew, hands that were calloused with labor, hands that clapped in rhythm to a dance. It will be my purpose, then, to speak about the person of John of the Cross, to tell the story of the man as a necessary prelude to reading the writings. The nature of the presentation will be primarily biographical, drawing attention to how some of the more important events shaped John's personal vision and his writings. For some this will be familiar territory, but I hope you will get some new insights. I found when trying to prepare that I had too much I wanted to say, but I have cut it down in hope of staying brief. Inevitably this means some things will remain unmentioned, other points only alluded to. I hope that you may be encouraged, though, to seek out more information on John yourself, to get to know the person.[2]

EARLY LIFE

He was born Juan de Yepes, third son of Gonzalo de Yepes and Catalina Alvarez, in Fontiveros, a small town near Avila, in 1542. In Gonzalo's and Catalina's story we find our first major lesson about John. Gonzalo was an orphan who lived with a wealthy uncle involved in the silk trade. In the course of working for his uncle, Gonzalo met Catalina Alvarez, a poor weaver. They fell in love, but to Gonzalo's dismay, his family greeted his engagement with anger, threatening to disown him if he were to marry below his estate. Their motives probably were more complex than mere class snobbery. The Yepes family had Jewish roots, a fact carefully hidden to avoid legal restrictions imposed on those who lacked *limpieza de sangre*, purity of blood. Catalina's background was obscure but the Yepes family feared that questions raised about her origins might lead to an investigation of their own. Better to wash their hands of the boy completely than to risk honor and money before the Inquisition.

Gonzalo was not swayed by threats of dishonor or of poverty. He married Catalina despite the objections of his family and the graphic predictions of disaster voiced by Catalina's own protector and landlady. It was probably 1529. The threats of the family were carried out; the warnings of the landlady were realized. Without resources of his own, Gonzalo learned to weave and they scraped out a living as a negligible part of the textile trade of Castile. In 1530, Catalina gave birth to her firstborn, Francisco. He was followed by Luis, date of birth unknown, and finally, in 1542, by Juan. In spite of hard work, the household was wretchedly poor and food scarce. Soon after John's birth, Gonzalo fell prey to one of the pestilences that swept through Spain during the sixteenth century and died, leaving a young widow with three starving children.

This background holds an important lesson about the family that produced John of the Cross: in the face of true love, everything else is cast aside. John grew up listening to his mother speak about her husband, hearing how Gonzalo had been raised in comfort with every expectation of material and social ease. Francisco, who for a short time was placed with one of his father's wealthy relatives, could describe the way Gonzalo could have lived had he not given it all up for Catalina. The young Juan would learn about priorities and would see firsthand the consequences of choosing love over all else. When he grows up and falls in love with God, John presses on with the spirit of Gonzalo, leaving all behind naturally, because it is love alone, love in Person, that matters.

Catalina attempted to obtain assistance from Gonzalo's family, appealing first to a brother-in-law who was an archdeacon in Torrijos near Toledo. This worthy person made excuses and closed the door in the widow's face. Another brother, a doctor in nearby Galvez, agreed to take Francisco in and adopt him. However, the doctor's wife began to abuse Francisco and Catalina finally took him back home.

Then Luis, the middle son, died, apparently of malnutrition. This convinced Catalina that she would never survive in the limited economy of Fontiveros, and she moved first to Arevalo and then in 1551 settled in Medina del Campo, a thriving market town in sixteenth century Spain. There she continued her weaving, assisted by Francisco.

Although the stay in Arevalo was brief, it was important for Francisco. A lively and sociable young man entering his twenties, Francisco did not let hard work at the looms during the day keep him from wandering the town streets at night, playing the guitar and singing with his companions until the small hours, often falling asleep in church not because he had gone there to pray, but because friendly sacristans would give him space to sleep off his revels. He was apparently guilty of at least minor vandalism and thefts. Following one episode in which some almonds he had stolen proved to be bitter, and apparently frightened that his trespassing had incurred an excommunication, Francisco sought spiritual guidance from a sympathetic priest. Under that man's wise direction, he gave up his nightly rambles with his companions and instead used the night hours to gaze silently into the sky, losing himself in prayer. Encouraged by Catalina, he married Ana Izquierda and settled down as a respectable member of a hardworking household.

In Arevalo and in Medina del Campo, these truly poor people began to be noted for their charity towards others in need. Francisco went out at night looking for the hungry and the homeless, bringing them back to share the little food and shelter he had or finding a place for them in one of the hospitals of the city. Besides working to earn a living for his own family, he begged alms to pay the expenses of those in greater need. He was sensitive to those who were ashamed to beg themselves and included them in his charity. Rather than ridiculing the impoverished nobility who were too proud to earn a living by labor, Francisco discreetly sought to help. Finally, this family that saw seven of eight children die in infancy and childhood made a special mission of rescuing abandoned babies, taking them into their own care or arranging for their placement and begging alms to pay expenses. The parish records of the city note many times where these infants received the sacraments with Francisco and his wife or mother for sponsors.

Note the contrast between the charity that marked this impoverished household and that of Gonzalo's well-to-do family. Juan entered adolescence witnessing a profound religious conversion in his brother whom we know he loved dearly. This conversion does not repress Francisco's high spirits but redirects them towards contemplation and an immediate practical care for those in need. This is a charity that extends itself to those who lack good name as well as those who lack good things. Juan's family bears witness to a Christian love that is not reserved for friends and family nor for the "deserving poor," but like the love and mercy of God pours out on all. It is a charity that touches and does not fear to get its hands dirty. It is a charity that gives on the basis of need, not on the basis of what it possesses. It is not a charity that parades itself for honor or recognition nor for the sake of increasing merit or adding to a celestial credit account. It is simply and purely love, springing from deep prayer and communion with God. It is against such a background that John will judge works of charity or ministry later, rooting out self-serving elements invisible to others, highlighting the essential connection between personal relationship with God in prayer and service rendered to others, exhorting to put love where one does not find love so as to draw love out, and so imitate the way God loves us.

In Medina, Juan was placed in the School *de la doctrina* (of doctrine), a sort of boarding school for poor boys that provided basic reading and writing, catechism and preparation for a trade. A farsighted policy at the time encouraged establishing such schools. "For it is certain," according to the Castilian court, or parliament, in 1548, "that by finding help for these lost children, robberies and serious and enormous crimes will be prevented. If these children are left to go free without a guide, such crimes will increase."[3] Note the implication of the social stratum from which John comes: poor, urban, illiterate and largely untrained, source of violence and danger to society at large. The remarkable virtues of his own family are not universal. We must recall this milieu when we read John's words about disordered appetites. He lived among the results of those disorders—selfishness, greed, oppression, violence—and he saw the difference in the quality of life in his poor family and those around him. He knew from this that the problem was not in things, possessed or unpossessed, but somehow in the human heart and mind.

Juan was rather incompetent at manual skills. Francisco testified that John's mother "tried to place her youngest son where he would learn a trade, and after trying carpentry, tailoring, carving, and painting, Juan did not settle into any of them; although he was fond of helping his mother with her work."[4] One happy result of this shuffling about from apprenticeship to apprenticeship is that Juan picked up a number of skills that would prove helpful later on, even if his dexterity was unremarkable. Francisco's remarks may indicate greater success for John as weaver, but I suspect it reflects a certain domesticity, a helpfulness with maternal tasks and nurturing that would characterize the John of later years who knew how to prepare meals to tempt ailing friars and who wrote easily of God, using images of a loving mother nursing, weaning and teaching children to walk.

Juan proved to be better at verbal skills, learning to read and write quickly. As part of the regimen of the school, he went out to beg alms for the children and served as acolyte at a nearby Augustinian monastery of nuns. There he was spotted by Don Alonso Alvarez de Toledo, administrator of one of the fourteen hospitals in Medina del Campo. This Hospital of the Concepción, popularly called *de las bubas,* was primarily for victims of plague and venereal diseases. Don Alonso gave Juan a job as an orderly in the hospital, with hands-on care of patients as well as responsibilities to beg alms for their support. Thus we find Juan in a situation that calls for sensitivity, tenderness and discretion. It says something about his background that he should have willingly gone to work in a place that might be compared to an AIDS hospice today. He distinguished himself by his gentleness with the sick and acquired an ease with them that reappears later in his care of ailing friars. He was seeing again firsthand the results of disordered living. Perhaps these images of disease and suffering in the flesh color his later vivid descriptions of the harm sinful or misguided desire does to the soul.

Impressed by the young attendant, Don Alonso helped him continue his studies at the newly founded Jesuit college in Medina, equivalent to a rather advanced high school specializing in the humanities. John spent four years there, taught by young Jesuits who were noted educators of their day. Attending classes in grammar, rhetoric, and philosophy went hand in hand with his duties at the hospital, meaning that the eager young student had to read well into the night. Thirsty for truth, charmed by the beauty of language, Juan considered the sacrifice of a few hours of sleep small to gain so much. Already he was learning some of the skills that would bear fruit in the poetry and prose of his maturity.

FIRST YEARS IN CARMEL

Don Alonso was pleased with the progress and promise of his protege and wanted to sponsor Juan for priesthood so that he could add the care of souls at the hospital to his other concerns. But Juan de Yepes had other ideas. In 1563, probably on February 24, he went secretly to the recently founded Carmelite monastery of Santa Ana, and asked to receive the habit of Our Lady of Mt. Carmel. Apparently it was his great love of Mary that drew him to her Order. Attracted by the contemplative traditions of Carmel and undoubtedly influenced by other natural motives, it is ultimately love that moved Juan de Yepes to leave all behind as his father Gonzalo had done. In the Order, he was known as Fray Juan de San Matía, John of St.Matthias.

The fervent young novice (and in this, John is hardly unique, although his family background probably intensified his response) flung himself wholeheartedly into the religious observance, internalizing the values of the Order readily. Noted even as a novice for his love of solitude, his devotion to prayer and to penance, John was admired but perhaps not particularly popular. Some considered his zeal extreme. Others smiled and expected him to grow out of it with experience. Juan no doubt would have quoted the motto of the Order: "With zeal have I been zealous for the Lord God of Hosts." His zeal would mature and some aspects of it would change, but the son of Gonzalo de Yepes was incapable of half measures.

In 1564, after making his profession, John went to the Carmelite College of San Andrés in Salamanca. There he studied the spiritual and theological tradition of his own order, and also attended the larger university itself. Appointed prefect of students by his superiors, he gave lectures to his companions and even took part in debates with senior faculty. This experience at one of the leading theological faculties of the world, including among its members men who had played a significant role at the recently concluded Council of Trent, prepared the disciplined mind that would write the precise analyses of the *Ascent of Mt. Carmel* and *Dark Night of the Soul.*

However, John of St. Matthias was not totally happy. Although he had obtained permission to follow the Rule of his community in what he thought was its primitive rigor, his behavior set him apart from his fellow students. His penitential way of life earned some admiration, but his love of solitude did not hide his sense of isolation. He began to consider transferring to the Carthusians, believing that their radical commitment to solitude and contemplation was what he wanted. Still he hesitated. In spite of his great love for solitude, John knew the need for companionship on the journey. He would write in later years, "The virtuous soul that is alone and without a master, is like a lone burning coal; it will grow colder rather than hotter.... Those who fall alone remain alone in their fall, and they value their souls little since they entrust it to themselves alone.... If you do not fear falling alone, do you presume that you will rise up alone? Consider how much more can be accomplished by two together than by one alone" (*Sayings of Light and Love*, 7-9). He was experiencing that he could not do it alone, but had not yet found the person to help him out.

In 1567 the newly ordained John of St. Matthias made a visit to his home monastery of Santa Ana to celebrate his first Mass for his community. While there, a brother student suggested he might want to visit a nun who was in Medina arranging for the foundation of a new monastery of Carmelite nuns. This was Teresa of Jesus, formerly Teresa de Ahumada y Cepeda, who in 1562 had established a reformed community of nuns in Avila and had now, with the blessing of the general of the Order, begun to establish more houses of strictly enclosed nuns who would follow the more primitive European Rule and devote themselves to contemplation and intercession for the Church. These sisters wore a simpler habit than the other nuns and like most reform groups of the day had adopted the sandals that were the footwear of the poor. This easily noted difference in dress led them to be called *las descalzas*, the discalced or barefoot Carmelites.

Teresa had met with the Carmelite prior of Medina, Anthony de Heredia, discussing with him a new project for which the general had given permission: the establishment of two houses for Discalced friars. These, while not cloistered like the nuns, would follow the ancient Rule of Carmel and be given to a more contemplative lifestyle than the other Carmelites. They would have some ministry, however, for one reason she wanted to found monasteries for men was to give the Church apostles whose active labors would be deeply rooted in personal prayer. To Teresa's consternation, Fr. Anthony offered himself as her first friar. Teresa suspected his age (he was then 57) would be against him, so she suggested he wait and practice living the stricter regimen for a while to see if he wished to pursue it.

Then came her visit with John of St. Matthias, a visit she describes in the *Book of her Foundations:* "And when I spoke with this young friar, he pleased me very much. I learned from him how he also wanted to go to the Carthusians. Telling him what I was attempting to do, I begged him to wait until the Lord would give us a monastery and pointed out the great good that would be accomplished if in his desire to improve he were to remain in his own order and that much greater service would be rendered to the Lord. He promised me he would remain as long as he wouldn't have to wait long" (F, 3, 17). With Teresa's assurances, John returned to Salamanca for one last year of studies. Teresa reported to her nuns, "We can begin. We have a friar and a half." Whether the half friar was the short John or the older and less certain Anthony we do not know.

This episode underlines again the passion of John of the Cross to give himself totally, without reserve. The refreshingly human and youthful extraction of a promise not to have to wait too long reminds us of John's remarks about young lovers of God being like new wine, full of fizz and bubbles. Old friends are like old wine, less bubbles but more faithful and no longer vulnerable to going sour (cf. C, 25, 10-11). Perhaps he is reflecting on his own experience that had shown him enthusiasms are not always the best guide for life decisions.

THE TERESIAN REFORM BEGINS AMONG THE FRIARS

In the summer of 1568, John went with Teresa to make a foundation of nuns at Valladolid. She taught him all she could about the way of life of the nuns and her vision for the friars. She desired that he "have a clear understanding of everything, whether it concerned mortification or the style of both our community life and the recreation we have together.... He was so good that I, at least, could have learned much more from him than he from me. Yet this was not what I did, but I taught him about the lifestyle of the sisters" (F, 13, 5). That Teresa was the teacher at this moment was important. While she had confidence in John, his reputation was for penitence; her vision of a way of life included community and recreation and she wanted to make sure he knew this.

In a letter to a friend about the experience, Teresa noted wryly that "the Lord seems to be leading him by the hand, for, although we have had a few disagreements here over business matters, and I have been the cause of them, and have sometimes been vexed with him, we have never seen the least imperfection in him. He has courage...."[5] A young, inexperienced friar with his ordination oils barely dry on his hands would have needed courage to disagree with Teresa of Jesus. She admired and loved John of the Cross, but when she chose someone to oversee the expansion of her movement among the friars, it was someone she found more manageable than John of the Cross. Yet the courage she praised was to stand him in good stead during his nine months of prison in Toledo in defense of her reform.

In the fall, John set out for the new monastery in Duruelo, little more than a tumbledown shack, miles from nowhere. On November 28, the first Sunday of Advent in 1568, he along with Anthony de Heredia and a brother put on the new habit of the discalced Carmelites, renounced the mitigated Rule and began a new life. They took new names, and he became *Juan de la Cruz,* John of the Cross.

These first friars gave themselves to a life of great simplicity and recollection. They were quite poor, but Teresa was greatly edified at the spirit of the new community and its obvious happiness. She continued to be concerned about possible excesses in corporal penance because she wanted to attract young men of learning who would be apostolically fruitful and did not want to frighten them off by unnecessary or unhealthy ascetical practices. She delighted to find that the friars were going to nearby villages to preach, to hear confessions and to teach.

John brought his family to live and work at the monastery. His mother and sister-in-law helped with cooking and cleaning and his beloved Francisco labored alongside the friars in setting the monastery in order. No doubt John was happy to have their companionship and support as he began this new endeavor. When reading his words about attachment and a too natural love for family, we must remember his love for his own and his willingness to bring them around him when he could. His doctrine about detachment is for the sake of purifying love and affection, not destroying them. His experience in his family and its practice of charity had helped purify his own love so that he was free to express and trust it.

The community soon outgrew its home, and in 1570 they moved to a new monastery in Mancera de Abajo. John, in his role as first novice master of the Reform, trained new members in accord with the vision outlined to him by Teresa. In October of the same year, he went to establish the novitiate at a new monastery in Pastrana that would become a central novitiate, where all new friars would get their initiation into the life of the reformed Carmel.

In spring of 1571 he went to Alcala de Henares to found a house of studies for friars preparing for ordination. John, because of his intellectual skills, his experience as prefect of students in Salamanca and his success in forming new Carmelites, was commissioned with establishing a house and directing the students who would also attend the nearby university. He continued forming the first generation of discalced friars, reminding them in the midst of their studies of their priorities: *religioso y estudiante, religioso delante* ("you are a religious and a student, but a religious first"). This is not a dismissal of scholarship, but rather a statement of John's personal principle that all goes well when things are done in proper order.

During the year John was in Alcala, a telling incident took place. He was sent back to Pastrana to moderate the excessive strictness and physical penances of the new novice master, a certain Angel of St. Gabriel. It is noteworthy that it was John of the Cross who was chosen to gently correct the erroneous overemphasis on self-inflicted pain and humiliations. Only a short while before, he had himself been considered excessively rigorous. John's personal experience and his interaction with St. Teresa had brought him to appreciate the limitations and possible misuse of corporal mortification. He was already aware that it is an evangelical interior mortification, a purifying of mind and will, that matters. When he wrote about the faults of beginners some years after this, he noted that "corporal penance without obedience is no more than a penance of beasts" (N, 1, 6, 2). Such experiences with misguided excess in the name of spirituality impressed on the young friar the necessity of a purification of spirit as well as of sense.

WITH TERESA IN AVILA

Meanwhile, in October of 1571, St. Teresa had been sent back to Avila, to the Monastery of the Incarnation that she had left to begin the reform. The superiors imposed her on the community as prioress to try to do something about the virtual collapse of the community, economically as well as spiritually. Teresa knew she could accomplish more with the support of a good confessor for the nuns, and she asked for John of the Cross. He arrived in late spring of 1572.

Both in the confessional and visiting in the parlor he assisted Teresa, winning the nuns over with his gentleness, guiding them firmly along the way of self-denial towards greater perfection. It was during the two years that they were both in Avila that he had his most intimate contact with Teresa, to their mutual benefit. She later wrote to Mother Anne of Jesus that after John left Castile, she had found no one comparable to him for inspiring souls with fervor.[6]

John proved himself a profitable guide for those as advanced as Teresa as well as others who were taking their first steps on the journey. There were over one hundred nuns, most of whom went to confession every week or every two weeks. John spent hours giving personal attention to the sisters, guiding them steadily toward a better following of Jesus Christ in their Carmelite vocation. Although they had been frightened of him at first (given that same reputation for strictness and rigor), again they came to love him dearly and mourned his departure. When John wrote about spiritual directors later in the *Living Flame of Love* (see F, 3, 29-62), he did so out of this intense experience of guiding people of varied temperament, experience and capacity. The great respect he had for the uniqueness of each person and the way the Holy Spirit moves was evident in his dealings with the nuns of the Incarnation.

Teresa's term ended in 1573 and she moved on, but John remained until 1577, living in a small hermitage near the convent with another of the discalced friars, rather than remaining at the nearby Carmelite friary. For now there was tension between the ancient observance and the fledgling reform.

IN THE PRISON OF TOLEDO

The details of the problem and all the personalities involved need not detain us here. Suffice it to say that it was a matter of confused jurisdictions, with each party appealing to different interpretations of the law.[7] Suffice it to say also that these conflicts involved the Holy See, the general of the Order, papal nuncios friendly and hostile, Dominican visitators appointed to reform Carmelites, a king and royal council who happily interfered with Rome's policies, and individuals who displayed lack of prudence (to put it mildly). Poor John of the Cross, quietly hearing confessions of nuns, would seem an unlikely target for the growing hostility. Yet as the first of the discalced, he was a symbol of the movement that many sincerely felt was destroying the Order. As confessor to the nuns of the Incarnation, he had replaced Carmelite friars of the ancient observance who saw him as a rival for that position.

On the night of December 2, 1577, a group of hostile Carmelite friars, laymen and armed guards broke into the hermitage where John lived with his companion. The two men were seized, and taken separately to places of hiding. John was carried off to Toledo blindfolded and under cover of darkness. He had no idea where he was, and the secret was remarkably well kept. He remained a prisoner until August of 1578 in spite of efforts to locate and rescue him. Teresa even appealed to the king, but to no avail. In the monastery, he was kept in a tiny room that had served as a latrine. It was scarcely large enough to lie down in, with no furnishings, no warmth against the cruel Toledo winter, only one window, a mere slit in the wall high up. He was not allowed to celebrate Mass nor to receive any visitors. Three days a week he was taken out to the dining room where he was threatened, cajoled and finally beaten in attempts to force him to renounce the reform. For the rest of his life he bore the physical scars of this treatment. Incredible as it sounds to us today, the friars were merely executing the sentence prescribed in the law for an incorrigible rebel. John was certain he was right, but so were they. It was a stalemate.

As a way of passing the time, he began to compose poems in his head, usually to fit popular romantic tunes he heard in the distance. A sympathetic jailer gave him writing materials, and he wrote down some verses that he probably took with him when he escaped. Here in the darkness of his cell, John consoled himself with images of woodlands and meadows. He composed part of the poem of the "Spiritual Canticle" and the "Romances on the Gospel." The former would develop into a love song of such power that it continues to be set to music in Spain. The latter poems, not of the same quality as John's great poetry, nonetheless reveal a powerful experience of the reality of the Triune God and of the goodness of creation brought to fulfillment in the Incarnation. It was amazing. He had been stripped of everything: health, friends, food, warmth, reputation. His enemies took everything from John but his God. In the darkness of the prison the son of Gonzalo de Yepes encountered his beloved, and that was enough to make him sing.

By August it was apparent that he was not going to be released and that no one was coming to rescue him. He managed to tie blanket strips together to make a rope, loosened the screws on the locked door, and one dark night managed to sneak out, throw the rope over the wall and slip away unseen. Ascertaining that he was in Toledo, he made his way to the convent of the discalced Carmelite nuns. He told them who he was and, on pretext of having him hear the confession of a nun who was ill, they took him inside and concealed him in the cloister. When the friars came to see if he was there, the nun at the door merely told them: "It would be amazing if you were to find a father in here." Suspicious but unable to do anything, the friars left, and with the help of a patron, the nuns got John out of town. Before he left, he recited some of his verses to them, and the nuns wept to see such an emaciated, cruelly treated man sing songs of pure love.

FREEDOM AND NEW BEGINNINGS IN ANDALUSIA

John then went to Almodóvar del Campo, where another discalced meeting was underway, this time trying more earnestly to come up with some resolution to the problems. At the chapter the discalced illegally elected their own provincial and sent delegates to Rome to try to straighten things out with the Holy See. They appointed John of the Cross superior of the monastery of El Calvario, far to the south, to remove him as soon as possible from the reach of the friars of the ancient observance who were still seeking their escaped prisoner. The chapter was unauthorized and the jurisdictional problems continued, but John was now out of the turmoil that raged for another two years and of which he had been the outstanding victim.

What a change from his prison cell was El Calvario, with the beautiful countryside of the Segura Sierra to enjoy, the peace and calm of a small hardworking community, and John's own labors. He used to take the friars out into the mountains, talk to them of the beauty of God, and send each off to pray in some place of natural beauty, himself often choosing the side of a stream that welled up not far from the house. He had learned in the purifying trial of Toledo that God is present everywhere, even when natural beauty is lacking. In the prison, it was the beloved who was the mountainside, the rivers, the forests, the fields enameled with flowers. John's love of natural beauty was not diminished but purified, and he rejoiced now to see the traces of the Beloved everywhere he looked. He had learned that nature could be a distraction from God, but that it could also, in its own creatureliness, speak profoundly of the Creator, not hiding God from sight but pointing beyond and through itself to the hidden Beloved. His writings reveal a deep appreciation of nature coupled with an awareness of the failings of the human heart until all is ordered properly towards God. John knew from his own experience that the person transformed by God sees and loves creation in its own full truth and beauty for the first time.

John served at this time as confessor for the discalced nuns in the nearby village of Beas de Segura. He had stopped there on his way to El Calvario, and although the nuns were touched by what he had undergone, the prioress, Anne of Jesus, was a bit offended that so young a priest should refer so casually to the great Teresa of Jesus as "my daughter." Shortly afterwards she wrote to Teresa about this and also complained that the nuns had no one capable of giving them adequate spiritual direction. Teresa promptly wrote back in no uncertain terms: "I am really surprised, daughter, at your complaining so unreasonably, when you have Padre Fray John of the Cross with you, who is a divine, heavenly man.... You would not believe how solitary his absence makes me feel.... I can assure you I should very much like to have Fray John of the Cross here, for he is indeed the father of my soul."[8]

Anne of Jesus, properly reprimanded, took Teresa at her word, and John came frequently to the nuns, hearing confessions and giving them instructions on the way of perfection. Anne became one of his closest friends and collaborators, and he wrote the commentary on the "Spiritual Canticle" for her.

In response to questions about the significance of some of his poems, which he would recite for the friars and nuns, John began to comment on certain passages, thus beginning the process that resulted in his major prose works. The books emerged, then, rooted first in his own experience of God expressed in the images of the poetry, then gradually commented on in the light of the life and experience of those he served. For all the philosophical and theological framework of the commentaries on his poem "One Dark Night," which he probably wrote remembering his escape from prison in the middle of the night, the originating experience is one of passion, and the questions addressed come from life, not speculation.

In 1579 John was again given the task of founding a house for students, this time in Baeza for the discalced Carmelites in southern Spain. He was rector there until 1581 and became a very popular figure in the town as a confessor to professors and to simple country folk as well. He continued to take care of the Beas nuns (although it was further to travel) and to expand his commentaries on his poetry. During the time John was in Baeza, on June 22, 1580, Pope Gregory XIII made the discalced a separate province of the Order, thereby resolving, at least for the most part, the conflict that had been going on for five years.

On March 3, 1581, the first real provincial chapter of the discalced was held, and in spite of his desire to get out of administration, John was elected prior of the monastery at Granada.

He was prior there from 1582 until 1584, after which he became vicar provincial (second in command) for Andalusia, remaining in residence in Granada until 1588. Not content with administrative duties, he worked as a manual laborer getting the monastery in better shape. One of his accomplishments was building a small aqueduct, which he designed and helped construct, to bring water from the mountain to the house. Although the friars are no longer there, the aqueduct remains as a witness to John's practicality as well as his eye for form and beauty.

It was in Granada that John completed his poems and major treatises. This is all the more amazing in that he was frequently on the road as vicar provincial, making foundations of friars and nuns throughout the territory.

Perhaps this is the answer to the problem of why John failed to complete either the *Ascent of Mount Carmel* or the *Dark Night of the Soul* commentaries. He may simply have put them at the back of his desk, planning to get to them if no one came to his door. For those with multiple duties pulling them in different directions, he might be a sympathetic ear.

FRESH CONFLICTS

Meanwhile, other things were developing that would embroil John in political difficulty again. In 1582 Teresa had died, and in 1585 Father Jerome Gracian, to whom she had wholeheartedly entrusted the success of the reform among the friars, was succeeded as provincial by an Italian, Nicholas Doria, a financial genius, penitential and legalistic to the core. Already he was convinced that the new order was in decline and he was determined to set things straight; that meant, basically, to recreate Teresa's order in his own image. Part of that involved getting rid of his rival, Jerome Gracian, who held more humane views and who was known to be Teresa's favorite. Doria set out to discredit Gracian and managed to have him deprived of all offices, eventually driving him out of the Order itself. Part of the irony of the situation was that Gracian had cast the deciding vote making Doria provincial, and John had told him at the time, "Your Reverence is making a man provincial who will strip you of the habit."

This rather scandalous political maneuvering was going on at the same time that Doria was working to have the new province made into a congregation, still under the general of the Order, but otherwise totally independent with its own vicar. Sixtus V, on June 27, 1587, approved Doria's Constitutions and the Discalced were now a congregation. In June of 1588 (a month after Gracian had been barred from holding any offices) the first general chapter met in Madrid. Doria was elected vicar general and John became first consultor, leader of a six member board that assisted the vicar in the government of the new congregation. This was despite John's open opposition to the treatment Gracian received.

As first consultor, he was superior of the central house at Segovia, where he moved in 1588. Whenever Doria was absent, John was head of the entire congregation. It is worth remembering that when he first talked to Teresa about his desire to withdraw to the Carthusians, she promised him all the solitude and recollection he desired. Yet from the time he was at Duruelo until a few months before his death, he was in a position of leadership in the Order, constantly dealing with matters of practical administration. Perhaps one reason he spoke of his time in prison as a singular grace was that it was the only respite from heavy responsibilities!

One consolation in Segovia was that John had his brother Francisco with him. He had brought him there to help with some building, and when Francisco started to move on, John detained him, protesting that they might not see one another again. He used to introduce his brother to guests as his dearest treasure on earth. They must have made an interesting pair, the simple illiterate laborer and his brilliant younger brother, now an important leader in a growing religious community. It was to Francisco that John told the story that would come to serve as a motto for him. John wanted to move a painting of Christ carrying his cross from the monastery to a more public location so others could benefit from it. After doing so, he had a vision that Christ spoke and asked him, "John, what reward do you desire for your labors?" John replied, "Lord, to suffer and to be despised on your account." I draw your attention to the "on your account." John's request was not masochistic self-loathing or a need to be punished; it was rather in the same spirit as the apostles in Acts who rejoiced that they suffered for the sake of the name of Jesus. John asked to be allowed to show his love to its fullest extent. And as with all such prayers, when sincere, his request was answered.

EXILE AND DEATH

Doria was displeased with his consultor, for John, whose courage and forthrightness Teresa noted when they were together in Valladolid, never failed to express his opposition to Doria's treatment of Gracian and his dealings with the nuns, whom Doria was seeking to reshape according to his own rigid and legalistic ideas. The other consultors were docile to Doria, but he would brook no opposition, especially since he knew that John represented the feelings of many of the friars and most of the nuns. At the chapter of 1591, John was appointed provincial of Mexico, with the hope that he would be no threat several thousand miles away. When his health began to fail, that appointment was revoked.

Instead he was sent to the tiny community at La Peñuela, where he gave himself up to prayer, to working in the fields and to his old apostolate of spiritual direction. Because of his reputation for austerity, some of the friars had been afraid of him, but they soon began to experience his gentleness and capacity to entertain, without ever leading them away from single-minded devotion to God. The community loved him and considered themselves blessed to be the site of his exile.

But not all was sweetness and light. With the knowledge of Doria, one of the consultors, a Diego Evangelista, began a campaign to discredit John and to have him destroyed. When Diego Evangelista was a young man, John had had occasion to correct him for taking pride in his success as a preacher. Having seen true charity expressed in the service of his family to the poor, John recognized self-importance masquerading as piety when he saw it. Lest we think John had been wrong, notice that the young man held the grudge and now set out to get his revenge, mounting a smear campaign against the first discalced friar with the express intention of driving him out of the Order. His friends wrote, warning of what was happening, but John remained undisturbed. Nothing was to come of the process, though not because of official reluctance to press it.

On September 12, John became ill with a fever. Nothing could be done to bring it down at La Peñuela and he had to go elsewhere for treatment. Given a choice of going to Baeza, where he had been superior and was still loved, or to Ubeda, he chose Ubeda where he would encounter another persecution. The prior, Fr. Crisóstomo, like Diego Evangelista, had been corrected by John years earlier and he was not at all pleased to serve as host for the ailing friar. John took the abuse calmly, but others in the community complained to the provincial— none other than Anthony of Jesus, the old prior of Medina who had begun the reform with John and about whom Teresa had had doubts because of his age! Anthony appeared, insisted that John receive better treatment, and stayed to console his old partner. Eventually John's charitable acceptance of everything won over the prior who had tormented him, and Crisóstomo became one of his greatest admirers and died himself with a reputation for great holiness. John's choice of the harder way for himself had opened a channel of grace for another.

John's condition worsened as the inflammation in the leg progressed and nothing could stop the spread of gangrene. Finally, on the evening of December 13, 1591, the end drew near. After listening to some verses from the Canticle of Canticles, he prepared himself for death. At midnight as the bells rang for the office of matins, John asked what they were for. When they told him, he exclaimed, "Glory be to God for I shall say them in heaven." He kissed his crucifix and murmured, *In manus tuas, Domine, commendo spiritum meum* (Into your hands, O Lord, I commend my spirit), and he breathed his last. He was 49 years old. The hands that had tended the sick, that had sketched Christ crucified, that had lifted stones from the garden, that had penned words of light and love, were still.

I must conclude with an apology for what is largely a biographical sketch, with only hints of implication. But I hope I have lifted at least a little the veil that history has slipped over the face of John of the Cross. No butcher saint, he, no saint of stone. A man of fire and love, warming and enlightening those he knew and offering that light to us as well. Next time you pick up his writings, remember first this man. See if it changes what you read, if it helps to understand. And remember these encouraging, exciting words from his "Prayer of a Soul Taken with Love":

> ...With what procrastinations do you wait, since from this very moment you can love God in your heart?
> Mine are the heavens and mine is the earth. Mine are the nations, the just are mine and mine the sinners. The angels are mine, and the Mother of God, and all things are mine; and God himself is mine and for me, because Christ is mine and all for me. What do you ask, then, and seek my soul? Yours is all of this, and all is for you. Do not engage yourself in something less or pay heed to the crumbs that fall from your Father's table. Go forth and exult in your Glory! Hide yourself in it and rejoice, and you will obtain the supplications of your heart. (*Sayings of Light and Love*, 26-27)

NOTES

1. "The Books of Saint John of the Cross," *Selected Poetry of Jessica Powers*, ed. Regina Siegfried and Robert Morneau (Kansas City, MO: Sheed & Ward, 1989), 132.

2. The material that follows is taken from a number of biographical sources. The standard Spanish biography, written by Crisógono de Jesús, has been translated into English by Kathleen Pond as *The Life of St. John of the Cross* (London: Longmans, Green & Co.,1958). An award-winning French biography, *St. John of the Cross*, by Fr. Bruno, O.D.C, is also available in English, edited by Benedict Zimmerman and with an introduction by Jacques Maritain, published by Sheed and Ward in 1932. Other sources of information in English include the translation of Leon Cristiani's *St. John of the Cross: Prince of Mystical Theology* (Garden City, NY: Doubleday & Co., 1962); Gerald Brenan, *St. John of the Cross: His Life and Poetry* (Cambridge: Cambridge University Press, 1973); Robert Sencourt, *Carmelite*

and Poet: A Framed Portrait of St.John of the Cross (New York, NY: Macmillan, 1940; E. Allison Peers, *Spirit of Flame: A Study of St. John of the Cross* (London: SCM Press, 1943); and most recently Richard Hardy, *Search for Nothing:The Life of John of the Cross* (New York, NY: Crossroad, 1982). Peers and Hardy are both still in print and readily available. No doubt the commemoration of the fourth centenary of John's death will result in new studies. The volume mentioned in the following footnote is one such.

3. See Federico Ruiz, et al., *God Speaks in the Night: The Life, Times and Teaching of St. John of the Cross*, trans. Kieran Kavanaugh (Washington, DC: ICS Publications, 1991), 54.

4. Ibid., 36..

5. *The Letters of Saint Teresa of Jesus*, trans. E. Allison Peers, 2 vols. (London: Sheed & Ward, 1980), 1:52 (Letter 10, end of Sept. 1568).

6. *Letters*, 2: 624-625 (Letter 261, Dec. 1578).

7. For a discussion of the jurisdictional complexities see Víctor de Jesús María, "Un conflicto de jurisdicción," in *Sanjuanistica* (Rome: Collegium Internationale Sanctorum Teresiae a Jesu et Joannis a Cruce, 1943), 413-528.

8. Teresa, *Letters*, loc cit.

FREE TO LOVE: NEGATION IN THE DOCTRINE OF JOHN OF THE CROSS

Daniel Chowning, O.C.D.

Daniel Chowning is a member of the Institute of Carmelite Studies, and currently serves as director of novices for the Washington Province of Discalced Carmelites.

I would like to begin with a true love story: Sometime around the year 1529, a young, wealthy, silk merchant from Toledo, Spain by the name of Gonzalo de Yepes was making his customary business trip through Castile either on the way to or from the prosperous trading village of Medina del Campo. Gonzalo was the orphaned son of noble parents. After his parents' death, he went to live under the guardianship of some wealthy uncles who owned a silk industry. Gonzalo's uncles incorporated him into the prosperous family business and appointed him manager or representative of the enterprise. Because of his position, he made regular trips to Medina del Campo where the plaza, among many other things, was famous for its silk commerce.[1]

On one of Gonzalo's trips he passed through the small Castilian village of Fontiveros in the province of Avila to visit a rich widow who operated a silk weaving business out of her home. Employed and living with this widow as a silk weaver was a beautiful young woman by the name of Catalina Alvarez. Like Gonzalo, Catalina was orphaned and a native of Toledo, but unlike him, she was poor and came from an entirely different social class. To use a twentieth century expression, she came from "the other side of the tracks." Her experience had been one of poverty, suffering, struggle, and abandonment. Gonzalo became enamored of Catalina's beauty, youthfulness, goodness and lovableness.

Despite their disparate social and economic backgrounds, they fell in love and decided to marry.

But Gonzalo's love for Catalina presented serious problems. According to the conventions and customs of the sixteenth century, a person did not marry out of his or her social class. People entered marriage by contract, arranged by their parents. Love had little, or in many cases nothing, to do with the purpose of marriage. The primary end of marriage was procreation and, at least for the noble classes, to keep their social class free of impure blood and their family heritage intact. To marry outside one's social milieu meant breaking the family lineage; it was simply not done.

The wealthy widow who had taken poor, orphaned Catalina into her home and business out of the sheer goodness of her heart, and who probably knew Gonzalo's relatives, warned him of the consequences of this marriage.[2] But Gonzalo loved Catalina passionately. She had stolen his heart. They must have shared a deep love because both were aware that their union could mean the loss of Gonzalo's secure position, inheritance, and family ties. This was no small matter in sixteenth century Spain, marked by widespread famine and poverty.[3] But the love they shared enabled Gonzalo to transcend himself and the economic and social considerations. Hadn't she stolen his heart? Wasn't his love so focused on her that nothing else really mattered? Thus, they married.

Of course, the widow's premonition came true. Gonzalo was thrown out on the street, disinherited and abandoned by his noble and rich family. A gifted accountant and writer, but unable to find work in his field of expertise, Gonzalo was forced to learn the trade of his young wife. He fell into poverty out of love. He must have been an extraordinarily free man to sacrifice all his material security and possessions out of love for his bride. His self-denial, his willingness to die to false securities for the sake of love, in itself was a supreme act of freedom and love that united him with Catalina. And her love for him empowered him to surrender all for the sake of their union. Within a few years, their love brought forth new life. They had three sons: Francisco, Luis (who later died of malnutrition), and Juan, who later became known as Juan de la Cruz, a canonized saint and Doctor of the Church, often referred to by his devotees and students as "the doctor of divine love."

St. John of the Cross, this great lover of God, was a "child of love" in the truest sense of the word. Although John never reflects directly upon his childhood in his writings, his humble origins marked by the deep love his parents shared and his father's sacrificial act of love must have shaped his profound understanding of love and union between God and human beings. Definitely, it must have given him an insight into the cost of love, that love is a self-emptying process. From where else, other than from the example of Jesus Christ, would the inspiration for such ideas as these come? "Love does not consist in feeling great things but in having great detachment and in suffering for the Beloved" (*Maxims*, 36).[4] Or again, "This is how we can recognize the person who truly loves God; if he or she is content with nothing less than God.... Satisfaction of heart is not found in the possession of things, but in being stripped of them all and in poverty of spirit" (C, 1, 14).

I cannot help but think that Gonzalo and Catalina's love adventure must have formed in some way John's teaching on the theme of my lecture: *Free To Love: Negation in the Doctrine of St. John of the Cross.*

Love is at the heart of the spirituality of St. John of the Cross. Oftentimes, however, people read his writings and become frightened by the absolute, stark, and radical language he uses, such as: *all or nothing, self-denial, mortification, emptiness, renunciation, nakedness, contempt for self and creatures,* and *detachment.* All these terms form a rich vocabulary to express the theme of negation and can appear repellent and inhuman if not understood correctly. They recur throughout John's works and are often the source of misinterpretation and fear that have distorted the beauty, depth, and humanness of his person and doctrine.

For instance, section 3 in chapter 13 of the first book of the *Ascent of Mount Carmel* contains a series of counsels that may seem disturbing and masochistic if not understood in the proper context:

> Endeavor to be inclined always:
>> not to the easiest, but to the most difficult;
>> not to the most delightful, but to the most distasteful;
>> not to the most gratifying, but to the less pleasant;
>> not to what means rest for you, but to hard work;
>> not the the consoling, but to the unconsoling;
>> not to the most, but to the least;
>> not to the highest and most precious,
>>> but to the lowest and most despised;
>> not to wanting something, but to wanting nothing.
> Do not go about looking for the best of temporal things, but for

the worst, and, for Christ, desire to enter into complete nudity, emptiness, and poverty in everything in the world.

For many of us in our North American culture whose experience of human love may have been broken and resulted in low self-esteem and self-hatred such statements may seem difficult to bear. In our culture we have a hard time distinguishing between appropriate and inappropriate self-love. Therefore, it is difficult to teach the spirituality of John of the Cross without hearing some negative response such as: "What do you mean, I have to die to selfishness? I need to take care of myself and love myself! I spent too many years hating myself as it is!"

Nevertheless, negation is the pillar of the system of St. John of the Cross and to misunderstand it is to miss out on the richness of his doctrine.[5] It is helpful, therefore, to have some comprehension of such terms as self-denial, all-nothing, mortification, renunciation, and emptiness, all of which comprise the theme of negation in John's works.

Let me begin by explaining what negation is not. First of all, Sanjuanist terms of negation have nothing to do with neoplatonic dualism or a denial of creation. John of the Cross is thoroughly Christian and incarnational. He exalts the beauty and dignity of creation and the purpose for which God created the world. For John, God is a mystery of self-emptying Love who created the world out of love to be "a palace for the bride" of Christ ("Romances," 4). In creating the world, God "looked at all things" with the image of his Son and thus communicated to them "their natural being and many natural graces and gifts" (C, 5, 4). Thus, creation reflects the presence, beauty, and excellence of God and increases love in the person who reflects upon it. "Since creatures gave the soul signs of her Beloved and showed within themselves traces of his beauty and excellence, love increased in her"(C, 6, 2). Images of creation abound in John's poetry.

> O woods and thickets
> planted by the hand of my Beloved!
> O green meadow,
> coated, bright, with flowers.... (C, 4)

> My Beloved, the mountains,
> and lonely wooded valleys,
> strange islands,

and resounding rivers,
the whistling of love-stirring breezes. (C, 13)

John would have us, therefore, love all of creation and regard it as the image of God's love and beauty, as the image of Jesus Christ.

Second, John's negation spirituality does not disparage the beauty and dignity of the human person. We were created in the image and likeness of God, created out of love to be the spouse of Christ, created for union with God thorough love (see "Romances," 3-4). Love is the reason we exist (C, 29). John writes: "the ultimate reason for everything is love" (C, 38, 5). God lives in the depths of our being imparting to us life, dignity, and love.

> Oh, then, soul, most beautiful among all creatures, so anxious to know the dwelling place of your Beloved that you may go in quest of him and be united to him, now we are telling you that you yourself are his dwelling and his secret chamber and hiding place. (C, 1, 7)

Furthermore, John's teaching on self-denial does not refer to a renunciation of material objects nor engagement in ascetical practices such as fasting, wearing tattered clothes, depriving oneself of all pleasures of life and performing extraordinary penances. John insists that what obstructs our relationship with God is not material reality as such, but the human heart when it craves, desires, and tries to possess material objects, people, and situations for selfish reasons.

> ...For we are not discussing the mere lack of things; this lack will not divest the soul if it craves for all these objects.... Since the things of the world cannot enter the soul, they are not in themselves an encumbrance or harm to it; rather, it is the will and appetite dwelling within that causes the damage.... (A, 1, 3, 4)

The problem, therefore, lies not in material reality but in the human heart when it becomes attached and inordinately desires created things for selfish motives. Definitely, ascetical practices may have a role in our effort to grow in union with God, but people have often concentrated too much on ascetical practices and the denial of material objects rather than on love and the interior, spiritual attitude that undergirds John's thinking. [6]

How, then, are we to understand the negation spirituality of John of the Cross without becoming discouraged or turned off by the absoluteness of his doctrine?

To begin with, the starting point for approaching John's negation spirituality is the experience of being loved by God—a God who desires to enter into a personal relationship of love with human beings—and our response to that love. Any notion of self-denial, detachment, renunciation, or emptiness that is not born of an experience of God's personal love makes no sense to John of the Cross. God always takes the initiative. "We love because he first loved us" (1 Jn 4:19). In the beginning of the *Spiritual Canticle*, which sings of and recounts the Christian journey toward union with God in terms of love, John writes that the soul is only able to begin the journey of love in search for union with God because she first had an experience of God's love, and as a fruit of that experience, came to an awareness that love is the purpose of existence (C, 1, 1). It is this experience of God's love that ignites the fire of love within a person so that one can begin the journey towards union with God through love.

> Where have you hidden,
> Beloved, and left me moaning?
> You fled like the stag
> after wounding me;
> I went out calling you, but you were gone. (C, 1)

For John, this experience of the transcendent but intimate loving nature of God, who takes the initiative and touches us with love, has a profound effect upon us; it begins a transformation process that frees us to love God, ourselves, creation, and all of life in the way God created us to.

This experience of God's love is pivotal for understanding some of the radical statements John makes about the "nothingness" of creation and all things in comparison to God who is All. For instance:

> All the creatures of heaven and earth are nothing when compared to God.... All the beauty of creatures compared with the infinite beauty of God is supreme ugliness.... All the grace and elegance of creatures compared with God's grace is utter coarseness and crudity. (A, 1, 4, 3-7)

> To possess God in all, you should not possess anything in all.
> For how can the heart that belongs to one belong completely to the
> other? (Letter 17—to Magdalena del Espíritu Santo, July 28, 1589)

A first reading of these comparisons without an understanding of the experience of God they reflect would lead us to believe that John is setting up an opposition between God and creatures, that he is denigrating created reality in writing that, compared to God, creation is "nothing," "ugly," and "crude." But this is far from his intention. God is not in competition with creation and human beings, for God is the source of all that exists. These statements reflect the experience of a person who has glimpsed the infinite goodness and beauty of God. John wishes to communicate a message about God. God is the Source of all life, goodness, and beauty. God is All; God is Everything. And no matter how good, wise, and beautiful creatures of this world may be, nothing can be compared to the goodness, wisdom, beauty, and love of God who is the author of all that exists and upon whom everything depends. In the light of God's tremendous love and goodness, all other things pale into insignificance without losing their value and worth. But isn't this the same when two people fall in love? A man and woman fall in love, and as a result, other men and women no longer attract their hearts as before. Their hearts have been stolen. Yes, others are beautiful and good, but all other loves and attractions are relative to their beloved. St. Paul expresses the same insight in his Letter to the Philippians: "I have come to rate all as loss in the light of the surpassing knowledge of my Lord Jesus Christ. For his sake I have forfeited everything; I have accounted all else rubbish so that Christ may be my wealth" (Phil 3:8). To have such an insight into the "Allness" of God is the fruit of a profound experience of being loved by God.

But John has another reason for making such radical statements: ultimately, only God can satisfy the human heart because God created us for a communion of life with God, created us for happiness and wholeness. And although the world and creatures are beautiful, made in the image and likeness of God, they cannot slake the deepest thirsts of the human spirit. Anything less than the infinite fails to satisfy us (F, 3, 18). This is a message that resounds throughout John's works. It is a truth he learned early in life. He grew up in misery and poverty; he knew hunger and abandonment. And like all the mystics of the great world religions, he was convinced that so much of human suffering comes from not realizing the truth that, ultimately, only God can satisfy the human heart.

The experience, therefore, of being deeply loved by God, God who takes the initiative and invites us to enter into a personal relationship of love, is the foundation for understanding John's negation spirituality. This is important because not only does it emphasize that it is God who takes the initiative but, in terms of any form of self-denial or renunciation or dying to self, we must view it in the context of a personal relationship of love with God.

The second foundation upon which John's negation spirituality is based is the human condition. Now when God's love begins to touch us deeply and we respond by entering into a personal relationship with God, pain is involved. It is the same in any love relationship. To enter into relationship with another is to allow ourselves to be wounded. When two people fall in love, there is a passionate, romantic period which is like a spark that sets off the fire of love. However, the more they grow in their relationship, the more they begin to experience all that is vulnerable and wounded within them, all that is contrary to mature love: fears, insecurities, hurts from the past, desire to control and dominate the other, and selfishness. In short, they begin to experience how unfree they are to respond fully to the demands of love, as they truly desire. In an analogous way, the same happens in our relationship with God. When God begins to communicate love to us on deeper levels , the light of God's love reveals the depths of our sinfulness, woundedness and selfishness; it brings to light all that prevents us from loving God and others according to the Gospel. It exposes our lack of freedom to love. As a result, we become painfully aware that we stand in need of a profound healing and liberation from all that blocks our capacity to love. John expresses this well in the *Living Flame of Love* :

> All the soul's infirmities are brought to light; they are set before its eyes to be felt and healed. Now with the light and heat of the divine fire, it sees and feels those weaknesses and miseries which previously resided within it, hidden and unfelt, just as the dampness of the log of wood was unknown until the fire being applied to it made it sweat and smoke and sputter. And this is what the flame does to the imperfect soul. (F, 1, 21-22)

John of the Cross has a profound insight into human nature and its

ills. Although we were created for a love relationship with God, ourselves, others, and creation, all is not well. Like all the mystics of the great
world religions, he recognizes that human nature is wounded and stands
in need of transformation and healing. Due to original sin, as well as our
own personal sin and fragmented personal history with all the factors
that make up our character and life stories, there is a profound disorder
or conflict within the human heart that makes it difficult to relate to
God, ourselves, others, and life in the way God intended at our creation,
and in the way we also desire in the depths of our being. Although we
have been redeemed by Christ, the roots of original sin lie deep within
us and we find it hard to love. John says we love in a "base manner" (N,
1, 8, 3). Therefore, the human heart stands in need of radical transformation and liberation.

How does the disordered heart or "base manner of loving" manifest
itself for John? He analyzes this in the first book of the *Ascent of Mount
Carmel* and in the *Dark Night*. At the risk of over-simplification, I'll try to
synthesize his analysis.

First of all, the disorder or conflict within the human heart manifests itself by our becoming enslaved or attached to things that ultimately
cannot satisfy us. At times, whether consciously or unconsciously, despite
our best desires and intentions we humans have this tendency to seek
satisfaction, peace, fulfillment, and love in something that can never
provide it for us, whether it be material possessions, riches, power, prestige, unhealthy relationships, and even spiritual experiences and consolations. We can see this not only in our personal lives but in society at
large, with all the addiction to drugs, alcohol, sex, food, co-dependent
relationships, and material possessions. According to John, our deepest
desire is really for God, who alone can satisfy us, but not being conscious
of this (or for some other reason such as fear or insecurity), we may give
our time and energy in an inordinate manner to other things that enslave us and prevent us from responding freely to that loving relationship with God and neighbor for which we were created and which alone
can fulfill us. Now an attachment for John of the Cross is a disordered
relationship, whether it be with a person, a material thing, an idea or
feeling, or even a religious image or experience, making it the source of
our love and happiness. It's when we say, "if only I had this car, I'd be
happy. If only I had this person living with me, I'd be happy. If only I
had nice clothes, I'd be happy." Instead of placing our relationship with

God as the source and object of our true longing, we become dependent on something else.

Another way this disorder within us manifests itself is through what John sees as an egotism rooted deeply in our hearts. He calls it "a base manner of loving" (N, 1, 8, 3). It is when we are motivated in our relationships with God, others, and objects by self-gratification, or what John calls "sensory satisfaction" (N, 1, 6, 6). Freud would call this living by the pleasure principle; other contemporary schools of thought might classify it as narcissistic behavior. It is when our motivation for doing things and relating to God and others is solely to get pleasure for ourselves, thus making our ego the center of attention. John gives a lot of attention to analyzing this type of behavior in the *Dark Night.* He maintains that this disordered way of loving is "childishness" (N, 1, 6, 6), contrary to true love, and is like a "stain" embedded in the depths of our being that prevents us from relating to and loving God and others in the way God created us to do, and from reaching our full potential as human beings (N, 2, 1, 1). It manifests itself in behavior such as condemning and judging others, wanting to be praised and esteemed as holy, the need to control and manipulate others in order to be liked, becoming angry when we don't receive sensory satisfaction in prayer and ministry, and impatience over the imperfections of others as well as our own.[7] Only God can heal this wound through the purification of the dark night.

With this perception of our broken human condition and our need for liberation and healing, we can better understand the fundamental and necessary role negation plays in John's doctrine. Renunciation, self-denial, detachment, and poverty are directed toward the process of healing and liberating the human heart in order to love God, others, and creation in the way we were created to love. It is the necessary process toward maturation and growth in love. For John of the Cross, negation is the Christian path towards freedom to love.

Now that we have looked at the foundation of negation, let us reflect on the various elements of this path as taught by John of the Cross.

The first aspect of John's teaching on dying to self and becoming empty for God is that it is modeled on Jesus Christ as the supreme example of self-emptying love. John's negation spirituality is thoroughly centered on the life and teaching of Jesus Christ. He writes:

A person makes progress only by imitating Christ, who is the Way, the Truth, and the Life. No one goes to the Father but through him, as he states himself in St. John [Jn 14:6]....

Accordingly, I would not consider any spirituality worthwhile that wants to walk in sweetness and ease and run from the imitation of Christ. ...He is our model and light. (A, 2, 7, 8-9)

His first counsel to beginners in the spiritual life is to have a habitual desire to imitate Jesus Christ and to make love for Jesus the motivation for one's self-denial. He writes in the *Ascent of Mount Carmel*:

First, have a habitual desire to imitate Christ in all your deeds by bringing your life into conformity with his. You must then study his life in order to know how to imitate him and behave in all events as he would. Second, in order to be successful in this imitation, renounce and remain empty of any sensory satisfaction that is not purely for the honor and glory of God. Do this out of love for Jesus Christ. (A, 1, 13, 3-4)

John's preferred image of Jesus is that of Jesus crucified (A, 2, 7, 7-11). Jesus crucified is his model of the Christian path. Now we must not view this symbol as something morbid, reflecting only the spirituality of the Spanish Baroque period. For John, Jesus crucified symbolizes a life of radical dependence upon God, of service, compassion, and self-giving love. Jesus is the one who reflected God's love perfectly in our broken world. His life was one of a continual death in order that others may live more fully (A, 2, 7, 9). He was totally committed to pleasing God in all things, the God whom he experienced as Father and who was the passion of his life (A, 1, 13, 4; 2, 7, 2). Jesus lived a life of mercy, compassion, and self-giving love that demanded a total surrender of false securities and self-gratification and resulted in death on the cross that concretized in a radical way his life of compassion and love for the reconciliation of humanity with God and with each other. According to John, in the love and poverty of Jesus crucified, God revealed his power, mercy, and goodness, and at the same time, revealed to us where we will experience the deepest communion with God, that is, in a life of compassion and self-emptying love for the love of God and in the service of others.[8] Jesus accomplished "the most marvelous work of his whole life," at the moment when he was poorest, weakest, and most empty of self-love and false securities (A, 2, 7, 11).

Jesus, therefore, is the model of the path of negation according to John of the Cross. To follow Jesus, to live according to the Gospel, implies by its very nature a life of loving dedication to pleasing God and a surrender of false securities and selfishness. It means treading the path of the cross, the way of service, compassion, and self-giving love. It means dying to self in order that others may live.

The second element of this path of negation is that negation for John of the Cross does not simply refer to some ascetical practice or form of renunciation that precedes love (in the sense of something I must do before I can love God, or some practice that prepares me to love); rather, negation is itself a form of love and union with God.[9] Now this is an important aspect of John's teaching, because if negation is directed toward freeing us to love, then love is the very essence of negation, since it is only love that liberates us. It is both the fruit of a love relationship with the Lord and also the way love manifests itself concretely.

There are three aspects of negation as a form of love and union with God we need to reflect upon. The first is that the whole process of maturation in love is born, as I said before, from a personal experience of God's love who takes the initiative and wounds us with love. Love is a response to a gift. In the first book of the *Ascent of Mount Carmel,* John analyzes the condition of the person enslaved by attachments and inordinate desires, and he tells us that the journey toward union with God entails a complete mortification of our inordinate desires and attachments (A, 1, 11, 6). We can easily become discouraged in reading that union with God and others requires a total renunciation of all our addictions, attachments and inordinate desires. However, John is very realistic and human. He is fully aware that this transformation process can only begin with a conscious experience of God's love that fires our will so we can do our part in liberating the heart from the obstacles to love. After having explained fully the extent of interior freedom from attachments God asks of us, John writes these consoling words:

> A more intense enkindling of another, better love (love of the soul's Bridegroom) is necessary for the vanquishing of the appetites and the denial of this pleasure. By finding satisfaction and strength in this love, it will have the courage and constancy to readily deny all other appetites. The love of its Bridegroom is not the only requisite

for conquering the strength of the sensitive appetites; an enkindling with urgent longings love is also necessary. (A, 1, 14, 2)

John knows that the only way we can begin to do our part in letting go of the false gods, attachments, and selfish patterns that keep us from loving according to the Gospel demands is the love of Jesus Christ and an ardent desire to respond to his love. God works with us according to the natural mode of human nature (A, 2, 17, 3-4). God knows that we would never undertake this path without a sense of God's love. It takes a greater love to conquer the obstacles to love. It takes, as John writes, "an enkindling of love for the Beloved." The same principle is at work in human love. When we love another person and then become aware of our need to control or dominate, or the selfish ways in which we relate to that person, what empowers us to begin to surrender these destructive tendencies is the love we feel for that person. When I love another I have the strength to let go of those things within me that harm our relationship. How else could a young married couple begin the renunciation process demanded by the intimate relationship of marriage without the *eros* of love? It is the same with God.

However, John's teaching may leave some of us perplexed. Perhaps we have never felt an "enkindling of love" for Christ the Bridegroom in any sensible manner. Yes, we love Christ; we seek God through prayer, but we have never felt that wound of love in any deep, vivid way. Quite the contrary, we experience the darkness of faith, struggle, and poverty.

Well, God wounds us in many ways. Some people begin their spiritual journey with a profound sense of God's love accompanied by ardent desires to love God in return. For others, God wounds them in other ways. For instance, through the love of another a person may enter into relationship with God. Still others, experience it through some illness or hardship that wakes them up and they begin to take their relationship with God seriously. This happened to a friend of mine who contracted viral encephalitis. He came out of the illness with a deep sense of God's presence in his life that initiated an intense search for God. Therefore, God wounds us in many ways. But the important element John teaches is that self-denial is born from an experience of being wounded by God's love.

The second aspect of negation as a form of love and union with God concerns an essential element of John's understanding of love. For John of the Cross, love is not some romantic, self-gratifying experience which leaves us in the clouds, nor is it an ephemeral feeling. Rather, love involves a process of conversion, of transcending one's own ego, of giving one's life for the Beloved. Love is a self-emptying process. "To love is to labor to divest and deprive oneself for God of all that is not God" (A, 2, 5, 6). As M. Scott Peck writes in *The Road Less Traveled*, love is self-disciplined. "If I truly love another, I will obviously order my behavior in a such a way as to contribute the utmost to his or her spiritual growth."[10] As a sign of my love, I will try to make those changes in my life that deepen and further the other's good as well as my own. In his own unique way, John teaches the same truth.

Stanza 3 of the *Spiritual Canticle* contains important teaching on John's notion of self-denial as a form of love. John says that many desire God. They say they long to love and serve God, but they don't want their desire for God to cost them anything (C, 3, 2). They won't even rise from a place of their liking, if they were not to receive some delight from God in their mouth and heart. They will not take one step to mortify their selfishness and to surrender some their useless desires and false securities. "But unless they rise up from the bed of their own satisfaction, and go in search of God, they will not find God, no matter how much they cry out" (ibid.).

> Those who seek God and yet want to find their own satisfaction and rest seek him at night and thus will not find him. Those who look for him through the practice and works of the virtues and get up from the bed of their own satisfaction and delight seek him by day and thus will find him. (C, 3, 3)

Love, therefore, is more a verb for John than a noun. It expresses itself by the self-discipline of actively seeking God through a life of prayer, service, growth in patience, generosity and the other virtues, and dying to selfishness. John gives concrete examples of the type of death to self that incarnates love: surrendering the need for selfish gratification and consolations in prayer and ministry, overcoming one's fears of what others may think of us if we earnestly follow the spiritual path, courageously facing the struggle of temptation and of integrating the dark side of our lives. For John, these are not simply the means that prepare us for love, but rather the concrete signs of maturing love. As the saying goes, "Love is as love does."[11]

The final element of negation as a form of love and union with God is that the more one's love grows the more one's heart becomes concentrated on the Beloved, and as a natural corollary, whatever impedes the growth of love or attention to the Beloved, or whatever is superfluous to this love, simply falls away. In this sense, detachment in St. John of the Cross is a natural outcome of an ever deepening and concentrated love of God. Negation has nothing to do with a depreciation of material or spiritual goods, other relationships, having fun, or created reality. It is about a relationship of love, of making an option for Jesus Christ the Beloved. John of the Cross was an ardent lover of God and his whole message is to make God the love and the center of our lives because we exist for Love, for God, who is the fulfillment of all human existence and who offers us the fullness of life, love, and happiness. He maintains that the more we are "won over to love," the more we concentrate our love and attention on God and God's reign, the more our attachments, selfishness, useless desires, and even very good but superfluous things, will fall away as a result. This is the mystery of Love that by its very nature transforms and frees us. He expresses this beautifully in stanza 29 of the *Spiritual Canticle.*

> The soul, indeed, lost to all things and won over to love, no longer occupies her spirit in anything else. She even withdraws in matters pertinent to the active life and other exterior exercises for the sake of fulfilling of the one thing the Bridegroom said was necessary [Lk 10:42], and that is: attentiveness to God and the continual exercise of love in him. (C, 29, 1)

We find this in everyday life and relationships. Psychologists such as Rollo May, Erich Fromm, and M. Scott Peck tell us that the principle work of love is attention or concentration on the one we love. When we love another, we give that person our full attention. This implies a setting aside of other preoccupations and concerns without in anyway disparaging them.[12] Individuals marry and things within their lives change that people think would never change. Other relationships and pastimes no longer take precedence. Their attention is on their beloved. Someone studies for a degree or sets out on the path for some spiritual quest or truth, and other material concerns, distractions, relationships pale into insignificance because one is lovingly attentive to the object of one's search.

An important element of this loving attention to God concerns our relationship to supernatural communications, consolations, and ideas about God. John reminds us over and over again in his writings that we must be very careful about such spiritual phenomena because God cannot be captured by spiritual consolations, ideas, images, or spiritual communications. Not only does God live in the depths of our being but God is also transcendent and far exceeds anything we can feel, think of, or imagine. John counsels us to renounce such phenomena. In the *Ascent of Mount Carmel* he writes:

> To reach this essential union of love of God, a person must be careful not to lean upon imaginative visions, forms, figures, or particular ideas, since they cannot serve as a proportionate and proximate means for such an effect; they would be a hindrance instead. As a result a person should renounce them and endeavor to avoid them. The only reason to admit and value them would be the profit and good effect the genuine ones bring to the soul....
> The eyes of the soul, then, should be ever withdrawn from distinct, visible, and intelligible apprehensions. Such elements are pertinent to sense and provide no security or foundation for faith. Its eyes should be fixed on the invisible, on what belongs not to sense but to spirit, and on what, as it is not contained in a sensible figure, brings the soul to union with God in faith.... (A, 2, 16, 10 & 12)

When John instructs us to renounce visions, ideas, spiritual consolations, and images concerning God he is not undermining or discrediting these phenomena, but he is telling us to love God for God, not for God's gifts. We may have beautiful thoughts about God, or God may give us consolations and spiritual delight. To cling to these or to go to prayer for this type of experience is self-seeking and manifests a lack of faith and respect for God as a person. We must receive consolation with gratitude but without clinging. John would have us respect God as a Person and not use God for the ideas and delights we may get from God. If we love a person just because the person gives us gifts, what type of relationship is that? It remains superficial. It is the same with God.[13] Self-denial, therefore, as a form of loving attention to God means loving God for who God is, not for God's gifts. This applies not only to God but to our relationship with creation, material goods, other people. Negation, therefore, implies a deeper respect for God which leads to "deeper communion" with God, other people and the world. When we love people for who they are there is a deeper relationship.[14] We love freely, with respect, without the desire to possess, control, or dominate. As a result, our union and appreciation grows. To do otherwise is against that loving attentiveness to God as Person that love requires.

This loving attention to God that grows ever deeper brings about an emptiness of self that leads to a fullness of life in Christ and freedom for the Kingdom of God. It leads us to lose ourselves in order to be found. John writes in stanza 29 of the *Canticle:*

> If, then, I am no longer
> seen or found on the common,
> you will say that I am lost;
> that, stricken by love,
> I lost myself, and was found.

John explains what it means to lose oneself and be found. To be lost is to be so much in love with Christ that we proclaim his Gospel without fear of what others might think (C, 29, 7). To be lost is to be so "stricken by love" that we forget ourselves and our own security and concentrate only on the Beloved and his affairs. To be lost is to be so taken up with the love of God and neighbor that we no longer seek our own selfish gain but live for love alone. To be lost is to live in the Beloved. In being lost this way, we find our true self in Christ. This is freedom to love.

Isn't this what happened to Gonzalo, John's father? For the love of Catalina he lost all things, all false security, his reputation, honor, wealth, comfort, and family. As a result of his loving attention on his beautiful bride, all things fell away, but in that he found his true self; and we for our part, reap the fruit of his loving negation, that is, we have John of the Cross, the "doctor of divine love," who teaches how to love freely by giving ourselves over to Love. All the rest will fall into place with God's grace and good time.

> The one who walks in the love of God seeks neither gain nor reward, but seeks only to lose with the will all things and self for God; and this loss the lover judges to be a gain.... The soul that does not know how to lose herself does not find herself but rather loses herself, as Our Lord teaches in the Gospel: *Those who desire to gain their soul shall lose it, and those who lose it for my sake shall gain it* [Mt 16:25].
> (C, 29, 11)

Negation in the works of St. John of the Cross, therefore, is essentially a gospel path of love. It is born out of an experience of being loved by God and is a response to God's invitation to live in union with God, others, and all creation. In this sense, it is a loving attentiveness to God as the source and center of our lives without in any way disparaging or denying anything created. It is dynamic self-giving love, exemplified in the life of Jesus, leading to self-transcendence and freedom. Negation is growing free to love.

> Take God for your bridegroom and friend, and walk with him continually; and you will not sin and will learn to love, and the things you must do will work out prosperously for you. (*Sayings of Light and Love*, 68)

Sum of Perfection

Olivido de lo criado,	Forgetfulness of created things,
memoria del Criador,	remembrance of the Creator,
atencion a lo interior,	attention turned toward inward things,
y estarse amando al Amado.	and loving the Beloved.

NOTES

1. Crisógono de Jesús, *Vida de San Juan de la Cruz* (Madrid: Biblioteca de Autores Cristianos, 1982), 14-16. See also Federico Ruiz, et al., *God Speaks in the Night*, trans. Kieran Kavanaugh (Washington, DC: ICS Publications, 1991), 3-10.
2. Crisógono de Jesús, *Vida de San Juan de la Cruz*, 15.
3. *God Speaks in the Night*, 26-28.
4. In the 1991 revised Kavanaugh/Rodriguez translation, the *Maxims* are included with the *Sayings of Light and Love* and renumbered accordingly. This particular maxim now appears as 115, on p. 93. Also, in this article, "Romances" refers to John's series of poems sometimes known as the "Romances on the Gospel text: *In principio erat Verbum,*" the heading of the first section.
5. See Frederico Ruiz (Salvador), *Introducción a San Juan de la Cruz* (Madrid: Biblioteca de Autores Cristianos, 1968), 415.
6. See Frederico Ruiz (Salvador), *Mistico y maestro: San Juan de la Cruz* (Madrid: Editorial de Espiritualidad, 1986), 87.
7. Examples of this "childishness" or "base manner of loving" can be found in the chapters where John describes the imperfections of beginners in the first book of the *Dark Night*, chapters 1-7.

8. See Frederico Ruiz, *Mistico y maestro,* 90-91.

9. Ibid., 89.

10. M. Scott Peck, *The Road Less Traveled* (New York, NY: Simon and Schuster, 1978), 155.

11. Ibid., 120.

12. Ibid., 120-121. See also Erich Fromm, *The Art of Loving* (New York, NY: Harper and Brothers, 1956), 108-109.

13. See Frederico Ruiz, *Mistico y maestro,* 94.

14. Ibid., 87, 94.

FAITH AND THE EXPERIENCE OF GOD IN THE UNIVERSITY TOWN OF BAEZA

Kieran Kavanaugh, O.C.D.

Kieran Kavanaugh is former chair of the Institute of Carmelite Studies, and a member of the Carmelite Forum. He is the author of numerous articles, translator of God Speaks in the Night: The Life Times and Teaching of St. John of the Cross, *as well as translator (with Otilio Rodriguez) of* The Collected Works of St. Teresa of Avila *and* The Collected Works of St. John of the Cross, *all available from ICS Publications. This article is based on a talk originally delivered at a conference on John of the Cross at Notre Dame, IN, in 1991.*

When John of the Cross escaped from his prison in Toledo in 1579, he was near death. For over a month he convalesced secretly in a hospital in that same city. Eager to get on with his life, he then insisted, against the advice of others, on leaving the hospital. His superiors, concerned for his safety, sent him south to the ebullient Andalusia where he could live without fear of being recaptured. There, John began another phase of his Carmelite life. He soon found himself in positions where he had to make greater use of his many gifts, those of mystic, poet, and spiritual director; theologian as well, and superior and builder of monasteries.

ASCETICISM

Assigned to El Calvario, a small, poor monastery in the wonderful, solitary mountains of Jaén, he discovered that the friars there, led by their previous superior, were identifying religious life with a life of physical penance. They seemed to be vying with one other on how much bodily deprivation and misery they could inflict upon themselves and

48

endure. They took seriously St. Paul's words in 1 Corinthians 9:27: "I punish my body and bring it into subjection."

St. Teresa's vivid descriptions of the asceticism of St. Peter of Alcántara provide a good example of this approach: "He told me that for forty years he slept only an hour and a half during the night and that in the beginning this was his greatest penitential trial, to conquer sleep, and that to do this he was always on his knees or standing. When he did sleep, he did so sitting up, with his head resting on a little log nailed to the wall" (L, 27, 17). She goes on to tell that he used to try to see how long he could go without eating. Her concluding remark neatly sums it all up: "it seemed he was made of nothing but tree roots" (L, 27, 18).

John of the Cross surely suffered severe bodily deprivation in his prison experience, more than any of the tough ascetics of those days inflicted on themselves. To help himself endure he fell back on his earlier education in the humanities and turned to poetry, composing his great poem, the *Cántico Espiritual* or "Spiritual Canticle." The verses sing about the way to seek God. "All your good and hope is so close to you as to be within you," John later wrote in his commentary of the same name. "You must seek him as hidden in faith and love.... Faith and love will lead you along a path unknown to you, to the place where God is hidden" (C, 1, 7 & 11). His theory was developing that bodily penances could never come near achieving the sanctity that only faith and love could bring about in purifying and uniting the soul with God.

John concluded quickly that these friars in the solitude of El Calvario were looking for salvation by an asceticism of dogged bodily penance. They were, perhaps implicitly, seeking a feeling of superiority and control through their penances. Only faith and love, through the poverty of spirit they create, can give a person the freedom necessary to follow the promptings of God's Spirit. But before discussing further John's understanding of this faith and love, some historical background is helpful.

SALAMANCA

A few months after John arrived in El Calvario, his superiors stepped in again and appointed him to found a monastery in the university town of Baeza, so that young Carmelites entering the new communities in the south of Spain could have a suitable place to undertake the studies required for ordination.

Entering Baeza must have brought back memories to John. Some fourteen years before, as a young Carmelite, he beheld for the first time the splendid university town of Salamanca in Castile. He had come to that city in its moment of glory to study philosophy and theology. The university of Salamanca had inherited the best qualities of the great medieval tradition. Bologna, Oxford, Paris, and Salamanca were centers of learning that inspired respect, even awe, throughout Europe.[1]

For almost a century the Carmelites had maintained in Salamanca a house of studies for philosophy and theology to take advantage of the classes and facilities of the university. Their house was situated in the lower part of the city, outside the walls, adjacent to the Dominican college of San Esteban. What a contrast there was between the small, rickety building of the Carmelites and the splendid Dominican monastery!

Salamanca was rich in culture and art, with magnificent examples of Romanesque and Gothic architecture bringing out the growth and dominance of Renaissance and Plateresque art. In fact there is an old saying, "In Salamanca, the museum is on the street." One of the marvels of this "museum" is the facade of San Esteban's, the Dominican monastery church, in classic Plateresque style. Its luster was a fitting accompaniment to the theological brilliance that the sons of St. Dominic brought to Salamanca. In John's time the Dominican monastery housed 200 students.

By contrast, the Carmelite monastery was so fragile that it collapsed in the St. Polycarp flood of 1626. There were no prominent Carmelite theologians at Salamanca, and there were only about twenty friars in the monastery, a mere eleven of them being students. Among this insignificant group, amid the 6,000 students attending the university, was the small and in many ways almost unnoticeable Fray Juan de Santo Matía, as John of the Cross was then called.

JOHN'S CRISIS

It did not take long, however, for John's superiors to recognize the sharp mind of this little friar, and perhaps to conjecture on the renown he could bring them as a university professor at Salamanca. Some said that in intellectual acumen he could have easily outshone the best at Salamanca. But this "little Seneca," as St. Teresa used to refer to him, was silently undergoing a vocation crisis.

In the past, historians have implied, if not actually stated, that the crisis stemmed from the laxity of the Carmelites he lived with, and that it was for this reason that John wanted to join the Carthusians. The problem with this explanation is that the Carmelites in Castile were not lax; this is evident from the latest research.[2]

John's crisis may well have sprung instead from the academic world, a crisis many have had to deal with. Perhaps he suffered a severe conflict between the task of theological speculation, for which he had a talent, and the mystical tendency that was inwardly pressing him to respond with total commitment to his contemplative vocation.

In his surroundings, there was the usual competitiveness, and many students set titles, promotions, offices, and professorships as their primary goal in life. Doctorates, contention over university chairs and promotion to them—everything had a public feature about it, celebrated with ornate parades, regional folklore, and bull runs on the main square. This competition for titles and professorships revealed the misguided priorities of many of his contemporaries. In his *Ascent of Mount Carmel,* John was later to write that when we give first place to such values as titles and positions, our relationship with God becomes darkened and our intellects clouded. This in turn leads to pride and a scornful attitude toward others; to flattery and vain praise, which conceal deception and vanity; to rivalries and quarrels (see A, 3, 19, 3; 22, 2-3). In his well-known chapter 7 in book 2 of the *Ascent,* he reveals his feelings when he complains that people of extensive learning and high repute, anxious about their rank, too often do not even know Christ (A 2, 7, 12).

St. Teresa, too, who certainly never hid her esteem for people of learning, had some complaints along the same line as John. Even monasteries did not escape the struggle for honors. "People," she noted, "ascend and descend in rank just as in the world." A professor of theology would consider it an affront if asked to teach philosophy. "And there will always be someone standing by to defend him and tell him that it's an insult" (W, 36, 4).

Of course, these human failings are found in most settings, and John's desire for more recollection, to go off and concentrate on the contemplative life in the quiet of the Charterhouse, may suggest his own inexperience and lack of integration at the time.[3]

The clash between spirituality and theological discourse shows its face in some poignant words from the Castilian Franciscan reformer Pedro de Villacreces: "St Francis often asserted that knowledge would be the downfall of the Order. And I learned more in my cell weeping in darkness than studying by candlelight at Salamanca, Tolouse, or Paris."[4]

But St. Teresa, as is well known, suffered much from spiritual directors who had not integrated learning with their spiritual lives (see C, 5, 1, 8). She probably would have admired Villacreces but not felt satisfied with him.[5] When John met Teresa before he had completed his studies at Salamanca, he found in her a deep contemplative spirit, at the same time desirous and capable of embracing many outward struggles for the Lord. She offered him inspiration but also the opportunity to follow her contemplative ideals and escape from the atmosphere of Salamanca, without having to leave the Carmelite order.

BAEZA

To return now to Baeza, at the time of John's arrival there in 1579 (after his escape from Toledo and brief assignment in El Calvario), it was a town of nearly the same population as Salamanca, with about 25,000 inhabitants.[6] Like the Montagues and the Capulets in *Romeo and Juliet*, two 15th century families, the Benavides and the Carvajales, forming two factions and backed by their respective followers, had converted the city into a violent battlefield. Only the preaching and efforts of St. John of Avila ("Juan de Avila" in Spanish) were able to quell somewhat this social discord.

In addition to his many other activities, John of Avila founded the University of Baeza in 1538. In prestige it was certainly no Salamanca, but Baeza did have an interesting personality of its own, infused by its founder. With a pastoral orientation, it was integrated into society. This integration began at the lowest level, with a school for children. Nurtured by John of Avila, the children's school actually began operating before the university. Along with reading (in Latin as well as the vernacular), the children learned writing, arithmetic, and Christian doctrine.

The presence of these schools in the city was a spirited one. The children assisted in the churches and at burials, and they enlivened the processions, above all the most popular and splendid one on the feast of Corpus Christi. St. John of Avila had composed a catechism in rhyme so that it could be sung in the streets. At least every Sunday, the children went about the streets and squares singing Christian doctrine as a permanent catechesis and sermon for others.

The faculty of arts (which included the humanities and philosophy) and the faculty of theology were the only two faculties that the university of Baeza had at the time; Salamanca also had faculties in canon law, civil law, medicine, and languages. At the university in Baeza, no degrees in theology were conferred without previous practice by the candidates in preaching, catechesis, and giving missions.

An incident recorded in John of Avila's life reveals much about this pastoral orientation: Diego Pérez de Valdivia, who had the lecture at Prime, would interrupt his class without the least problem when informed that there were many people in the marketplace shocking others by their bad example. Ordering the beadle to ring the bell, he and all the students would rush into the streets singing Christian doctrine until arriving in the market square. There the professor would mount the platform of the town criers and begin his fiery sermon. When the crowd was reduced to tears and sighs, the university people, singing their song, would march back to the campus.

Almost all of the professors at the university were cleric disciples of St. John of Avila; they all loved the pulpit, and in their teaching gave a prominent place to preparing for this ministry.

The fact is, then, that Baeza in John of the Cross's time was a city living in a permanent atmosphere of religious enthusiasm. Children shouting or singing the catechism through the streets, preachers declaiming their loud, ostentatious sermons anywhere and everywhere. Dominating the city were churches, monasteries, and shrines. In fact, one of John of the Cross's companions noted that all that was needed for Baeza to be a monastery was to keep the gates of the city closed.

RECOGIDOS AND BEATAS

Apart from the many priests, friars, and nuns were a host of *recogidos*. Recogidos were those who practiced the prayer of recollection. Women who lived in their houses and devoted themselves to this recollection were called "beatas." It was they in great numbers who nurtured this form of life.

Some historians have asserted that the number of beatas could have reached 2,000. Exaggerations aside, beatas were everywhere. The large number was perhaps due to the obligatory celibacy imposed by the emigration of men to the Indies. It was due also to a certain economic independence made possible through the employment of many in the textile industry.

The beatas had their own entourage of devotees, confessors, and admirers. In the presence of such groups they made their vow of chastity and narrated their spiritual experiences. Confessors often urged them, at least indirectly, to think that the stranger and more flamboyant their austerities, graces in prayer, struggles with the demon, and diabolical possessions, the better.

BILCHES'S DESCRIPTION

There is an interesting description of the beatas in Francisco Bilches's work on saints and shrines in the dioceses of Jaén and Baeza:

> The women lived recollected in their own houses, in a room set apart, weighed down with hairshirts and garments of rough wool, without anything more satisfying than some bread and herbs earned through their own manual work, even though some of them were from rich backgrounds and the highest nobility in the city.... They spoke seldom, and then only out of necessity; they prayed a great deal, almost without ceasing, day and night; they did not leave their houses except on feast days for the purpose of hearing Mass, confessing their sins, and receiving communion, without waiting to receive compliments or signs of courtesy, or to visit with others, as though they were dead to the world. In this way they spent their lives in voluntary poverty, obedience to their spiritual fathers, and in angelic purity. These were the *beatas* of those times, daughters of the Holy Master Avila.... Many of them lived a life more admirable than imitable. Baeza at that time attained such perfection that its inhabitants seemed very much like the Christians of the early Church.[7]

VALDIVIA'S ADVICE

Professor Pérez de Valdivia, in a book of advice for people practicing recollection entitled *Aviso de gente recogida* (Barcelona, 1585), is a good source of information about the kind of spirituality in vogue among these groups. Undoubtedly he wrote the book with Baeza and its beatas in mind. In the following words he addresses and exhorts them:

> I ask and warn these brides of Jesus Christ...that they earnestly beg him not to give them visions, revelations, raptures, transports, or anything similar that would make them stand out among the others.... And if nevertheless he should give them some of these ex-

traordinary experiences, they should hold them suspect and never feel safe about them but always think that some bad snare is or may be lurking there, and they should in no way make it known to anyone among the people. Ecstasy and other graces of the sort, even supposing they are authentically supernatural—which is supposing very much—can engender spiritual pride.... The recipients can begin to think that others do not have any spirituality, or not as much as they themselves, and that the Spirit of God is governing them while others are being governed by their learning or pure human reason.... Recollected people should understand that sanctity consists mainly in self-denial, taking up one's cross, in being meek and humble and in serving one's neighbor and practicing the works of mercy and charity. I have come into contact with many people who have experiences of this sort.[8]

Valdivia then goes on to say that, even when these ecstasies, visions, and revelations are authentic, they make him wary because the person is rare who can deal with them prudently and humbly.

DOCTOR HUARTE

A doctor from Baeza (1529-1588), an esteemed physician named Juan Huarte, gives some interesting counsel in his book on discernment of spirits, *El Examen de Ingenios*. His advice is closer to the spirit of the Enlightenment than to the credulity of his times. With scientific criteria and biblical support, he sought to uncover the natural causes of spiritual phenomena, especially the many ecstasies and revelations that stirred the emotions of the people in those years.

With regard to preachers Huarte notes:

The preacher by the force of his imagination, allied with the memory, is capable of speaking for one and even two hours in succession, enchanting and holding his listeners in suspense.... They do not use their intellects, which is the faculty by which one verifies whether a spirit is Catholic or depraved. Through an excess of imagination and rhetoric, and a lack of scholastic theology, those in Northern Europe fell into error and corrupted the people.[9]

Huarte's golden rule was that we should not seek from God or attribute to him what can be done through secondary causes. He insisted that God rules the world, but that his doing so doesn't imply a miraculous or

preternatural intervention; God ordinarily lets secondary causes do
their work. He complained about the growing interest in raptures and
revelations, and attributed the public raptures and revelations of the
beatas to their empty stomachs. At times he sounds so much like St. John
of the Cross that one would be inclined to think that he influenced John
with passages like the following:

> The common people do not know that God does natural and
> prodigious works to show those who are unaware of it that he is
> omnipotent, and that he uses these as an argument to confirm his
> teaching and that when this is not needed, he never performs them.
> This becomes manifest if we consider that he no longer performs
> those singular works that he did in the New and Old Testaments.
> And that is why he made every effort possible so that people could
> not claim ignorance as an excuse. And to think that he will turn to
> arguing again with new miracles so as to prove anew his doctrine is a
> great error. For God teaches what humanity needs to know once,
> and he proves it with miracles; and he does not repeat: *Semel Deus
> loquitur, et secundo idipsum non repetit* (God speaks once, and never
> repeats it a second time).[10]

THE TEACHING OF JOHN OF THE CROSS

Though it is even possible that he knew Doctor Huarte personally,
John of the Cross had more to offer the beatas than a warning about
pride and empty stomachs. In fact, he strongly encouraged them along
the path of recollection they were following. But first, if God teaches
once that which humanity needs to know, as Dr. Huarte affirmed, where
do we find this teaching? John of the Cross would direct us to the Bible,
where he searched for and found truth. He points out in his prologues
that Scripture is his guide and that the Holy Spirit speaks to us through
it. So familiar had he become with the Bible that some of those who
knew him claimed he knew it by heart. Whatever we may think of that,
he was a contemplative by vocation and was taught in the Carmelite Rule
to meditate on God's word and to love it—in contrast to much post-
Tridentine Catholic spirituality—and to use it in lectio divina as the way
into God's mystery. In the Bible, John discovered the true face of God,
and he discovered as well his own destiny as a human being.

Now when John wrote the *Ascent of Mount Carmel,* he was drawing
upon his experience in Baeza. He recognized the bad results of contem-

plative living without sound theological grounding, as did St. Teresa previously.[11] Using his theological, philosophical, and literary background, he started to explain the process of divinization, pointing out the mistakes being made by many of the practitioners of recollection. In book 2, chapter 22 of the *Ascent*, in a vein similar to Dr. Huarte's, John writes: "In giving us his Son, his only Word (for he possesses no other), [the Father] spoke everything to us at once in this sole Word—and he has no more to say." Or again, a few sentences later, he says: "Hear him because I have no more faith to reveal or truths to manifest" (A, 2, 22, 3 & 5).

How can John, speaking for the Father, say "I have no more *faith* to reveal?" This is to equate faith with Christ the Word. When John speaks this way he is identifying faith with its content, and so speaking of faith's object, what the scholastics called the material object.

Christ and Faith

In this same chapter (A, 2, 22), we also find, relative to faith's object, the key to John's interpretation of Scripture. God spoke to us definitively, says John, when he spoke Christ, his Word. Everything that he spoke before Christ "through words, visions, and revelations, sometimes through many types and figures, at other times through many other kinds of signs" was for the sake of the promise, who is Christ. By turning to Christ, we find what was incomplete now complete.

Looking at this another way, we can say that Christ is also the personal, active Subject of the revelation, before being the passive object of our search. It is he who first looks at us, loves us, and speaks, offering us his friendship.

If faith is Christ, and he is the answer to all the longings and petitions of the people in the Old Law and in him we obtain every good, then there must be something about faith that would draw us. But Christ, our risen Lord, is not seen by us. How can we be drawn by him? This brings us to the believer, or the subject of faith.

The aspect John heavily underscores in speaking of the subject of faith is "darkness." The reason behind his insistence on darkness lies in his experience of contemplation, which he also calls faith. Faith is a "dark night" for a human being, and so is contemplation.

Why is this so? Because their content, who is Christ the Light, shines like the blinding sun, and, in John's words, "so obscures all other lights that they do not seem to be lights at all when it is shining" (A, 2, 3, 1).

The comparison of faith to a light was taken from the analogy the scholastics and others used in speaking of human knowledge, in which understanding was like seeing by means of light, and this light was the intellect.

The Symbols of Faith

The symbols John selects in speaking of faith usually suggest his fascination with its obscure character. Faith is a "dark night," a "dark cloud," "dark water," a "blind person's guide." He leans toward the quotation from St. Paul's Letter to the Romans (Rom 10:17) that faith comes through hearing, and so not by sight (see A, 2, 3, 3). In the Old Testament, John noticed, whenever God communicated at length with someone, he appeared in darkness: after Solomon finished the temple, God filled it with darkness; appearing to to Moses on Mount Sinai, God was covered with darkness; he spoke to Job from the dark air (A, 2, 9, 3).

There is paradox here: the dark cloud illumines. "How wonderful it was: A cloud, dark in itself, could illumine the night! This was related to illustrate how faith, a dark and obscure cloud to souls...illumines and pours light into their darkness by means of its own darkness" (A, 2, 3, 5).

Faith involves communication between God and the human person. The object of faith, Christ the blinding light, is also a Subject who communicates a loving knowledge, pours light into the person, who is blinded by the reception of the light. In varying degrees, there is always this darkness in the receiver of God's communication.

This symbolism of light and darkness does not explain all the aspects of faith, but John of the Cross's main interest in speaking of faith was its capacity for uniting us immediately with God. To put it another way, faith is the proximate means to divine union. John's own mystical experience of faith and its dynamism was certainly a source for his teaching.

Faith and Love

The articles of faith, expressed in the Creed and coming to us through hearing in explicit propositions, are like veils covering the light, or like silver plating that covers the gold, according to John of the Cross. Our assent of faith does not arise out of any light of understanding that we have of the articles, but by bringing our intellects into submission.

Submitting in faith, surrendering ourselves to what we hear, we are carried into God.

Faith, then, is never for John a matter of intellect alone, but an activity of the whole person. Now since a person cannot submit in faith by reason of what is understood, many a theologian has raised the question of how we can defend this submission to God that takes place in darkness, without seeing.[12] Why should anyone enter this dark night, this cloud, this dark water? For John the answer would lie in who God is. We know who he is through Christ, who is Truth, Goodness, and Beauty.

When Christ, seeking our friendship, communicates the light of faith, which is himself, one is secretly and mysteriously drawn to him. When John speaks of faith, he is not excluding love. The theological virtues may be analyzed separately, but in the life of the believer they are so interconnected that where the one is present the others are also (see A, 2, 24, 8; 29, 5-6; 3, 1, 1).

Love is an indispensable factor in the life of faith. God's activity in Jesus Christ cannot be accepted first of all by the mind (in belief), in order to elicit then a corresponding return of love. Faith receives the mystery and becomes certain of it to the degree in which it affirms the mystery in love.

Dynamism of Faith

Faith is not static, an act we make now and then. As Walker Percy has tried to show in his novels, we human beings are best described as wayfarers or pilgrims. John of the Cross gave his teaching for the wayfarer. He envisioned this life of faith in us as a journey, a pilgrimage. One's loving belief in God's love enfleshed in Jesus Christ is not strictly speaking merely a repeated act. Loving belief is a way of progressing, as on a journey from one extreme to the opposite.

Comparing God's grace to a ray of light that penetrates into the deep caverns of our darkness, John of the Cross observes that with the experience of this light comes the desire for more light. This faint light in the abyss of the soul calls to another abyss of light and is not satisfied until it is transformed into that light (see F, 3, 71).[13]

The journey is through a night into an abyss of light. One begins with a faint illumination, moving away from the world in which we live (A, 1, 2, 5). This does not mean physical separation from the physical world. The world John of the Cross was thinking of is the one found in

1 John 2:16: "the concupiscence of the eyes, the concupiscence of the flesh, and the pride of life" (see A, 1, 13, 8). The world, in this sense, is a darkness that merely seems like a light. Only God's self-communication can draw us out of this darkness. But grace itself is darkness for us by reason of faith, a light strong enough to blind.

Faith may be said to be a journey in darkness toward light. John uses Hebrews 11:6 as a starting point: "Whoever would draw near God must believe that he exists." But he interprets this "drawing near" as moving toward union with God. He then explains:

> Those who want to reach union with God, you should advance neither by understanding, nor by the support of their own experience, nor by feeling or imagination, but by belief in God's being. For God's being cannot be grasped by the intellect, appetite, imagination, or any other sense; nor can it be known in this life. The most that can be felt and tasted of God in this life is infinitely distant from God and the pure possession of him. (A, 2, 4, 4)

This was the mistake of the beatas of Baeza. They thought their ecstasies, visions, and revelations were the journey's end. They gauged the quality of their spiritual lives by these phenomena, and felt no need of reason as an instrument of right thinking and action. They could find their answers in their revelations.

John urged them to press on and not stop on their journey. They must adapt in faith to the mode of God, who is simple and speaks his only word in simplicity and silence (F, 3, 34). In pure contemplation there is neither the discourse of Salamanca nor the visions of Baeza.

In urging us to journey to God in faith, then, John is reminding us that the mystery of God cannot be identified with our ideas or experiences. Our ideas and experiences ought to direct us to the mystery that always lies further ahead and is welcomed by a faith steeped in confidence and love. We do not reach the fulfillment of faith by overtaking it, or leaving it aside, or doing away with any of its characteristics, whether of object or subject.

Recollection in Faith

John's concern about the spiritual seekers in Baeza, despite their high religious ideals and their lifestyle centered in God, was that they were shortchanging themselves in their pursuit of particular lights from heaven. Even when authentic, as many of their experiences may have been, recollection in faith, John insists, is more fruitful. Particular lights may convey wisdom concerning a few truths; but through recollection in faith that does not stop in any particular idea or experience "all of God's Wisdom is communicated in general, that is, the Son of God, who communicates himself to the soul in faith" (A, 2, 29, 6-7). John does not urge them to go back to what some considered the safer ground of vocal or discursive prayer, but to go further into the recollection of faith. In the *Living Flame,* he has hard words for spiritual directors who opposed this quiet mode in prayer, erroneously thinking that contemplative prayer was the equivalent of illuminism, the "heresy" of the *alumbrados* (F, 3, 30-62).[14]

This illumination in faith has a transforming effect on its recipient, and in a mysterious way changes a person; after all, it is God's life in us. "In this faith," says John of the Cross, "God supernaturally and secretly teaches the soul and raises it up in virtues and gifts in a way unknown to it" (A, 2, 29, 7).

Rational Control and Reaction

It may well be true, also, that the atmosphere in Baeza was a reaction to the effort of authorities to control religious experience by keeping it within well-defined limits. This was one of the tasks the theologians of the Inquisition set out for themselves. As we learn from St. Teresa's accounts, a number of them distrusted interior recollection.

Today, science, technology and mass culture can also make people feel controlled and exploited. In the New Age movement we sometimes find practices similar to those used by the *recogidos* in Spain. There are meditation techniques that make one both more susceptible to suggestion and more likely to undergo spiritual experiences.[15] Furthermore, spiritual leaders can take advantage of people by using techniques that lead them into passive states and thereby make them more vulnerable to the leaders' suggestions.

John sees his way of faith as a protection against such deceptions for those practicing interior recollection. It frees them from the need to get involved in the complexities of discerning the authenticity or inauthenticity of their experiences.

Faith and Community

One final point about faith: we do not journey alone. We need at least one other friend. This is another important aspect of John of the Cross's approach to faith. As loving faith grows, rugged individualism in one's dealings with God decreases. The person of faith cannot be completely satisfied without human counsel and direction. Surprisingly, after all that we have said about his teaching on faith, John exalts human reason. He explains that "to declare and strengthen truth on the basis of natural reason, God draws near those who come together in an endeavor to know it." When we seek truth with others, the light of reason must be our guide.

Christian mystics, in John's thought, never reach a stage in which they move beyond the community of the Church. His norm is that "God will not bring clarification and confirmation of the truth to the heart of one who is alone" (A, 2, 22, 11). Trying to go it alone, we grow cold in faith. Two can communicate warmth to each other.

John demonstrates his thought here with different examples from Scripture. He marvels at how Paul after his exalted revelations of Christ felt he had to go and consult with Peter. And John becomes so moved by this that he forgets his readers and addresses Paul himself: "O Paul! Could not he who revealed the gospel to you also give security from any error you might make in preaching its truth?" (A, 2, 22, 12). Yet even when God does give an authentic revelation, John points out, there are still many aspects of it and related matters that we can know only within the community of the Church, and through the use of our own reasoning powers. John asserts firmly that all matters must be regulated by reason save those of faith, which transcend but are not contrary to reason (A, 2, 22, 13). We receive the faith from those who believed before us, and in faith we are supported by the whole community of believers. One always believes in and with the Church.[16]

Our wayfaring in faith is not without its difficulties, needs, and tests. Many times we get lost, or the community doesn't agree; things get muddled, and we don't know what to do. It would be nice in these cases to receive some direct revelation from above, or find someone else who receives one. But John again exhorts us to the use of reason. We must not look for answers through personal revelations. What do we do when our minds can not find a satisfying answer? When we cannot agree and do not know not what to do, he says, our recourse within the bounds of faith are prayer and hope that God will provide by the means he desires (A, 2, 21, 5). We can see here how closely united are faith, reason, recollection, and poverty of spirit.

To sum up, then, John of the Cross brought Salamanca and Baeza together: Christ's communication draws one to recollection in prayer, and this recollection is good when it is recollection in faith. Theology need not oppose this recollection, but should in fact lead to silent awe in this very recollection. The use of reason in theological discourse is a service to the community of faith, helping its members communicate Christ's mysteries with each other and make decisions in their wayfaring; the wayfaring is in faith and love toward God, who is always higher and deeper than anything we can reach. "Never pause to love and delight in your understanding and experience of God, but love and delight in what you cannot understand or experience of him. Such is the way...of seeking him in faith" (C, 1, 12).

NOTES

1. For further details on Salamanca and John's university years there, see chapter 3 in Federico Ruiz, et al., *God Speaks in the Night*, trans. Kieran Kavanaugh (Washington, DC: ICS Publications, 1991), 61-92.

2. See Joachim Smet, *The Carmelites* (Darien, IL: Carmelite Spiritual Center, 1976) 2:1-22.

3. See *God Speaks*, 82.

4. See *God Speaks*, 121. In the houses of Villacreces's reform an anti-intellectual spirituality was imposed: external, affective, abounding in ceremonies, devotions to the saints, and many hours of vocal prayer in common. See Daniel de Pablo Maroto, "La oración teresiana en su entorno histórico," *Teresa de Jesús* (January, 1984): 17-28.

5. Teresa often speaks glowingly of *letrados* (learned men), and she thinks they can be a great help even when they don't have experience of prayer themselves; see, for example, her *Life*, 13, 18.

6. See *God Speaks*, chap. 7, for further information on Baeza in John's day, especially Teófanes Egido's "Baeza and Its Spiritual Milieu," 216-220.

7. Francisco de Bilches, *Santos y Santuarios del obispado de Jaén y Baeza* (Madrid: García y Morrás, 1653), 170-171.

8. Valdivia, *Aviso de gente recogida* (Barcelona, 1585); published in Alvaro Huerga, *Historia de los Alumbrados: los Alumbrados de la Alta Andalucia (1575-1590)* (Madrid: Fundación Universitario Española, 1978), 383-384.

9. Huarte, *El Examen de Ingenios* (Madrid: Rodrigo Sanz, 1930), 220; see also Huerga, 356. John of the Cross likewise admits that a preacher's good style, gestures, and well-chosen words may be moving, that such sermons can please the senses and even the intellect, and that they can have an effect similar to a musical concert or sounding bells. But he thinks that such effects will all be soon forgotten unless there is a living spirit behind them capable of enkindling fire (see A, 3, 45, 4-5).

10. Huerga, 356-369.

11. Regarding Teresa's unfortunate experiences with unlearned confessors, see her *Life*, 5, 3; 13, 19; 25, 22.

12. See Walter Kasper, *Transcending All Understanding: The Meaning of Christian Faith Today* (San Francisco, CA: Ignatius Press, 1989), 7-76.

13. See also Ps 42:7 and Georg Muschalek, "Faith, Freedom and Certitude," in Avery Dulles, ed., *Toward a Theology of Christian Faith* (New York, NY: P. J. Kenedy & Sons, 1968), 199.

14. See Eulogio Pacho, "Escenario histórico de Juan de la Cruz: su entorno religioso-cultural," *El Monte Carmelo* 98 (1990): 225-241.

15. Because of this, for example, Dr. Herbert Benson, in his research with meditation techniques at Deaconess Hospital in Boston, tries to give people meditation techniques in keeping with their own religious background, for the major religious traditions usually have a sound body of doctrine to protect people from delusions that may result from inner passivity. See Herbert Benson, *Beyond the Relaxation Response* (New York, NY: Berkley Books, 1984), 5-6; Idem, *Your Maximum Mind* (New York, NY: Avon Books, 1987), 31-59.

16. See George Morel, *Le Sens de l'Existence selon St. Jean de la Croix*, vol. 1, (Paris: Editions Aubier Montaigne, 1960), 198-205.

QUALITIES OF A GOOD GUIDE: SPIRITUAL DIRECTION IN JOHN OF THE CROSS'S LETTERS

Kevin Culligan, O.C.D.

Kevin Culligan is a psychologist, a member of the Carmelite Forum and former chair of the Institute of Carmelite Studies. He is currently superior of the desert community of the Washington Province of Discalced Carmelites. He is the author of numerous articles, and editor of Spiritual Direction: Contemporary Readings *(Locust Valley, NY: Living Flame Press, 1983).*

On February 4, 1987, the American psychologist Carl R. Rogers died after a long and distinguished career as a psychotherapist, researcher, educator, and writer. He was 85. His professional interests ranged widely, but perhaps his most significant contribution to contemporary psychology was his work in understanding the psychotherapeutic relationship and determining the necessary and sufficient conditions under which people can be expected to change and grow in counseling and psychotherapy.

In this article, I review those qualities in a psychotherapist which Rogers maintained make for a good therapeutic relationship and promote positive personal growth in a client. Then I examine John of the Cross's letters of spiritual direction to demonstrate that these and other important personal qualities can be found in his spiritual direction ministry. Following this review and examination, I conclude with a suggestion for spiritual directors today.

THE THERAPEUTIC RELATIONSHIP

On the basis of his extensive practice and research, Rogers maintained that three qualities—genuineness, caring, and understanding—

must be present in a therapeutic relationship if positive change is to occur in a client. Assuming a person truly desires to change and grow, positive change and growth are predictable for that person when these qualities are present in the therapeutic relationship, regardless of the method of psychotherapy followed in the relationship—psychoanalysis, behavior therapy, client-centered counseling, rational-emotive therapy, or any of the other established therapies. On the other hand, if genuineness, caring, and understanding are absent in a therapeutic relationship, enduring positive change is not likely to occur in a person, regardless of the therapeutic method used, the fame of the therapist, or the time and money spent in the treatment.

Genuineness, the first quality, describes a condition in which therapists are being themselves as fully as possible in the therapeutic relationship. This means that the therapist is continually aware of what is happening within his or her own organism, especially attitudes and feelings that arise in the course of the relationship with the client. It involves, further, the ability to communicate this awareness to the client when it is appropriate to do so, particularly if the same attitudes and feelings persist in the course of their relationship. Genuineness in a therapist means, quite simply, being real with oneself and one's client.

Some years ago, I found myself frequently drowsy in the early stages of my work with a priest client. I had to fight hard to stay awake as he told me about his problems. After this had persisted for some weeks I finally said to him: "When were together, I have difficulty staying awake when you're talking. Maybe it's just me, or the hour, but I wonder too whether you're telling me what really bothers you the most?"

Hesitatingly, but noticeably reassured, my client acknowledged his avoiding telling me about the increasing frequency and strength of his homosexual impulses. When I asked why, he said he was afraid of what I might think of him. After some discussion about his fear of my opinion, we began discussing the meaning of his sexual urges.

From that point on, our meetings changed significantly. He talked about himself in a lower, more personal tone, more slowly, often groping for the words to express his troubled feelings. For my part, I was wide awake. It is hard to fall asleep when others tell you their deepest concerns. He felt reassured that I could recognize his resistances and help him through them to get to his real problem; but that meant my willingness to be honest both with myself and with him. My genuineness at that moment in our relationship helped to move our dialogue from surface exchange to a more intimate—and more therapeutic—interaction.

The second quality is caring. In his early work, Rogers called this "unconditional positive regard" and described it as an experience within the therapist of unqualified acceptance of the client as a person. Caring means prizing or valuing clients in all their uniqueness, with all their strengths and weaknesses, placing no conditions that they must fulfill to merit the therapist's esteem. Caring implies respectful, non-possessive, non-romantic love for persons just as they are. Rogers believed that New Testament *agape* best expresses what he meant by caring.

Understanding, the third quality, is an experience by the therapist of the client's inner world of meaning as if it were the therapist's own, but without losing the "as if" character of the experience. Understanding is the therapist's ability to see life as the client sees it, from his or her own internal frame of reference, to understand accurately and sensitively the experiences and feelings of the client and the meanings he or she attaches to them. A therapist's response, like "It saddens you that your father never really lived up to your expectations for him," conveys to the client that the therapist understood both the client's feeling of sadness as well as the meaning he or she gives to the feeling. Empathic understanding enables the therapist "to get inside the skin" of a client and "to walk in his or her own shoes for a while." It is to understand the client's subjective world as though it were the therapist's own.

Rogers insisted that genuineness, caring, and understanding must be real experiences within the therapist. You cannot fake them and hope thereby to be therapeutic. To pretend nonchalance when you are experiencing threat or discomfort with a client is not genuine; to pretend total acceptance when you are experiencing deep hostility toward a client is not caring; to formulate a diagnosis of a person based solely on psychological tests and intake interviews is not an experience of empathic understanding.

Moreover, the therapist must be able to communicate these experiences of genuineness, care, and understanding to the client, either verbally or nonverbally, and the client must be able to perceive them, at least to some minimal degree. Unless this experiencing, communicating, and perceiving are present in a therapeutic relationship, enduring positive change is not likely to occur in the client.

I once worked with a young physician who suffered from deep self-hatred. Very early in our relationship I was conscious of experiencing caring feelings for him; moreover, I believed I was accurately communicating to him my understanding of his inner world. However, his extreme low self-esteem blinded him to my experiences. Instead, he denied them, challenging them with statements like: "You care for me because I pay you to, not because you like me. And why should you? Why are you even interested in understanding me? No one else ever took the time to see how I really feel. Why are you any different, except that you get paid for it?"

Then one Saturday morning, after months of such struggle, he said: "I've been thinking a lot about us, and you know something? I think you really do care for me." Finally, he was beginning to perceive what I had been experiencing for months. As his ability to perceive my caring increased, his self-evaluation gradually become more positive, not dramatically so, but at least enough to provide hope for the continued strengthening of his self-concept.

INTERPERSONAL RELATIONSHIPS AND SPIRITUAL DIRECTION

Although Rogers derived his conclusions from his practice and research in psychotherapy, he soon realized the significance of genuineness, care, and understanding for other interpersonal relationships. These three qualities enhance human relationships everywhere—in friendship, family life, business and industry, government and international relations. They especially foster other professional helping relationships, such as patient care in medicine, pastoral ministry in the church, and teacher-student relations in education. Wherever these qualities are found in interpersonal relationships, and to the degree they are present, one can predict positive change and growth for those involved; where they are lacking, and to the degree they are lacking, dysfunction and breakdown in human relations can be anticipated.[1]

Spiritual direction—like psychotherapy, teaching, counseling, parenting, industrial relations and friendship—is an interpersonal, helping relationship. Rogers's findings would suggest that genuineness, caring, and understanding ought also to characterize good spiritual direction. And indeed these very qualities do appear in the spiritual direction of Saint John of the Cross, one of the world's most reliable spiritual guides, as we can see in his letters.

JOHN OF THE CROSS'S LETTERS

We have today only 33 letters, either whole or in part, from the pen of John of the Cross, covering a mere 28 pages in his *Collected Works.*[2] Ironically, the people who benefited the most from his spiritual guidance destroyed his other letters. St. Teresa of Jesus, for example, following a familiar practice, routinely destroyed letters after she answered them. That John wrote to Teresa may be seen in his July 6, 1581 letter to Catalina de Jesús, a discalced Carmelite nun in Palencia. This letter, the first in our present collection, was apparently included with another letter that John wrote to Teresa, for he says: "I…write these lines trusting that our Madre [Teresa] will send them on to you if you are not with her" (Letter 1, 736).

Teresa highly regarded John's skill as a director, stating that "our Lord has given him special grace for that purpose." In fact, he guided her own soul during a crucial period in her spiritual journey when they were both in Avila from 1572 to 1574. Forever after, she regarded him as "the father of my soul."[3] It is a lamentable loss to the history of spiritual direction that the correspondence between these great spiritual teachers has not survived.

More tragically still, the communities of Carmelite nuns in Granada, Málaga, and Sevilla, for whom John was a spiritual guide, burned his letters to protect against their falling into the hands of one of his fellow discalced Carmelite friars, Fray Diego Evangelista. Diego, retaliating for reprimands received years earlier when John was his religious superior, was determined to drive him from the Order during the last year of John's life on the grounds of indiscreet relationships with the Carmelite nuns.[4]

Nevertheless, the letters we do have were written during the last ten years of his life when he was at the height of his effectiveness as a spiritual director; some twenty of these can be considered letters of spiritual direction, to Carmelite friars and nuns (both individuals and communities) and laity. These letters reveal John's genuineness, caring, and understanding.

LETTERS TO MADRE LEONOR AND JUANA DE PEDRAZA

These three qualities appear in a fragment of John's letter to Madre Leonor de San Gabriel, a Carmelite nun in the convent of Córdoba who felt deeply misunderstood by her Father Provincial. John writes to her in the summer of 1590 from Madrid in these words:

> Jesus be in your soul, my daughter in Christ.
>
> In reading your letter *I felt sorry for you in your affliction, and I grieve over it* because of the harm it can do your spirit and even your health. *But you ought to know that I don't think you should be as afflicted as you are.* For I do not see in Our Father [Provincial] any kind of dissatisfaction with you or even any recollection of such a thing.... I certainly believe it is a temptation the devil brings to your mind so that what should be employed in God is taken up with this.
>
> *Be courageous, my daughter,* and give yourself greatly to prayer, forgetting this thing and that, for after all we have no other good or security or comfort than this, for after having left all for God, it is right that we not long for support or comfort in anything but God....
> (Letter 22, 757-758)[5]

In this passage, John empathically understands her affliction and expresses his care in the grief he feels over the potential harm it can do her; nonetheless, he genuinely shares his assessment of her situation and counsels courage in her commitment to God, reminding her that she lives for God, not the provincial.

These three qualities appear again in his letters to Doña Juana de Pedraza, a single woman in her early 30s, living in Granada. John had been her spiritual director when he was stationed there from 1582 to 1588. In June 1588, John was transferred hundreds of miles to the north to Segovia, but continued to guide her through the mail.

We do not have Juana's letters to John, but we have two of his to her. These suggest that she was undergoing prolonged periods of spiritual darkness and had complained that he was too far away and his letters too infrequent to help her, and she wanted the help of other spiritual directors to whom she might have more ready access.

On January 28, 1589, John wrote from Segovia to Juana in Granada. He opens with both caring and understanding:

> Jesus be in your soul.
>
> A few days ago I wrote to you through Father Fray Juan in answer to your last letter, which, as was your hope, *I prized.* I have answered you in that letter, since I believe I have received all your let-

ters. And I have *felt your grief, afflictions and loneliness*. These, in silence, ever tell me so much that the pen cannot declare it.

Then, in the body of the letter, John speaks genuinely to her concerns:

> In what concern the soul, it is safest not to lean on anything or desire anything. A soul should find its support wholly and entirely in its director, for not to do so would amount to no longer wanting a director. And when one director is sufficient and suitable, all others are useless or a hindrance. Let not the soul be attached to anything, for since prayer is not wanting, God will take care of its possessions; they belong to no other owner, nor should they....

Finally, John concludes his letter, reassuring Juana, that he cares for her:

> ...I am well, although my soul lags far behind. Commend me to God, and, when you can, give your letters to Fray Juan or to the nuns *more often—and it would be better if they were not so short.*
> From Segovia, January 28, 1589.
> Fray John of the Cross (Letter 11, 744-745)

Juana continued through most of 1589 writing to John, complaining that her darkness was not lifting and accusing him of forgetting her because she had not received any letters from him. On October 12, 1589, John again wrote her from Segovia. He begins with genuineness and care:

> Jesus be in your soul and thanks to Him that he has enabled me not to forget the poor, as you say, or be idle, as you say. For *it greatly vexes me* to think you believe what you say; this would be very bad after so many kindnesses on your part when I least deserved them. That's all I need now is to forget you! Look, how could this be so in the case of *one who is in my soul, as you are?*

Noting the difficulty of translating accurately the phrase *harto me hace rabiar* in the Spanish original of the above paragraph, E. Allison Peers suggests that the words might also be rendered "makes me absolutely furious."[6] The passage thus indicates John's ability to express strong negative emotion to his directee when he judges it appropriate to do so. Yet, at the same time the very next line conveys how he truly prizes her.

After a prolonged exhortation to walk in her "darknesses and voids of spiritual poverty" with trust in God, John concludes his letter, as he began it, with genuineness and care.

> Desire no other path than this and adjust your soul to it (for it is a good one) and receive Communion as usual. Go to confession when you have something definite; you don't have to discuss these things with anyone. Should you have some problem, write to me about it. Write soon, and more frequently. ...Commend...me also to God, my daughter in the Lord.
>
> From Segovia, October 12, 1589.
>
> Fray John of the Cross (Letter 19, 754-55)

OTHER LETTERS OF DIRECTION

John's letters to Madre Leonor and Doña Juana de Pedraza contain examples of all three qualities of genuineness, care, and understanding. Other letters of direction, too, show genuineness and caring.

For example, in a letter to Madre Leonor Bautista, a Carmelite nun in Beas, John shows both these qualities to a woman who was quite upset because her community did not reelect her as their prioress. He writes:

> Jesus be in your Reverence.
> Do not think, daughter in Christ, that I have ceased *to grieve for you in your trials* and for the others who share in them. Yet, in remembering that since God called you to live an apostolic life, which is a life of contempt, he is leading you along its road, I am consoled. *After all, God wishes religious to be religious*—in such a way that they be done with all and that all be done with them. For it is God himself who wishes to be their riches, comfort, and delightful glory. God has granted Your Reverence a great favor, because truly forgetful of all things you will be able to enjoy his good in solitude, and for love of him have no care that they do to you what they will, since you do not belong to yourself but to God. (Letter 9, 742-3)

John demonstrates the same genuineness and caring in a letter to Madre Ana de Jesús Jimena, distraught over his transfer from Segovia where he had been her director for three years. On July 6, 1591, he wrote to Ana:

...If this cannot be [that I remain in Segovia], Madre Ana de Jesús will not be left without my direction, as she fears, and thus *she will not die of this sorrow* that the opportunity, in her opinion, of being very holy has come to an end. But whether leaving or staying, wherever or however things may come to pass, *I will neither forget nor neglect you,* as you say, *because truly I desire your good forever.*

Now, until God gives us this good in heaven, *pass the time in the virtues of mortification and patience, desiring to resemble somewhat in suffering this great God of ours, humbled and crucified.* This life is not good if it is not an imitation of his life. May His Majesty preserve you and augment his love in you as his holy beloved. Amen.

From Madrid, July 6, 1591

Fray John of the Cross (Letter 25, 759-60)

These examples from his letters of spiritual direction show John's genuineness, caring, and understanding with his directees. True, they are only letters; we do not know what he was like when he sat down face-to-face with these persons in a spiritual direction session. However, "one recipient of his letters, a Carmelite nun in Toledo, testified that a letter from him had the same effect as hearing him speak."[7] Presumably, John was as genuine, caring, and understanding with his directees when he met with them in person as when he wrote to them from a distance.

At the same time, his letters suggest that John was capable of pursuing his own agenda rather than responding directly to the person's expressed issues and needs. In a letter to Ana de Jesús and the Carmelite sisters at Beas, for example, John defends the long absence of his letters with an eloquent statement on the value of "silence and work" over "writing or speaking"(Letter 8, 741-742).

On another occasion, he writes the following to a young Castilian lady who desired to be a Carmelite nun:

A great deal could be said about the three points you raised [in your letter], more than my lack of time and paper now permits. But I shall speak to you of *another three* that you will find a help. (Letter 12, 745-746)

John then proceeds to give apparently unsought advice about sin, the Lord's passion, and seeking true glory, ending the letter with a prayer that God will grant her his spirit.

LEARNING, DISCRETION, AND EXPERIENCE

Nowhere does John himself explicitly say that genuineness, caring, and understanding are indispensable for a good spiritual director. In fact, in the *Living Flame of Love,* he insists rather that a spiritual director should be learned, discreet, and experienced. He writes further: "Although the foundation for guiding a person to spirit is knowledge and discretion, directors will not succeed in leading a person onward in it when God bestows it, nor will they even understand it if they have no experience of what true and pure spirit is" (F, 3, 30).[8]

We find these qualities in John's letters also. His learning, for instance, may be seen in his combined use of Sacred Scripture, the theology of divine transcendence, and the psychology of attachment or addiction to challenge persons to journey to God, not by pleasant feelings, but in deep faith, concerned only with living in union with the divine will. Accordingly, John responds to one of his fellow Carmelite friars who sought his advice on how to occupy one's will in God alone "by loving God above all things." John's long reply to the friar includes the following passage:

> ...Loving God purely, above all things...means centering all the strength of one's will on God. In being bound and attached to [a] creature by means of the appetite, the will does not rise above it to God, who is inaccessible. It is impossible for the will to reach the sweetness and delight of the divine union and receive and feel the sweet and loving embraces of God without the nakedness and void of its appetite with respect to every particular satisfaction, earthly and heavenly. This is what David meant when he said: *Dilata os tuum et implebo illud* ["open wide your mouth and I will fill it"—(Ps 81:10)].
>
> It is worth knowing, then, that the appetite is the mouth of the will. It is opened wide when it is not encumbered or occupied with any mouthful of pleasure. When the appetite is centered on something, it becomes narrow by that very fact, since outside of God everything is narrow. That the soul have success in journeying to God and being joined to God, it must have the mouth of its will opened only to God himself, empty and dispossessed of every morsel of appetite, so God may fill it with his love and sweetness; and it must remain with this hunger and thirst for God alone, without desiring to be satisfied with any other thing, since here below it cannot enjoy God as he is in himself. And what is enjoyable—if there

is a desire for it, as I say—impedes this union. Isaiah taught this when he said: *All who thirst, come to the waters* [Is.55:1]. He invites to the abundance of the divine waters of union with God only those who thirst for God alone and who have no money, that is appetites.

It is very important and fitting for Your Reverence, if you desire to possess profound peace in your soul and attain perfection, that you surrender your whole will to God so that it may this be united with God and that you do not let it be occupied with the vile and base things of earth.

May His majesty make you as spiritual and holy as I desire you to be.

From Segovia, April 14.
Fray John of the Cross (Letter 13, 748-749)

John's discretion—a word that implies "both a practical, natural judgment of internal realities ('discretion') and...the virtue which moderates external behavior ('prudence')"[9]—may be seen in his letter to his dear friend, benefactor, and directee, Doña Ana de Mercado y Peñalosa, the "very noble and devout" laywoman for whom he wrote his masterful poem and commentary, the *Living Flame of Love* (see F, Prologue, 1). Writing to Doña Ana, by then a widow in Granada, from the "holy solitude" (Letter 31, 763) in La Peñuela, "six leagues north of Baeza," on August 19, 1591, four short months before his death, John advises:

Take care of your soul and do not confess scruples or first movements or imaginings in which the soul does not desire to be detained. *Look after your health,* and do not fail to pray when you can. (Letter 28, 761)

Doña Ana's condition at the time of this letter is unknown; but there appears to have been a health problem, possibly a lingering depression related to the successive deaths of her husband and daughter, together with other family misfortunes over the previous ten years.[10] As a general rule, John would have been the first to insist on continuous prayer; in particular cases, he also knew that illness can adversely affect one's ability to pray.[11] Therefore, with this particular woman at this time in her life he counsels her to take care of her health first and pray when she is able.

Evidently, Doña Ana was also prone to scruples, a neurotic and often very painful obsession with religious and/or moralistic ideas. Because these obsessive thoughts (e.g., images or "first movements" of attraction or revulsion toward objects) are not voluntary, there is no sin in such mental activity, regardless of its content. Therefore John directs Doña Ana not confess to them in sacramental penance.

He gives the same counsel to a discalced Carmelite nun suffering from scruples to whom he wrote a year or so earlier, shortly before Pentecost:

> If you could put an end to your scruples, I think it would be better for your quietude of soul not to confess during these days. But when you do confess, you should do so in this manner:
>
> In regard to thoughts and imaginings (whether they concern judgments, or other inordinate objects or representations, or any other motions) that occur without being desired or accepted or deliberately adverted to: Do not confess them or pay attention to them or worry about them. *It is better to forget about them no matter how much they afflict the soul.* At most you can mention in general any omission or remissness as regards the purity and perfection you ought to have in the interior faculties: memory, intellect, and will.
>
> In regard to words: Confess any want of caution in speaking with truthfulness and rectitude, out of necessity, and with purity of intention.
>
> In regard to deeds: Confess any lack of the proper and only motive—God alone without any other concern.
>
> By such a confession you can be content and need not confess any other particular thing, however much it may battle against you.

Clearly, John does not regard frequent sacramental confession as the cure for scruples. Constantly reiterating the same troublesome thoughts, images, and affective movements to a confessor only reinforces, rather than heals, obsessional thinking. Instead, he counsels "forgetting," his method for healing the memory described in the *Ascent of Mount Carmel* (see A, 3, 15, 1). In her case that means letting go of emotional attachment to specific involuntary thoughts, fantasies, and movements, and confessing only in the most general terms failures in purity of intention and truthfulness.

After acknowledging with empathic understanding how difficult it is to break the obsessional process, John recommends some practices to help her do just that. The first is not to allow her obsessional thoughts of sin or unworthiness keep her from the communion rail. "Receive communion on Pentecost in addition to those days on which you usually receive." Next, he recommends the practice of silence to break the tendency in scrupulous persons to talk compulsively about their obsessions: "When something distasteful or unpleasant comes your way, remember Christ crucified and be silent. Live in faith and hope, even though you are in darkness, because it is in these darknesses that God protects the soul."

Finally, he directs her to practice trust in God.

> Cast your care on God, for he watches over you and will not forget you. Do not think that he leaves you alone; that would be an affront to God.
>
> Read, pray, rejoice in God, both your good and your salvation. May He grant you this good and this salvation and conserve it all until the day of eternity. Amen, Amen.
>
> Fray John of the Cross. (Letter 20, 755-756)

Unfortunately, we do not know how the woman responded to John's therapy of forgetting. Possibly, in advising her to confess only in general terms her lack of truthfulness and proper motivation, he merely introduced two more religious concepts for her to obsess about, and her problem worsened. But possibly too, she perceived his belief in her ability to change her way of thinking and found strength in this perception to make a determined effort to do so.

Regardless of the outcome, we see clearly John's approach in spiritual direction. He counsels persons to let go of inordinate emotional attachment to specific desires, thoughts, memories, images, and interior movements, no matter how religious or spiritual, and instead to center their mental energies on the incomprehensibly good God present in the depths of their being, a process he summarized in his little verse, *Suma de la perfección:*

Olvido de lo criado,	Forgetfulness of created things,
memoria del Criador,	remembrance of the Creator,
atención a lo interior,	attention turned toward inward things,
y estarse amando al Amado.	and loving the Beloved.[12]

Finally, John's remark to the scrupulous Carmelite nun about God protecting persons in darkness comes, I believe, from his own experience of spirit. In his October letter to Juana de Pedraza already quoted, he confidently encourages her to be at peace and to trust interior darkness, a security he himself has gained from years of walking by faith alone.

> Those who desire nothing else than God walk not in darkness, however poor and dark they are in their own sight.... You are making good progress. Do not worry, but be glad!...

Speaking from personal experience, John reassures Juana about the fruits of contemplative darkness—humility, detachment, and a deeper understanding of God, self, and the world:

> You were never better off than now because you were never so humble or so submissive, or considered yourself and all worldly things to be so small; nor did you know that you were so evil or God was so good, nor did you serve God so purely and so disinterestedly as now, nor do you follow after the imperfections of you own will and interests as perhaps you were accustomed to do.

Next he describes with genuineness the reality of the contemplative life, pointing out the psychological benefits of letting go of attachment to "experiences" and of embracing instead the emptiness demanded by the inner journey.

> What is it you desire? What kind of life or method of procedure do you paint for yourself in this life? What do think serving God involves other than avoiding evil, keeping his commandments, and being occupied with the things of God as best we can? When this is had, what need is there of other apprehensions or other lights and satisfactions from this source or that? In these there is hardly ever a lack of stumbling blocks and dangers for the soul, which by its understanding and appetites is deceived and charmed; and its own faculties cause it to err. And thus God does one a great favor when he darkens the faculties and impoverishes the soul in such a way that one cannot err with these.

Finally, he reassures her of the inner security that results from living daily in utter simplicity and emptiness of spirit:

And if one does not err in this, what need is there in order to be right other than to walk along the level road of the law of God and of the Church, and live only in dark and true faith and certain hope and complete charity, expecting all our blessings in heaven, living here below like pilgrims, the poor, the exiled, orphans, the thirsty, without a road and without anything, hoping for everything in heaven? (Letter 19, 754-755)

By his own criteria, then, John was a good guide: wise, discreet, experienced. Moreover, by criteria developed in contemporary therapeutic psychology, he appears to have been even more effective because he was able to bring the qualities of genuineness, caring, and understanding into his relationships with his directees.

THE SPIRITUAL DIRECTOR AND THE HOLY SPIRIT

But specifically, why, in addition to learning, discretion, and experience are genuineness, caring, and understanding so valuable in the helping relationship of spiritual direction? The answer, I believe, is that these qualities create an interpersonal atmosphere between the director and directee that promotes the Spirit's guidance of the directee.

John maintains, after all, that the Holy Spirit is a person's primary guide; the human director is merely the Holy Spirit's instrument in this guidance. In the *Living Flame of Love,* he writes:

Directors should reflect that they themselves are not the chief agent, guide, and mover of souls..., but the principal guide is the Holy Spirit, who is never neglectful of souls and they themselves are instruments for directing these souls to perfection through faith and the law of God, according the spirit given by God to each one.

Thus the whole concern of directors should not be to accommodate souls to their own method and condition, but they should observe the road along which God is leading one; if they do not recognize it, they should leave the soul alone and not bother it. (F, 3, 46)

Psychologically, Rogers observed that a person's inner potential for self-direction, behavioral guidance, and value formation is ordinarily released through relationships with other persons who experience and communicate genuineness, caring, and understanding to the individual.

Similarly, with a director who is genuine, caring and understanding in their relationship, and who is communicating these in a perceptible way, directees experience the freedom, indeed the encouragement, to explore, express, and discern the interior movements of the Holy Spirit. They are enabled to discover the road along which God is leading them, and to live more consciously under the Holy Spirit's guidance.

Persons on extended retreat or in individual on-going direction, for example, often come with an agenda for discussion and discernment: what to do about this particular situation, or with this particular relationship. Very soon, however, in the freedom of the direction relationship where these qualities are present, they often experience the delicate movements of the Holy Spirit within themselves and their own unique relationship with the risen Lord. These experiences enable them to re-commit themselves to the risen Lord and open themselves anew to the daily guidance of the Holy Spirit. Thus, the "agenda" has not necessarily been resolved point by point, but the renewed relationship with the Holy Spirit of the risen Lord has strengthened them to live more fully in each moment as Jesus' disciples, following wherever his living Spirit leads them.

John's reminder that the Holy Spirit is the ultimate guide and that spiritual directors are instruments in bringing directees into contact with the Holy Spirit also helps us to situate the many counseling tools available today within the overall work of spiritual direction. Undoubtedly John would welcome journaling, dream work, guided imagery, the Enneagram, the Myers-Briggs Type Indicator, focusing, and other similar methods as helpful for self-understanding and discovering the particular road one is called to walk; but he would also firmly remind us that the Christian spiritual journey itself is one of personal transformation through dark faith and self-transcending love. He would caution us not to substitute these methods for the daily self-emptying of disordered desires, thoughts, memories, and behavior necessary for continued growth in faith and love.

John similarly cautioned the Carmelite community at Beas de Segura where he served as both confessor and spiritual director following his first assignment to Andalusia in 1578:

> The waters of inward delights do not spring from the earth. One
> must open toward heaven the mouth of desire, empty of all other

fullness, that thus it may not be reduced or restricted by some mouthful of another pleasure, but truly empty and open toward God who says: *Open your mouth wide and I will fill it* [Ps 81:11].

Accordingly, those who seek satisfaction in something no longer keep themselves empty that God might fill them with his ineffable delight. And thus just as they go to God so do they return, for their hands are encumbered and cannot receive what God is giving. May God deliver us from these evil obstacles that hinder such sweet and delightful freedom.

Serve God, my beloved daughters in Christ, following in his footsteps of mortification, in utter patience, in total silence, and with every desire to suffer, becoming executioners of your own satisfactions, mortifying yourselves, if perhaps something remains that must die and something still impedes the inner resurrection of the Spirit who dwells within your souls. Amen.

From Málaga, November 18, 1586

Your servant,

Fray John of the Cross (Letter 7, 740 741)

CONCLUSION AND IMPLICATIONS

The qualities that John exemplifies in his letters of spiritual direction—genuineness, caring, understanding, wisdom, discretion, experience—provide an excellent checklist for those of us who do spiritual direction today. Being a good spiritual guide requires continual growth in each of these six areas.

Obviously, we must be praying contemplatively if we are to know "true and pure spirit" from firsthand experience; otherwise, we easily become like uncertain guides who try to lead others through a terrain they do not know themselves. We must be faithful to our study of Sacred Scripture, theology, Christian spirituality and psychology, as these are the basic foundational sciences for our applied ministry. We must hone our skills in applying general principles of the spiritual life to the specific requirements of individual persons, a process fostered through regular participation in case conferences, peer supervision, and consultation with other spiritual directors and helping professionals.

Perhaps not so obvious, but nonetheless crucial for creating an intimate interpersonal atmosphere, is our need to grow continually as persons who can experience and communicate genuineness, caring and understanding in human relationships. These qualities are not unmerited gifts (*gratia gratis data*) like healing, tongues, prophecy and miracles in the New Testament; they are human attitudes that can be developed with practice. We can learn to be more real with ourselves and with others, to prize others unconditionally, and to listen with empathy.

This, of course, is an agenda for a lifetime. But as we grow in experience, wisdom, discretion, genuineness, caring and understanding, our effectiveness as spiritual directors increases, for these qualities are particularly suited to helping directees dispose themselves for the completely gracious action of the Holy Spirit, who alone transforms persons in God.

NOTES

1. This summary of Rogers's teaching on the qualities that make for successful psychotherapy is based on his following writings: "A Theory of Therapy, Personality, and Interpersonal Relationships, as Developed in the Client-Centered Framework," in *Psychology: A Study of a Science*, vol 3, *Formulations of the Person and the Social Content*, ed. Sigmund Koch (New York, NY: McGraw-Hill, 1959), 184-256; "The Interpersonal Relationship: The Core of Guidance," in Carl R. Rogers and Barry Stevens, *Person to Person: The Problem of Being Human* (Layfayette, CA: Real People Press, 1967), 89-103; "Client-Centered Psychotherapy," in *Comprehensive Textbook of Psychiatry—II*, 2nd ed., vol. 2, ed. Alfred M. Freedman, Harold I. Kaplan, and Benjamin J. Sadock (Baltimore, MD: Williams and Wilkins, 1975), 1831-1843; "Empathic: An Unappreciated Way of Being," *The Counseling Psychologist* 5 (1975), 2-10. See also my "Toward a Contemporary Model of Spiritual Direction: A Comparative Study of St. John of the Cross and Carl Rogers," in *Carmelite Studies*, vol. 2, ed. John Sullivan (Washington, DC: ICS Publications, 1982), 95-166.

2. Using the system of abbreviations indicated on page vii above, all quotations from John of the Cross are taken from *The Collected Works of John of the Cross*, rev. ed., trans. Kieran Kavanaugh and Otilio Rodriguez (Washington, D.C.: ICS Publications, 1991). The letters appear on pages 736-764 of this new edition, and will be cited both by letter and by page number. Thus, "Letter 4, 738" refers the reader to John's Letter #4, on page 738 of the new revised edition.

3. Letter of Teresa of Jesus to Ana de Jesús, December, 1578 (#261), in *The Letters of Saint Teresa of Jesus*, trans. and ed. E. Allison Peers, 2 vols. (Westminster, MD: Newman Press, 1950) 2: 625.

4. See Federico Ruiz, et al., *God Speaks in the Night: The Life, Times, and Teaching of St. John of the Cross*, trans. by Kieran Kavanaugh (Washington, DC: ICS Publications, 1991), 297, 343, 362-364.

5. Except for Scriptural citations, the italics used in the quotations from John's letters are my own, to indicate instances of his genuineness, caring and understanding.

6. *The Complete Works of St. John of the Cross,* trans. and ed. E. Allison Peers, 3rd rev. ed., 3 vols. (Westminster, MD: Newman Press, 1953), 3: 265.

7. See *Collected Works,* rev. ed., 735.

8. A thorough discussion of John's three recommended qualities for a director may be found in Dennis R. Graviss, *Portrait of the Spiritual Director in the Writings of Saint John of the Cross* (Rome: Institutum Carmelitanum, 1983).

9. Graviss, *Portrait,* 176.

10. Ruiz, et al, *God Speaks in the Night,* 324-325.

11. See, for example, N, 1, 9, 1-9, where John acknowledges the disturbing effects of "bodily indisposition," "bad humor," and "melancholia" in one's prayer life.

12. See *Collected Works,* 73.

JOHN OF THE CROSS FOR CARPENTERS: THE ORDINARY WAY OF THE DARK NIGHT OF FAITH

Denis Read, O.C.D.

Denis Read is a moral theologian and member of the Institute of Carmelite Studies .In recent years he has devoted much of his efforts to Hispanic ministry and to the Secular Carmelites.

In these pages I simply want to mediate that part of the Carmelite tradition first codified by John—the great and ancient tradition of Carmelite mysticism. Karl Rahner has said that "the devout Christian of the future will either be a 'mystic,' one who has 'experienced' something, or he [or she] will be nothing."[1] Either we live by theological faith, out of which true mysticism grows, or we diminish to nothing. But people today are afraid of mysticism—and some of this fear is cultural.

From many years in the Hispanic ministry, I have discovered that when we translate the Hispanic idiom into English, we add something positive to our American culture: what Hispanics call *la caridad de la vida,* the environment of love that permeates all life; and a certain warmth (*el calor*) of the community of Hispanidad that chases out the *frio,* the coldness, that comes to people who are not living by love as the mystics do.

So let us look at John of the Cross, the theologian of a warm, loving, living faith.

> One dark night,
> fired with love's urgent longings
> —ah, the sheer grace!—
> I went out unseen,
> my house being now all stilled.

In darkness and secure,
by the secret ladder, disguised,
—ah, the sheer grace!—
in darkness and concealment,
my house being now all stilled.

On that glad night,
in secret, for no one saw me,
nor did I look at anything,
with no other light or guide
than the one that burned in my heart.

This guided me
more surely than the light of noon
to where he was awaiting me
—him I knew so well—
there in a place where no one appeared.

O guiding night!
O night more lovely than the dawn!
O night that has united
the Lover with his beloved,
transforming the beloved in her Lover.... (N, Prologue)

As St. Paul says, "The just man lives by faith" (Rom 1:17). It is the light and life of this simple Christian faith that John celebrates, and faith is the key to his spirituality, as it is to St. Paul's: *pure faith*, unadulterated and unsophisticated, such as Joseph the carpenter lived, and Jesus the carpenter—and John of the Cross, another carpenter. We risk misunderstanding John's entire message if we misunderstand the centrality of this faith, and what it means to him. "Faith" he constantly repeats, "is the only adequate means to union to God" (see, e.g., A, 1, 2, 1; 2, 2, 1ff; 8, 1-7; 9, 1; 16, 12; 19, 14; 24, 8; 30, 5).

It is a *resurrection faith,* for John is celebrating the Paschal Mystery here, the Easter Vigil, a night "more lovely than the dawn." The cross is the instrument of resurrection.

It is the *Catholic faith,* not some new gnosticism; there is nothing in John's works about a "new age," or a "creation spirituality" or any popular pseudo-spirituality, but only a spirituality of Jesus, crucified and risen, living in his church.

INTRODUCTION: THE SEARCH FOR A LAY THEOLOGY

The title of this reflection may sound paradoxical. What could St. John of the Cross—the Mystical Doctor, poet, theologian of the dark nights and spiritual marriage—possibly have to do with carpenters, and with the nitty-gritty of manual labor, earning a paycheck, meeting deadlines, dealing with the unions, and facing the rat-race of daily hard work? Surprisingly, a great deal, as we shall see. Let us look for a moment at the circumstances of his own life, and perhaps lay to rest certain myths about the Carmelite way that have made John himself seem unapproachable and unintelligible for the majority of Christians.

First, John *was* a carpenter, and a stone-mason. He spent more time building monasteries for the friars, and helping the nuns set up a wall here or a room there, than he did writing books. He spent more hours serving the poor souls who came to him than he did in the library. As a poor boy from a poor family with a widowed mother, he did his apprenticeship in carpentry, and perhaps helped add to the meager family income. He learned a great deal from work. I would offer him as a patron for the working man and woman. The carpenter is a symbol of all working people.

Second, carpentry, and many other occupations, open people up to the movement of the Spirit. In carpentry, much quiet time is spent alone, time that can be spent in contemplation and intimate interaction with God. The carpenter's work is much like the work of a spiritual director. The carpenter strips away the rough exterior bark of the tree, and lays bare the heart of the wood. He or she reveals whether the heart is decayed, whether termites and insects have weakened the sinews of the tree, whether the wood is sound, strong and beautiful, or weak, decayed and useless. The carpenter takes the wood as it is, and then transforms it into something new in the form of chairs, pianos, doors, houses, and such. Spiritual directors do similar work with people who seek their counsel, accepting them as they are, then assisting in their transformation.

Third, the Carmelite Order, which Teresa of Avila and John of the Cross called to renewal, back to its roots, was originally a community of lay people who gathered together, after the Crusades, "to live in the service of Jesus Christ with pure hearts and a steadfast conscience"; this is their goal and purpose, as articulated in the original Carmelite *Rule* given by Albert of Jerusalem. Theirs was a life of perpetual prayer, work, and study in community. The *Rule* enjoins "work of some kind, so that the devil may always find you busy. ...Earn your own bread by silent toil. This is the way of holiness. Follow it." This whole "formula of living" is the silent presupposition of all Carmelite and Christian spirituality. It is a vocation to hard work, the work of sanctification. Mysticism, poetry and theology only make sense when built upon the foundation of daily hard work. The call to total generosity "in the service of Jesus Christ," and its concomitant call to total self-denial, is simply the practical working out of the Gospel call to conversion: "Repent and believe in the Good News" (Mk 1:15).

But we humans can get overinvolved in work as an end in itself. The successful worker can become blind to the world of the Spirit. We fail to "lift up our hearts to the Lord," because we often don't know how to live a spiritual, Christian life in this workaday world. John of the Cross shows us, step by step, how we all need a second conversion in adulthood, to foster our receptivity to the guidance of the Holy Spirit. He leads us through the purification of our souls from the spiritual vices, into the light of faith that unites us with Jesus, the Lord.

Jesus urged his followers to "see with their eyes, hear with their ears, and understand with their hearts, so they might be converted, and [he] might heal them" (Mt 13:15). This Gospel "understanding of the heart" is the fruit of contemplative prayer, to which John of the Cross is constantly inviting his disciples and directees. It is, essentially, the awakening of the Spirit, already within the Christian by baptism, to the living faith involved in following the Lord wherever he leads. John calls the fulfillment of such faith "transforming union" of the human will with and within the will of God.

My topic is the the *ordinary* way of the dark night of faith, because the situation of feeling marginalized, and the necessity of living by faith, have never been more widespread. Why?

1) We need such living faith *because we are living in a church suffering the birthpangs of a new Christian culture*—a "renaissance" just as real as the spiritual renewal and reform that St. Teresa of Jesus began, and St. John of the Cross lived and helped to shape. They brought Spanish Catholicism—and eventually European Catholicism—out of the feudal culture of a Spain "more Catholic than Rome" into a worldwide missionary movement that began the thrust of the Roman Catholic Church to become catholic in fact, as well as in theory.[2]

Today we are witnessing the emergence of a *global* church. We have the potential at this moment to become truly "catholic" in the original sense, i.e., transcultural, ecumenical, and universal, "people of every race, language and way of life." But this new birth, after Vatican II, involves a crisis of transition to renewal and conversion. This is the "dark night" we are undergoing today. John of the Cross would say: On the road to communion with God and one another, the night of faith shall guide us. Faith tells us of things we have never seen, and cannot come to know by our natural senses. It is like the light of the sun which blinds our eyes, because its light is stronger than our powers of sight. So the light of faith (with hope and love) transcends our comprehension (see, e.g., A, 2, 3, 1-4).

John of the Cross also said, "We cannot come to a place we do not know except by journeying in a way we do not know" (cf. A, 1, 13, 11; 2, 4, 2-7), and on the way, we need someone to believe in—the Lord Jesus.

And there are so many contrary lights that beckon us, saying, "Christ is here!' or "The Gospel is there!" Almost everyone is confused by the noisy voices of our mass media culture. John of the Cross is a sure guide for the working man and woman, a "Christian Classic" for the spiritual life.

2) We also need this spirituality of the ordinary way of living faith because *ordinary working men and women have been forgotten.* Today, I believe, the university typically does not see the need for a doctrine of living faith. Theology has become so specialized, so compartmentalized, that the simple knowledge of Jesus Christ is fragmented and divided up beyond recognition. Perhaps our Lord foresaw that this would be the case, when he praised his Father: "for although you have hidden these things [the knowledge of God and God's reign] from the wise and learned, you have revealed them to the childlike [including carpenters].... Come to me, all you who labor and are burdened, and I will give you rest" (Mt 11:25, 28). The knowledge of Jesus is not front page news; it has never been a best seller. Rather, it is mysterious, only available to those who work and suffer for it. Jesus has made it so.

The working man and woman need help finding a deeper meaning for their labors. We need to be working *with God,* and John of the Cross shows us how to do this, daily. He does not pamper us, does nothing to feed the fires of envy or resentment; instead, he shows us how all the ups and downs of ordinary living are purifications of an all-too-human faith, that must be transformed into pure, naked searching for the God who is our Ransom and our Reward. We need to learn not to envy the rich, nor to be beholden to the powers of this world, but to take charge of our own feelings so as to turn them towards the imitation of Christ. He is our only Lord; all the rest of us are brothers and sisters, in the same human condition.

3) We need St. John of the Cross's doctrine of faith *because of the broken nature of our Catholic solidarity*. The Roman Catholic Church in this country used to be the church of the immigrant poor. Now after Vatican II another reality has emerged. As Catholics have become wealthy, educated and upwardly mobile, we have lost a great deal of the earlier solidarity with the poor that used to characterize our religious life. John of the Cross speaks to this cultural growth process and progressive liberation because he himself was the Doctor of both a liberated intelligence and of the asceticism needed in order to use our liberty wisely. Wealth and capitalism are not our problems, but rather what do to with them. Education and technology are not our problems, but rather what we do with our added knowledge and scientific progress. John of the Cross was the most cultured of all the Spanish mystics, but that did not prevent him from engaging in pastoral ministry with the laity, including carpenters and other ordinary people.

We need intellectual humility, and the wisdom that begins with obedience to the one true God for the great mission God has entrusted to us workers in his vineyard. "You too go into my vineyard, and I will give you what is just" (Mt 20:4), says the Lord to the layman and laywoman of today. This mission of the laity is to keep the church both simple and balanced, because today the health of the church is in the hands of the laity, in the hands of the carpenters, homemakers, nurses, other lay people who make up the church.

But our laity also need solidarity, instruction and direction from their pastors and spiritual directors. Spiritual direction is the art of arts. Especially in times of division and controversy, we have a greater need for the light of Catholic wisdom and spiritual theology to find our way to living faith, amid all the trouble and misunderstanding around us. John of the Cross is the church's acknowledged "Doctor of Spiritual Theology."

PART I: JOHN OF THE CROSS, PRACTITIONER OF SPIRITUALITY

The tradition of Teresian Carmelite spirituality, with its roots in Teresa of Jesus and John of the Cross, was developed and systematized after John by spiritual theologians who emphasized *practicality* as the aspect of Christian wisdom most needed in the direction of souls. Let us begin from this same insight and reconstruct several key theses of this "school" now so widely accepted that they can be rightly called *fundamentals of Catholic spirituality*.[3] This Catholic science has several notes that commend it to contemporary laymen and laywomen:

1) It is *Biblical*, described as "wisdom" in the Book of Wisdom (Wis 7) and in the writings of St. Paul as the gospel of "Jesus Christ crucified" (1 Cor 2:2).

> We speak wisdom to those who are mature, but not a wisdom of this age, nor of the rulers of this age who are passing away. Rather we speak God's wisdom, mysterious, hidden, which God predetermined before the ages for our glory. As it is written: *Eye has not seen, ear has not heard, and it has not entered the human heart, what God has prepared for those who love him.* But this [wisdom] God has revealed to us through the Spirit." (1 Cor 2:6-10)

2) It is *short, concise,* like the Gospels. Because this spirituality is not mere speculation, but a living, practical guide, it *uses* the conclusions of speculative theology but *applies* them. It is applied Christianity.

This shows the dependence of spirituality on the teaching of the church. John of the Cross uses the church's teaching to show his readers "a short way" to the perfection of the Christian life.

3) It is *spiritual*, a doctrine of "spirit speaking to spirit," or, in the words of Cardinal Newman, "heart speaking to heart."

4) It is *progressive*, involving a process—beginning with the purgative way, continuing with the illuminative way, towards the fulfillment in the unitive way—which are all included in John's expression, "the way of transforming union with God."

5) It is a science of *human, psychological health.* Holiness is true wholeness, of the human incarnate spirit. John of the Cross has become a sourcebook for the integration of spirituality and psychology, because

he deals with the care and cure of the mind and spirit.

PART II: KEY THESES IN JOHN'S SPIRITUALITY

Among the fundamental principles of John's spirituality are the following:

First Principle: *The grace of the Holy Spirit is the Christ-Life in us.* John is rooted in the spirituality of St. Paul and St. John the Evangelist. From Paul he received the master-principle: "I have been crucified with Christ; yet I live, no longer I, but Christ lives in me; ...I live by faith in the Son of God who has loved me and given himself up for me" (Gal 2:19-20). John the Evangelist proclaimed the great promise of the indwelling Trinity: "Those who love me will keep my word, and my Father will love them, and we will come to them and make our dwelling with them" (Jn 14:23).

This indwelling of God engenders the dynamism of grace-life in all the baptized:

a) The life of God, knowing and loving us always, sanctifying and activating us;

b) Our response to the living God, in living faith, hope, love (a response that is the result of God activating us);

c) The gifts of the seven virtues of the Christian disciple (faith, hope, love, justice, temperance, fortitude and prudence);

d) Our response to these gifts, the struggle to grow in these virtues and to overcome their contrary vices. We are engaged in a spiritual combat against pride, greed, lust, anger, addiction, envy and laziness. Thus, the Christian life is a journey through a "dark night of faith" towards "the light of contemplative insight and intuition." But, this contemplative peace and rest is prepared by the practice of the theological and moral virtues. Christian formation is the "science of the Cross," learned through work.

e) The gifts of the Holy Spirit, direct interventions of the Spirit of Jesus always active within us, working on our passivity, gently and sweetly, in our daily labors.

f) The fruits of the Holy Spirit, the joyful experiences of the acts of Christian living (many more than the traditional twelve).

g) the practice of the eight beatitudes, through which Jesus illuminates us with the gifts of His Spirit, and thus builds up our faith, hope and love for God and each other. (These works of love are the synthetic theme of the Christian life, and the proximate means to union with God.)

Second Principle: *The Christian community—the church—is the social form of our life in grace.* John of the Cross is a man of the church. For him, the concrete ecclesial community in which he lives and works is the supreme validator of religious experience.

One of John's most famous shorter works is called the *Precautions,* in which he instructs novices on how to live community life in such a way that they can "attain in a short time holy recollection and spiritual silence, nakedness and poverty of spirit, where one enjoys the peaceful comfort of the Holy Spirit, reaches union with God, is freed of all the obstacles incurred from the creatures of this world, defended against the wiles and deceits of the devil, and liberated from one's own self" (*Precautions,* 1). He goes on to counsel his young religious to mind their own business, "for should you desire to pay heed to things, many will seem wrong, even were you to live among angels, because of your not understanding the substance of them" (ibid., 9). Pessimistic? No, utterly realistic about the necessity of letting go of judgmental inclinations, for these are the source of the vices of envy, self-aggrandizement, and misunderstanding all through the church. This advice is valuable for *all* church members, including carpenters, business people, and so on.

John of the Cross does not explicitly speak at great length about the church, because the doctrine of the church (i.e., ecclesiology) was still underdeveloped in his time. But he does show us how to be liberated from the habits of rash judgment that were the cause of so much destruction within the church, and among individuals in and outside of the church. He helps liberate our judgment from illusion, from patronizing and superior attitudes, so as to allow the *Holy Spirit* to be the guide of the Church, for us and for our salvation. It is the Holy Spirit who is "the principal guide, agent and mover of souls," not spiritual directors or self-appointed saviors. The Spirit is "never neglectful of souls"; humans can only be "instruments for directing these souls to perfection through faith and the law of God, according to the spirit given by God to each one" (F, 3, 46). The Spirit speaks directly to the heart of each individual.

John was a good community man. He taught his students how to "get along well in the community" and to "overcome your sensitiveness and feelings," "rejoicing in the good of others as if it were your own, ...thereby [to] possess a happy heart" (*Precautions*, 13 & 15). Lay people usually find their community in the workplace and in their families. The advice of John of the Cross is excellent counsel for carpenters and for any others working in groups where feelings and resentments often run high, due to the competition for the desired promotion, higher paycheck or more prestigious title. Being able to rejoice in the success of others is one key to a happy life.

Third Principle: *The Christ-Life is given and nourished in our communities through the liturgy, sacraments and personal prayer.* John of the Cross is a "liturgical mystic" and his spirituality is a liturgical spirituality, because the Carmelite community in which he was formed, and the Spanish Catholicism within which he was brought up, were liturgical communities in a liturgical church. One of his lesser known poems is "The Song in the Soul that Rejoices to Know God by Faith," especially faith in the Blessed Sacrament:

> ...Aquesta eterna fonte está escondida
> en este vivo pan por darnos vida,
> *aunque es de noche.*

> Aquí se está llamando a los criaturas,
> y de esta agua se hartan, aunque a oscuras,
> *porques es de noche.*

> Aquesta viva fuente que deseo,
> en este pan de vida yo la veo,
> *aunque es de noche.*

> ...Even though it is night, I know
> That this eternal spring [of faith] is hidden
> In this living Bread, to give us life.

> And because it is night,
> Here it is, in hiding, crying to all creatures,
> And they are filled with this living water.

> This living spring which I so desire,
> I see now in this Bread of Life,
> Even though it is night. (my translation)

a) For John of the Cross, *the prayer of the church represents the faith of the church.* He used to quote from the liturgical books of the church to illustrate his spiritual doctrine. The hymns, the antiphons of the Divine Office and the *Roman Ritual* are so many sourcebooks for him, along with Scripture, to explain the things of God. His conferences attest that he lived a thoroughly liturgical life, in tune with the different seasons of the church year, so much so that we may say he was *socialized in the life of the liturgy.*

He would have rejoiced to pray the renewed liturgy of Vatican II! And today, even some readings from his own works are included in that liturgy. The point is evident enough: He simply takes the liturgy as the starting point for growth in the contemplative life of prayer, a starting point that every carpenter, baker, investment banker and seamstress can relate to, because the liturgy is the place where we have easiest access to the experience of God and the church's spiritual tradition.

b) *Liturgical prayer is a preparation for personal prayer.* John of the Cross observed a practical principle that any working person can appreciate: Prayer is for union with God, and the very purpose even of the beautiful prayer of the liturgy is to foster personal "conversation alone with Christ, who we know loves us" (Teresa's definition). John had his priorities clear; while he, Teresa, and the others of her reform dedicated two hours daily to "mental prayer" (meditation and contemplation), he counseled his penitents and students to learn, first, meditation on the life of Christ, and second, passive or contemplative prayer responding to Christ himself within us. The carpenter of our title might find it easy, while spending hours silently sanding and painting a piece of furniture or the woodwork in a home, to meditate at the same time on the many hours the Lord must have spent in similar work. The carpenter might also meditate on the miracle of creation, on the beauty, strength and unique characteristics of each kind of wood that has been created by God. A carpenter becomes a ""spiritual director," bringing out the beauty of each individual piece of wood, just as the spiritual director of souls help bring out the spiritual beauty of each person.

All prayer is indispensable for transforming union with Christ, whether one is in the stage of beginners when meditation usually predominates, or in the stage of proficients when the contemplative inflowing of the Holy Spirit begins to take over. It is in his treatment of the arts of meditation and contemplation that John's most original contribution, on the "dark nights" of faith, of sense and of the spirit, can be found.

c) For John of the Cross, *spiritual direction is a pastoral and sacramental ministry.* His whole reason for writing his masterworks—the *Ascent of Mt. Carmel* and the *Dark Night*—was to educate spiritual directors about the ways of God with souls. We need to understand the meaning of spiritual direction in a sacramental church to understand John of the Cross's doctrine.

After the Council of Trent, the practice of confession in the confessional (also called "auricular confession") became standard. But confession did not displace guidance of souls by pastoral counseling, which had endured from the beginning of Christianity. Because it typically involves a private one-on-one encounter, spiritual direction has yet to find the historian who can fully document the development of guidelines for this pastoral ministry. Gregory the Great in his *Pastoral Rule* gives many examples of how to guide souls toward overcoming their vices and practicing Christian virtues, but not until John himself do we really have a doctrine of spiritual direction for the guidance of souls on the way to perfection and mystical union. He teaches us that the Holy Spirit is the principal agent in the spiritual life; spiritual directors are instrumental agents only. The spiritual life is a journey of the "spirit" (with a small "s") toward the great "Spirit" (with a capital "S"). The Spirit of God intervenes directly in the lives of God's people. Let God be God, and let directors be human, guiding souls according to the spirit God gives directly to each one.

John of the Cross's principles for developing the living faith in Jesus include:

1) *The following of Jesus Christ, crucified, as the norm for all spirituality,* "bringing our lives into conformity with his" (see A, 1, 13, 3).

2) *Studying his life* "in order to know how to imitate and behave in all events as he would" (ibid.; here we see the need for spiritual reading).

3) *Undergoing the dark nights of sense and spirit* "in order to be successful in this imitation" (see A, 1, 13, 4; note that the night of faith is a blessing, not a curse).

4) *Experiencing these dark nights as a "second conversion," divinizing our own human thinking, expectations and affections,* first by conforming our conduct to our consciences, and then by conforming our consciences

to the Spirit of God. In practice, this means learning how to deny ourselves and take up our daily crosses, an energetic program of asceticism
that subordinates our desires to our reason (as John eloquently demonstrates in the first seven chapters of the *Dark Night*, on the need for
purification of the spiritual roots of the seven capital sins). This invitation into the purgative way consists in the development of the virtues of
adult love and friendship, liberation from habitual sins, and humble self-
knowledge, the beginning of humility (as St. Teresa explains in the *Way
of Perfection*).

5) *Living out the cross and resurrection of the Lord in a practical way.* This
means dying to our own desires, living by "faith alone, which is the only
proximate and proportionate means to union with God" (A, 2, 9, 1).

6) *Receiving the gifts of the Holy Spirit* as the necessary and sufficient
interventions by God himself to provide his people with the light and
love for a connatural growth into transforming union, "for the Holy
Spirit enlightens us according to our recollection."[4] One of these gifts is
"right judgment" or "counsel." In the way of perfect love, proper to all
Christians, the "evangelical counsels" of poverty, chastity and obedience,
as well as the message of the eight beatitudes, are the "counsels," the
practical guidelines, offered by Christ himself. He proposed them to the
rich young man, if the latter wanted "to become perfect." They are lived
out by Secular Carmelites and by religious communities. But they are
also the ordinary way to perfection in every Christian life, i.e., for carpenters as well. They represent the very essence of what it means for a
Christian to be a *Christian,* rather than something else.

To follow these counsels of the Lord, we need individual spiritual
direction—Christian doctrine, the guidance of moral theology, but also
the applied Christianity represented by these six principles of St. John
of the Cross. They coincide with the *Spiritual Exercises* of St. Ignatius of
Loyola, the *Introduction to the Devout Life* of St. Francis de Sales, and the
Imitation of Christ by Thomas à Kempis.

They are all meant to bring us into what the church today, in the
renewed "Rite of Christian Initiation of Adults," calls the *Mystagogia* or
spirituality of the Holy Spirit. The principles, and the practical application of them in self-direction, group direction and private direction
comprise *a spirituality for everyone to follow in the footsteps of the Lord,* one
which issues in the apostolic action of the working man and woman. May
we follow our Lord, through his cross, to his (and our) resurrection.

CONCLUSIONS

What would John of the Cross say if he were living in the church today? Perhaps his doctrine could be summarized as follows: 1) *Love one another, and work for unity,* against polarizations, party spirit, and factions. John of the Cross had memorized Jesus' "high priestly" prayer for unity at the Last Supper, and prayed it often—daily, some biographers say—for the splits in the Carmelite Order. The church is always being crucified by her own members—but love is a unitive force. 2) *Learn the art and science of conflict resolution.* Management and labor have found ways to make conflicts positive. Carpenters and their employers do this as a matter of course, but they struggled long and hard to develop ways to solve workplace disputes equitably, and are still grappling with new issues as they arise. Conflict resolution helps a working team to achieve a wider synthesis of two opposing views. The theological disputation of John's day and age taught this same kind of holy common sense, the reconciling of two apparently antithetical positions. And finally, as John wrote to one of his directees at the end of his life: 3) *Where there is no love, put love, and you will draw out love* (Letter 26—to María de la Encarnación, July 6, 1591). This is the lesson of the cross. Love is more necessary than ever, and much more real when it is selfless and pure. "For a little of this pure love is more precious to God and the soul and more beneficial to the church, even though it seems one is doing nothing, than all these other works put together" (C, 29, 2).

NOTES

1. This famous statement is repeated in various forms throughout Karl Rahner's works. This particular version may be found in "Christian Living Formerly and Today," in *Theological Investigations,* vol. 7: *Further Theology of the Spiritual Life* (New York, NY: Crossroad, 1977), 15.
2. Several of the "second-generation" Discalced Carmelites of the Italian Congregation, especially Thomas of Jesus, O.C.D., played an instrumental role in the establishment of the Propaganda Fidei. See Peter-Thomas Rohrbach, *Journey to Carith: The Story of the Carmelite Order* (Garden City, NY: Doubleday & Co., 1966), 233ff.
3. I use the term "spirituality" here as a synonym for the technical term "spiritual theology," commonly used of this subdivision of moral theology.
4. Cf. for example, the outline of the growth process inside the front cover of Fr. Marie Eugene's *I Want to See God* (Westminster, MD: Christian Classics, 1978).

JESUS CHRIST IN THE WRITINGS
OF JOHN OF THE CROSS

Regis Jordan, O.C.D.

Regis Jordan is publisher of ICS Publications, chair of the Institute of Carmelite Studies, and superior of the community of Discalced Carmelites in Washington, DC.

Implicitly, at least, all the works of St. John of the Cross speak to us of Jesus Christ. John was passionately in love with Jesus Christ, the center, the focal point, of his life. He writes in the "Prayer of a Soul Taken with Love":

> You will not take from me, my God, what you once gave me in your only Son, Jesus Christ, in whom you gave me all I desire....
> Mine are the heavens and mine is the earth. Mine are the nations, the just are mine, and mine the sinners. The angels are mine, and the Mother of God, and all things are mine; and God himself is mine and for me, because Christ is mine and all for me. (*Sayings of Light and Love*, 26 & 27)

"Because Christ is mine"—this is what John believed. Christ was his, given him by the Father. Christ is the Father's ultimate gift, to John and to all of us. John's firm belief that in Christ he was gifted with all that the Father could give him is essential for understanding his message.

Everything John teaches concerning the journey of the human person toward union with God in love, everything he asks of those who begin this journey, is based on the fact that "God so loves us that he gave us his only Son" (see Jn 3:16). He gave us his Son to be to be our possession. Christ now belongs to John, to us.

THE INCARNATION AND THE PASCHAL MYSTERY

But how and when was this ultimate gift of God given to us? John directs our attention especially to two moments of Christ's life: his Incarnation and his death.

The Incarnation

The moment the Word became flesh and dwelt among us he became God's gift to us, our possession. At this instant, the Father gave us all that he could, and now has nothing more to give us. Jesus, the "God-man," the Word made flesh, is the outpouring of the Father's love for us. John viewed the Incarnation as the triumphal entrance of Christ into the world, and as the uplifting of all creation. He writes in the commentary on the *Spiritual Canticle:*

> Not only by looking at [creatures] did [God] communicate natural being and graces..., but also, with this image of his Son alone, he clothed them in beauty by imparting to them supernatural being. This he did when he took on our human nature and elevated it in the beauty of God, and consequently all creatures, since in human nature he was united with them all. Accordingly, the Son of God proclaimed: *Si ego exaltatus a terra fuero omnia traham ad me ipsum* (If I be lifted up from the earth, I will elevate all things to myself) [Jn 12:32]. And in this elevation of all things through the Incarnation of his Son and through the glory of his resurrection according to the flesh, not only did the Father beautify creatures partially, but...he clothed them entirely in beauty and dignity. (C, 5, 4)

Clearly, John considers the Incarnation (and the Resurrection) the means by which all things are clothed with beauty and dignity.

Again, in stanza 37 of the *Spiritual Canticle* John adds that:

> One of the main reasons for the desire to be dissolved and to be with Christ [Phil 1:23] is to see him face to face and thoroughly understand the profound and eternal mysteries of his Incarnation, which is by no means the lesser part of beatitude. ...The first thing the soul desires on coming to the vision of God is to know and enjoy the deep secrets and mysteries of the Incarnation and the ancient ways of God dependent on it. (C, 37, 1)

In John's teaching, the mystery of the Incarnation is one of the most important reasons for the soul to undertake the long, difficult ascent to the mount of perfection.

> One reason urging the soul most to enter this thicket of God's wisdom and to know its beauty from further within is her wish to unite her intellect with God in the knowledge of the mysteries of the Incarnation, in which is contained the highest and most savory wisdom of all his works. (C, 37, 2)

It is in her knowledge of the Incarnation that the soul will come to know all the beauty and wisdom of things, including her own beauty. In eternity, when the soul's union with its Beloved will be complete, when she will see Christ face to face, the soul will delight in coming to know and enjoy the deep secrets and mysteries of the Incarnation. It will be an eternity of exploring the deep, unfathomable caverns of this mystery.

The Paschal Mystery

Within the totality of the Paschal Mystery, John places special emphasis on the cross (as one would expect from his religious subtitle). He bases his approach to the theme of *absolute negation*—one of the key elements in his doctrine (see Daniel Chowning's essay in this volume)—on the death of Christ. Christ's death is the motive and model for own death. This accounts for John's radical teaching on the so-called *negative way:* the death, the self-abasement of the soul in the sensual and spiritual nights must correspond to the death of Christ, so that the soul may be united to him and, through him, with the Trinity. (We will see this more clearly in a moment, when we consider Christ as the Way.)

The mystery of the Incarnation and the Paschal Mystery, therefore, are the two key Christological touchstones in the doctrine of St. John of the Cross. They are the mysteries before which John stood in awe and wonder. The divine love revealed in Christ's Incarnation and Passion overwhelmed him, and was the source of his love for God, for Christ. It is almost as if we can hear John saying: "My God, what have you done? Do I dare believe what you have done for me? Can it be true that you have sent, not just any messenger, but your only Son? Can you love me so much, my God, that this could be so?" We can almost see him trembling with wonderment and joy, as the implications of these mysteries flowed over him.

CHRIST THE WAY, THE TRUTH AND THE LIFE

What implications did John draw from meditating and reflecting on the mystery of the Incarnation? What specific role does the Word-made-flesh, the God-man, Jesus Christ, play in John's spiritual doctrine? How is he involved in the various phases of our spiritual journey?

John considers Christ's role in the *Ascent.* Turning to Scripture, as usual, he writes: "A person makes progress only by imitating Christ, who is the Way, the Truth, and the Life. No one goes to the Father but through him, as he states himself in St. John [Jn. 14:6]" (A, 2, 7, 8).

For John, then, Christ is the *Way,* the *Truth,* and the *Life.* Christ, and Christ alone, is the one chosen by the Father through whom we can come to the union of love with God.

Taking our lead from the passage just cited, let us consider John's teaching on the role of Christ in the spiritual journey, by reflecting on Christ as the Way, the Truth, and the Life.

Christ the Way

John talks about Christ as the Way in terms of our call to imitate him. He writes: "I would not consider any spirituality worthwhile that wants to walk in sweetness and ease and run from the imitation of Christ" (A, 2, 7, 8). When giving counsels on how to conquer one's appetites upon entering the night of sense, or as one begins the journey, John advises:

> ...have a habitual desire to imitate Christ in all your deeds by bringing your life into conformity with his. You must then study his life to know how to imitate him and behave in all events as he would. (A 1, 13, 3)

The imitation of Christ is, for John, the way to make progress on the journey toward loving union with God.

There are three things worth noting in the last quotation. First, one has to have a *desire* to imitate Christ. Second, the *goal* is to bring of one's life into conformity with his. Third, the *means* to this goal is study of the life of Christ.

Desire

The first thing St. John of the Cross says we need for imitating Christ is the *desire* to do so. Without this desire, we will make no headway. We know this from our own experience in other areas of life. If we want to achieve something worthwhile in any field we have to be motivated. If we do not really desire it, we know that, no matter how good the goal might be, we will not invest the necessary effort. How many times have we said to ourselves and others that we want something, only to find out later that we really didn't desire it, at least not enough to do what was necessary to get it? Often the difference between success and failure is not our lack of talent, intelligence, or physical strength, but our lack of desire, our unwillingness to pay the price necessary to achieve the goal. John of the Cross, keen observer of human nature, knew that the same dynamic applies to the spiritual journey. If we believe that Christ is truly the Way, then we must desire with all our being to imitate him. The first requirement, then, is *the desire to imitate Christ in all our deeds.*

Study

For John, studying Christ's life does not mean merely acquiring an intellectual knowledge of him. Rather, it involves a reflective, "prayerful" pondering. It is not enough for us simply to read the New Testament or some life of Christ occasionally. It means that we must constantly read and reread Sacred Scripture, both the Old Testament and the New Testament. We must make every effort, according to our abilities, to understand everything we can about Christ, his times, his society and its various institutions (such as Judaism as it was practiced then, who the Pharisees and Sadducees were, and whatever else will give us insight into his life situation). Christ did not live in a vacuum. He was a Jew, living under the Roman domination of his homeland, and schooled in the Judaism of a certain historical period. All of these things can give us insights into the attitudes he brought to the various situations in his life.

Included in study, of course, is need for constant meditation on what we learn about Jesus' life, desires and attitudes—not simply speculative theorizing, but prayerful reflection on our own life in the light of Christ's, analyzing and comparing our desires and attitudes with his, asking constantly whether or not our our desires and attitudes are in conformity with Christ's, and if not, why they differ, and what we must do to make Christ's desires and attitudes our own. Our prayer is one of surrender to the will of God, as his Spirit reveals to us the deeper desires and attitudes of Christ that he wants us to make our own.

Conformity with Christ's Life

What does this imitation of Christ involve? For John, it consists in bringing our life into conformity with Christ's, "behaving in all events as he would" (ibid.).

As we have seen, this means, first of all, that we must make the desires and attitudes of Christ our own. We must rid ourselves of our own disordered desires and attitudes, the effects of our sinfulness and self-ishness. Whether the desire or attitude has to do with material or spiritual things, it must be brought into conformity with Christ. Some of the obvious desires of Christ as found in the New Testament are: to announce and help establish the reign of God; to do the will of the Father in all things; and to unite all people into one in himself. The attitudes he displayed in his life include: a radical openness to others, especially the outcasts of his society, those considered sinners, sick, and downtrodden; a spirit of forgiveness, not seven times but seventy times seven; his simple and direct approach to prayer; his attitude of total availability to others, even to giving up his own life for their sake. These, of course, are just some of the more obvious attitudes of Christ that we must make our own.

For John, bringing one's life into conformity with Christ's goes even deeper. He notes: "Because...Christ is the way and...this way is a death to our natural selves in the sensory and spiritual parts of the soul, ...this death is patterned on Christ's, for he is our model and light" (A, 2, 7, 9).

Thus, imitation of Christ involves renunciation, annihilation, self-emptying, dying to our natural selves; it is the way of the cross. In a very powerful passage, John sums up his teaching on Christ the Way:

> David says of [Christ]: *Ad nihilum redactus sum et nescivi* (I was brought to nothing and did not understand) [Ps 73:22], that those who are truly spiritual might understand the mystery of the door and the way (which is Christ) leading to union with God, and that they might realize that their union with God and the greatness of the work they accomplish will be measured by their annihilation of themselves for God in the sensory and spiritual parts of the soul. When they are reduced to nothing, the highest degree of humility, the spiritual union between their souls and God will be an accomplished fact.... The journey, then, does not consist in consolations, delights, and spiritual feelings, but in the living death of the cross, sensory and spiritual, exterior and interior. (A, 2, 7, 11)

This is the way, because it was the way Christ walked. Christ himself calls us to this when he says: "If any one wishes to follow my way, let him deny himself, take up his cross and follow me. For he who would save his soul shall lose it, and he who loses life for me and for the gospel shall gain it" (Mk 8:34-35). This is how Jesus himself did the will of his heavenly Father, giving him honor and glory. To imitate Christ, to conform one's life to his life, to pattern one's life on Christ's is to follow this same way, the way of the cross. "He is our model and light."

Christ the Truth

That Jesus is the *Truth* for John is clearly seen in chapter 22 of the *Ascent.* There he shows how, with the coming of Christ, it is no longer permissible to petition God for further revelations through supernatural means, that is, through visions, locutions, extraordinary messages, etc. In section 5, John imagines a dialogue between God and a person desiring a vision or an extraordinary revelation. To such a person:

> ...God could answer as follows: If I have already told you all things in my Word, my Son, and if I have no other word, what answer or revelation can I now make that would surpass this? Fasten your eyes on him alone because in him I have spoken and revealed all and in him you will discover even more than you ask for and desire.... For he is my entire locution and response, vision and revelation, which I have already spoken, answered, manifested, and revealed to you by giving him to you as a brother, companion, master, ransom, and reward. (A, 2, 22, 5)

In other words, God has already revealed all in Christ, and has no other word or revelation. In the following section, John continues:

> If you desire me to answer with a word of comfort, behold my Son subject to me and to others out of love for me, and afflicted, and you will see how much he answers you. If you desire me to declare some secret truths or events to you, fix your eyes only on him and you will discern hidden in him the most secret mysteries, and wisdom, and wonders of God.... (A, 2, 22, 6)

John repeatedly tells us to fix our eyes on Christ. He is the complete revelation of the Father. He has been given to us as "brother, compan-

ion, master, ransom, and reward." By fixing our eyes on Christ, by imitating Him in all we do, we "will discern hidden in him the most secret
mysteries, and wisdom, and wonders of God." We will possess the Truth.

How does Christ, as Truth, exercise his role in today's world? John
goes on to say, in sections 7 and 9 of the same chapter, that:

> We must be guided humanly and visibly in all by the law of
> Christ, who is human, and that of his Church and of his ministers.
> Any departure from this road is not only curiosity but extraordinary
> boldness. One should not believe anything coming in a supernatu-
> ral way, but believe only the teaching of Christ, who is human, as I
> say, and of his ministers who are human....
>
> ...God is so pleased that the rule and direction of humans be
> through other humans and that a person be governed by natural
> reason that he definitely does not want us to bestow entire credence
> on his supernatural communications, or be confirmed in their
> strength and security, until they pass through this human channel
> of the mouth of another human person. (A, 2, 22, 7 & 9)

The Truth is to be found in "Christ, who is *human.*" Note how the
Incarnation again comes into John's thought. "We must be guided
by...the law of Christ, who is human.... One should believe only the
teaching of Christ, who is human...."

Then John, the mystic, says something we might not expect: Because
God revealed everything to us in Christ, who is human, he wants "the
rule and direction of humans to be through other humans." All spiritual experiences, ordinary and extraordinary, must be confirmed
"through...the mouth of another human person." Christ, the Word-
made-flesh, continues his role through the ministers of the church.
Here we find echoed the great truth that Christ remains with his people,
the church, in each of its members. Christ continues to exercise his
salvific work in and through other men and women. To find Christ, to
be sure that we have his truth, we simply have to turn to one another
with the eyes of faith. It is in one another that we will find Christ,
through one another that Christ speaks to us.

Christ the Life

Throughout the Gospel Christ affirms that he is the source of eternal life. Talking to the Samaritan woman, Christ tells her that anyone

drinking the water that he will give will never thirst again, that this water
will become a spring of water welling up to eternal life (Jn 4:13ff). Elsewhere the Gospel of John says: "Jesus answered them: Do not labor for
the food that perishes, but for the food that endures to eternal life,
which the Son of man will give to you" (Jn 6:27). Or again: "I am the
bread of life.... I have come down from heaven, not to do my will, but
the will of him who sent me.... This is the will of my Father, that everyone who sees the Son and believes in him should have eternal life; and
I will raise him up at the last day" (Jn 6: 35ff.).

Taking his cue from such Scriptural passages, St. John of the Cross
speaks of Christ as the *Life* throughout his works. All the various aspects
of the journey he describes—i.e., mortification, detachment, the dark
nights of sense and spirit, annihilation—have one purpose, the transformation of one's life into the divine life of Christ. This is the union of
love to which John is guiding us. Commenting in stanza 12 of the *Spiritual Canticle* on the line "Which I bear sketched deep within my heart,"
John writes:

> When there is union of love, ...it is true to say that the Beloved
> lives in the lover and the lover in the Beloved. Love produces such
> likeness in this transformation of lovers that one can say each is the
> other and both are one.... Thus each one lives in the other and is
> the other, and both are one in the transformation of love. (C, 12, 7)

In the union of love, the Beloved (Christ) and the lover (the soul)
are so transformed into one another that now there is only one life.
John, commenting St. Paul's statement in Galatians 2:20—"I live, now
not I, but Christ lives in me"—notes in this same stanza:

> In saying, "I live, now not I," he meant that even though he had
> life it was not his because he was transformed in Christ, and it was
> divine more than human. He consequently asserts that he does not
> live but that Christ lives in him. In accord with this likeness and trans-
> formation, we can say that his life and Christ's were one life through
> union of love. (C, 12, 8)

At every level the transformation is so complete that the life of the
person is more divine than human. As John writes in the *Living Flame of
Love:*

In this new life that the soul lives when it has arrived at the perfect union with God..., all the inclinations and activity of the appetites and faculties—of their own the operation of death and the privation of the spiritual life—become divine. (F, 2, 33)

The Beloved and the lover now live in each other; both are one in the union of love. Even a person's most basic operations have their source in the life of the Beloved, in the life now shared with the Bridegroom, with Christ.

CONCLUSION

John of the Cross speaks to us from the summit of the mountain, as one who has experienced the most intimate union of love with God possible in this life. He himself has tasted and come to the knowledge of the mysteries of God, especially those of Christ's Incarnation and Passion. He has explored the deep caverns of Christ described in the *Spiritual Canticle*. The infinite mysteries of Christ have been revealed to him from within the life of the Trinity itself. He sees all things now, not from a merely human point of view, but from God's own point of view. He comes to see that in the divine plan, Christ is, indeed, the only way to the Father. Christ is the Way, the Truth, and the Life.

In speaking of Christ the *Way*, John speaks in terms of imitation. We are to imitate Christ in all things, but especially in emptying ourselves as he did. As Christ accepted the Father's will that the way to life was through the cross, through annihilation and death, so too must we imitate Christ in this, the surest and safest way to union with God in this life and the next.

Christ is the *Truth*, because in him the Father has spoken his unique Word, his only begotten Son. Out of love he has sent his Son to reveal everything he, the Father, desires us to know, everything that we need know to come to him. We have no need for any other extraordinary revelations. In Christ, the Father has given us the Truth.

By uniting ourselves to Christ, through imitation, through listening and accepting his revelation, his truth, we already possess divine *Life*. This life, which we now possess through grace and adhere to in faith, will be the same life we will enjoy when we see God face-to-face. And one of the greatest joys of this face-to-face encounter with God will be the satisfaction of knowing and experiencing the deep mysteries of the

Incarnation and Passion.

We see, therefore, that the entire doctrine of St. John of the Cross rests on Jesus Christ, the Word-made-flesh. Whatever John asks of us, as we journey toward union, no matter how difficult, has but one purpose: to bring us to this union of love with God through Jesus Christ, the Way, the Truth and the Life.[1]

NOTES

1. For further material on John's doctrine in general, and his Christology in particular, see: Norbert Cummins, *An Introduction to St. John of the Cross* (Darlington Carmel, 1986); E. W. Trueman Dicken, *The Crucible of Love: A Study of the Mysticism of St. Teresa of Jesus and St. John of the Cross* (New York, NY: Sheed & Ward, 1983); Thomas Dubay, *Fire Within:St. Teresa of Avila, St. John of the Cross, and the Gospel—On Prayer* (San Francisco, CA: Ignatius Press, 1989); Marie-Eugene, *I Want to See God* (Westminster, MD: Christian Classics, 1978); Idem, *I Am a Daughter of the Church* (Westminster, MD: Christian Classics, 1978); Florencio Garcia Muñoz, *Cristologia de San Juan de la Cruz: Sistematica y Mistica* (Madrid: Universidad Pontificia de Salamanca y Fundacion Universitaria Española, 1982); Federico Ruiz, *St. John of the Cross: The Saint and His Teaching* (Darlington Carmel, 1988); Tomas de la Cruz (Alvarez), "The Carmelite School: St. Teresa and St. John of the Cross," in *Jesus in Christian Devotion and Contemplation*, trans. Paul J. Oligny (St. Meinrad, IN: Abbey Press, 1974).

MARY AND THE HOLY SPIRIT
IN THE WRITINGS OF JOHN OF THE CROSS

Emmanuel J. Sullivan, O.C.D.

Emmanuel Sullivan is a member of the Institute of Carmelite Studies and a past president of The Mariological Society of America. He is an associate professor of philosophy and religious studies and chair of the Religious Studies Department at St. Joseph's College in North Windham, ME.

MARY IN THE CARMELITE TRADITION

In the history of the Church, the Order of Carmel has come to be known for its dedication to a life of prayer and to Mary, the Mother of Jesus. From its very earliest days near the end of the twelfth century, the hermits who gathered together on Mount Carmel to lead a life of prayer built in the midst of their cells a small chapel dedicated to Mary. Soon they became known as "The Brothers of Our Lady of Mount Carmel," and that little chapel became the focal point of their daily existence.

As the Order migrated to Europe and adopted a life-style similar to that of the mendicant friars, on more than one occasion the Carmelites successfully defended their right to be known as the "Brothers of the Most Blessed Virgin Mary of Mount Carmel." In the thirteenth and fourteenth centuries, in the writings of Carmelites, we find many statements to the effect that the Order was founded to honor and serve Our Lady. While some would question the historical precision of such statements, still the fact remains that the earliest hermits did dedicate their chapel to Mary and that there developed a growing awareness that Mary was in truth the patroness of the Order.

While Carmelites gathered together for "a life of allegiance to Jesus Christ" (*in obsequio Jesu Christi*, according to the *Rule* given them by

Albert of Jerusalem), they looked to Mary as their model and guide in this gift of their lives to the service of Christ and his church. Wherever a Carmel came into existence, it was almost always with a church dedicated to Mary under the title of her Annunciation, Immaculate Conception, or Assumption.

Because of Mary's patronage of the Order, Carmelites looked upon themselves as belonging totally to her; likewise Mary their patroness and Mother belonged in a very special way to the Order of Carmel and to each of its members. In the fourteenth and fifteenth centuries, it was Mary the Most Pure Virgin who became the focus of Carmel's Marian devotion. What was stressed was not so much Mary's bodily chastity as her purity of heart and total dedication to God.

This understanding of devotion to Mary was in complete accord with Carmel's contemplative ideal, as clearly expressed in the famous work known as *The Institution of the First Monks*, which speaks of the goal of Carmelite life in the following terms:

> In regard to that life we may distinguish two aims, the one of which we may attain to, with the help of God's grace, by our own efforts and by virtuous living. This is to offer to God a heart holy and pure from all actual stain of sin.... The second aim of this life is something that can be bestowed upon us only by God's bounty, namely to taste in our hearts and experience in our minds, not only after death but even during this mortal life, something of the power of the divine presence, and the bliss of heavenly glory.

This work and the consequent spirituality that it engendered had a tremendous influence, centering Carmelite spirituality on Mary as the model, personification, and embodiment of its contemplative ideal. The goal and the ideal of Mary's life came to be seen as the goal and ideal of the life of every Carmelite. While Albert's *Rule* for the Carmelites does not mention Mary by name, it does call all Carmelites to a continual meditation and living assimilation of the word of God, "pondering the Law of the Lord day and night." Carmelites were quick to realize that no one ever heard or kept that divine word better than did their Patroness and Mother, Mary.

It should also noted that during this same period Mary the Most Pure Virgin became increasingly known as Mary, the sister of each and every Carmelite. The Order had always been known as the Brothers of our Lady of Mount Carmel, but now a deeper consciousness emerged of what that title meant. Mary our Patroness, Mary our Mother, is also our Sister. Our very home is her home, and the habit we wear unites us in a most intimate way to her. Carmelites began to appreciate as never before that Mary is not just above and beyond us in so many ways, but is also one with us. She is our sister, and as our sister she is with us always and everywhere.

MARY IN THE LIFE OF JOHN OF THE CROSS

It was to Carmel thus permeated with the presence of Mary and the call to imitate her in her total response to God that Juan de Yepes came at the age of twenty in the year 1563. Just as Carmel was totally Marian before John's entrance into the Carmelite novitiate, with equal truth it could be said that John was totally Marian before joining Carmel. All his biographers attest to his great love and devotion to Mary, the Mother of Jesus. Without exception, these same biographers recount how on more than one occasion Mary had intervened in an extraordinary way to save John from almost certain death. There seems to be little doubt that it was Mary who attracted John to Carmel. John would certainly have felt very much at home in the distinctively Marian atmosphere that was and is so much a part of life in Carmel.

In his years of Carmelite formation, John's love and devotion to Mary would grow even deeper and more intense. We know that very soon after his ordination to the priesthood in 1567, John came in contact with Teresa of Jesus and learned of her intention to extend the reform of Carmel to include friars as well as nuns. At this particular time, John informed her that he was on the verge of leaving Carmel to join the Carthusians. Just why he was considering this move is not known, but had he carried it out, he would have had to give up much that he deeply appreciated, not the least of which was Carmel's deep and pervasive Marian tradition. At any rate, as she testifies in the *Book of Foundations,* Teresa urged John to reconsider, and "pointed out the great good that would be accomplished if in his desire to improve he were to remain in his own order" (F, 3, 17).It has been suggested that Teresa prevailed on John's great love for Mary, and that it was this that attracted him to join her in the work of the reform of Carmel. If this is true, then we could say that Mary not only brought John to Carmel, but also kept him in Carmel.

In November of the following year, 1568, John became one of the founding members of the first monastery of discalced Carmelite friars, in Duruelo. From this time and until his death in December of 1591, John played a very important role in the life of the new and growing family of discalced Carmelites. He held many important offices among the discalced and was of great assistance to Teresa of Jesus and her Carmelite nuns. He also endured many difficulties and misunderstandings, especially in his later years. But since these have already been described by other contributors to this volume, let us turn now to John's texts, which have earned for him the title of "Doctor of the Church."

JOHN'S MARIAN DOCTRINE

All of John's writings, his prose and even more his poetry, tell us of what God will accomplish in us through prayer, as well as what wonders God has already accomplished, in our lives and in our world. John is constantly urging us to make room within ourselves for God, to empty ourselves, that God may live and act in and through each one of us. Mary is ever present in John's thoughts. She more than anyone else exemplifies that self-emptiness within that calls forth the very fullness of God's self-communication, presence and love. For John, it is Mary who teaches us what constant intimate union with God means. It is Mary who shows us how to be responsive to the work of the Holy Spirit molding us in the image of her Son. And it is Mary who teaches us how to pray, and who helps us to learn and grow spiritually from our sufferings, so that we might more readily respond to and ease the sufferings of others.

A question often asked is why John wrote so little directly about Mary. The truth is that while the explicit references to Mary are very few, all of John's writings are really centered on Mary. Actually, there is little about Mary that John has left unsaid. His whole spiritual doctrine conveys an implicit Mariology.

John's writings are all concerned with the union of the soul with God. In his mind, the prime exemplar and perfect model of the soul united in union of love with God is Mary, the Mother of Jesus. All that John teaches about that union finds its focus not just in doctrines and principles but in the very person of the Virgin Mother. For him, Mary is the living embodiment of all that he has come to know and experience about union with God.

While prayer and devotion to Mary are the two distinctive characteristics of Carmelite life, in John's case these two characteristics merge into one. For him, Carmelite life is not a life of prayer *and* devotion to Mary, but rather a prolongation, a continuation of Mary's own life of prayer. The goal of Carmelite life and the goal of every Christian life is that very same union with God that John sees so clearly present in the life of Mary.

In an excellent recent article on "The Marian Gospel of Saint John of the Cross," Father José Vicente Rodriguez examines all the texts in the writings of Saint John where there is an explicit reference to Mary.[1] He lists a total of twelve such instances. When we examine these, we find that Rodriguez, like so many before him, identifies only four references to Mary in the major works of Saint John. The first is found in chapter 2 of book 3 of the *Ascent of Mount Carmel,* and is considered the most fundamental and significant of John's Marian texts. In the commentary on the *Spiritual Canticle,* we find two more explicit references to Mary: one in stanza 2, which treats of Mary at the wedding at Cana; and another in stanza 20, which treats of suffering in the life of Mary. The fourth Marian reference from John's major works is in the commentary on stanza 3 of the *Living Flame of Love,* and treats of the meaning of Mary's overshadowing by the Holy Spirit.

Other significant references to Mary occur in two of John's poems: "The Romance on the Gospel Text: *In Principio Erat Verbum,*" and the little poem entitled: "Del Verbo Divino." The final important Marian reference is found in the "Prayer of a Soul Taken with Love," included among the "Sayings of Light and Love." All the remaining references are incidental invocations of the name of Mary in John's letters and counsels to various religious.

Before considering the four major Marian references, it would be well to recall some of what Fr. Rodriguez has to say in his introductory remarks. First, he reminds us that for Saint John of the Cross, Mary is encountered not as a theological problem but as a real person clearly present in the history of salvation. He notes that John always sees Mary in relation to Christ and in relation to his Mystical Body.

It is in the two poems mentioned above (i.e., the "Romances" and "Del Verbo Divino") that we discover something of the depth and intensity of John's own personal love and devotion to Mary. In the major treatises, however, because of his immediate preoccupation with pastoral concerns and his general goal of discussing union with God, John's references to Mary are more restrained. Yet even here, says Rodriguez,

"John is a master in situating Mary at strategic points and in key contexts, in order to shed light on his doctrine and to encourage us on our way by Mary's example and her docility in allowing herself to be formed by the Holy Spirit."

Ascent of Mount Carmel

In chapter 2 of book 3 of the *Ascent,* we find the following passage, considered (as we have said) the principal Marian text of Saint John of the Cross.

> ...God alone moves these souls [who have reached habitual union with God] toward those works that are in harmony with his will and ordinance, and they cannot be moved toward others. Thus the works and prayer of these souls always produce their effect.
>
> Such were the prayer and the works of our Lady, the most glorious Virgin Raised from the very beginning to this high estate, she never had the form of any creature impressed in her soul, nor was she moved by any, for she was always moved by the Holy Spirit. (A, 3, 2, 10)

The context in which John make this statement is a discussion of the purification of the memory and its union with God. The soul must be purified of all natural knowledge, all such knowledge as can be formed from the objects of the five corporal senses. For the memory cannot be united both with God and with sensory forms and distinct kinds of knowledge, inasmuch as God has no such form or image naturally comprehensible to the memory. Divine union empties the memory of all particular forms and kinds of knowledge and elevates it to the supernatural.

John affirms that in the state of union:

> ...all the operations of the memory and the other faculties...are divine. God now possesses these faculties as their complete lord because of their transformation in him. And consequently it is he who divinely moves and commands them according to his divine spirit and will.... [In this state] the operations of the soul united with God are of the divine Spirit and are divine. (A, 3, 2, 8)

For John, souls in this state "perform only fitting and reasonable works and none that are not so. For God's Spirit makes them know what must be known and ignore what must be ignored, remember what ought to be remembered—with or without forms—and forget what ought to be forgotten, and makes them love what they ought to love, and keeps them from loving what is not in God." Precisely because "God alone moves these souls" to do the works in harmony with his will and ordinance, they cannot be moved toward other works. "Thus the works and the prayers of these souls always produce their effect" (A, 3, 2, 10).

According to Rodriguez, when we view this principal Marian text in its context, the following points should be noted:

1. The Virgin Mary was elevated to perfect union with God from the first instant of her existence.

2. This initial union implies without question the Immaculate Conception.

3. Mary, the perfect pre-redeemed one, remains always at the summit of perfection, and for John of the Cross the efficacy and excellence of her life and actions derive from the fact that she remains forever so empowered by God.

4. This passage clearly identifies the source of the effectiveness of her prayer and petitions. If we recall here the intervention of Our Lady at Cana and in other circumstances, the positive and efficacious response of Christ and his heavenly Father will not surprise us, for they together with the Holy Spirit were encouraging this very prayer that they desired to grant.

5. In the light of these considerations, it is evident that John of the Cross sees Mary as one who prays, as the perfect one who prays, one more perfect than her prayer. In Mary's case, as in no one else's, the Spirit of the Lord aids human weakness; dwelling in her, he pleads with unspeakable groanings in order to manifest the spiritual yearnings she can neither fully express or comprehend (cf. Rom 8: 26-27).

6. Besides the petitions and the prayers of Mary, the text mentions Mary's works as full of efficacy. We can think of her cooperating with Christ in the history of salvation, yet knowing that "the total salvific influence of the Blessed Virgin on men originates, not from some inner necessity, but from the divine pleasure. It flows from the superabundance of the merits of Christ, rests on his mediation, depends entirely on it and draws all its power from it" (*Lumen Gentium,* #60).

7. Without in any way forcing John's text, it is clear that the passage does not reserve the efficacy of her works, prayers and petitions to the more solemn moments in Mary's life, such as the Annunciation, the birth of Christ, her presence at the cross and in the Cenacle. "All her works, prayers and petitions" means exactly that: *all*, including those which humanly speaking we call less important. When the Second Vatican Council spoke of Mary's collaboration, it stated precisely: "This union of the Mother with the Son in the work of salvation is made manifest from the time of Christ's virginal conception up to his death" (*Lumen Gentium*,57). But Rodriguez asks:

> Was the involvement of Mary in the work of salvation blocked or frozen before the Annunciation? This is certainly the impression we might get from reading the Council [document]. Yet we can ask (and in the question is found our positive response): Was the Spirit active in the world before Christ was glorified, and even before he was conceived by the work of the same Holy Spirit, and is the Spirit present and active in Mary even before the Incarnation? Was she not enjoying by anticipation and for always the fruits of the redemption?
>
> Should we not consider all her works, prayers and petitions an involvement in the future redemption of all humanity? Why cannot we call this anterior world of Mary, and all that proceeds from the action of the Spirit within her, an intimate collaboration with the Son and Redeemer? Is the category of space and time an insuperable impediment?

8. Just as Mary with the Apostles implored the gift of the Spirit, could not Mary moved by the Spirit have implored anteriorly the coming of the Messiah? There is nothing unusual in this notion, for John in his poetry has already told how the prophets and men of God had done precisely this. Nevertheless, to petition or request is not yet always "impetration" in the technical sense, which includes *obtaining* through prayer that which is requested or petitioned. If for the reasons given we believe in John's doctrine concerning the efficacy of Mary's prayer then, in her case, to pray and to implore is the same as to impetrate; in her case, to make a request is to obtain that which is requested.

9. In this text, John recalls the most pure docility of Mary to the action of the Holy Spirit. At the end of the same chapter, although he does not name her explicitly, John does seem to have her clearly in mind when he writes:

Although it is true that a person will hardly be found whose union with God is so continuous that the faculties, without any form, are always divinely moved, nevertheless, there are those who are very habitually moved by God and not by themselves in their operations, as Saint Paul says: The children of God (those who are transformed in God and united to him) are moved by the Spirit of God (that is, moved to divine works in their faculties) [Rm 8:14]. It is no marvel that the operations are divine, since the union of the soul with God is divine. (A, 3, 2, 16)

Mary is the creature always moved by the Holy Spirit, and in her this divine adoption is realized in a perfect manner.

10. If we apply some of John's descriptions of God's generous self-communication to souls (wherever there is room), we would find the basis for an interior biography of our Lady, cooperating with the inhabitation of the Holy Trinity. John assures us that in the soul faithful in love, the promise of the Son of God will be fulfilled: that the Most Blessed Trinity will come and dwell in anyone who loves him (see Jn 14:23ff.). God takes up his abode in us by making us live the life of God and dwell in the Father, Son, and Holy Spirit.

11. Finally, we should note John's own doctrine, that the most holy Virgin, elevated to the state of perfect union with God from the very beginning, did not experience that same forgetfulness and purification of the memory that we suffer who are still on the road to perfection.

* * *

Many years ago, in an article on "The Mariology of Saint John of the Cross," Otilio Rodriguez noted that: "This one citation of the Mystical Doctor is the equivalent of an entire volume of Mariology."[2] More recently (1981), in an article in Spanish entitled: "The Holy Spirit and the Virgin Mary According to Saint John of the Cross", another distinguished Carmelite scholar, Father Ismael Bengoechea, has many very interesting things to say about this basic text. He begins by observing that this brief Marian passage from the *Ascent of Mount Carmel* tells us all that John needs to tell us about Mary, and adds that "John of the Cross has succeeded in condensing in this one utterance his entire system of spirituality, and has made of it a radically pneumatological vision. No modern charismatic writer has expressed with greater profundity the unlimited action of the Paraclete in Mary." In fact, says Bengoechea, "I do not believe that it is possible to say more about the perfection of Mary in fewer words."[3] He goes on to say that while John has written much on the Holy Spirit and little explicitly on Mary, yet if we were to speak of a Mariology according to Saint John of the Cross, it would be essentially a pneumatological Mariology, one in which the role of the Holy Spirit would be clearly and emphatically stressed.

Spiritual Canticle

On two occasions in the *Spiritual Canticle,* John brings the example of Mary to our attention. In the commentary on stanza 2, he tells us that:

> The discreet lover does not care to ask for what she lacks or desires, but only indicates this need, so that the Beloved may do what he pleases. When the Blessed Virgin spoke to her Beloved Son at the wedding feast at Cana in Galilee, she did not ask directly for the wine, but merely remarked: *They have no wine* [Jn 2:3]. (C, 2, 8)

John then lists three reasons why it is better to merely show our need to the Lord, rather than tell him how to fulfill those needs.

> First, the Lord known what is suitable for us better than we do; second, the Beloved has more compassion when he beholds the need and the resignation of a soul that loves him; third, the soul is better safeguarded against self-love and possessiveness by indicating its lack, rather than by asking for what in its opinion is wanting. (ibid.)

Here Mary is presented to us as the perfect model of the prayer of petition.

In stanza 20, John is treating of the preparation of the soul for spiritual marriage. Part of that preparation consists in the subduing of the passions, which John (following Boethius) lists as joy, sorrow, hope, and fear. When the preparation is complete, sensible sorrow is no longer felt, though the effects of such sorrow are experienced on a higher level. John tells us: "Sometimes, however, and at certain periods, God allows [the soul] to feel things and suffer from them so she might gain more merit and grow in the fervor of love, or for other reasons, as he did with the Virgin Mother, St. Paul, and others" (C, 20 & 21, 10).

While the experience of sensible sorrow would otherwise have been incompatible with our Lady's state of intimate union with God, John tells us that God allowed her to experience such sorrow, precisely that she might grow in love; and, we could add, that she might increase in her compassion for all of us. Thus Mary is presented to us as the Mother of Sorrows and as one who knows by experience what it means to endure intense sorrow.

Living Flame of Love

Finally, in stanza 3 of the *Living Flame of Love*, John once again refers to Mary's intimate union with the Holy Spirit. He is describing the state of transforming union with God, and likens the graces God bestows on a soul in this state to an "overshadowing." For John:

> ...when a person is covered by a shadow, it is a sign that someone else is nearby to protect and favor. As a result the Angel Gabriel called the conception of the Son of God, that favor granted to the Virgin Mary, an overshadowing of the Holy Spirit: *The Holy Spirit will come upon you and the power of the most High will overshadow you.* (F, 3, 12).

John goes on to tell us that when the Holy Spirit casts his shadow on a soul, he is so close that he not only touches but is united with it, and the soul understands and experiences the power, wisdom and glory of God (see F, 3, 15). Thus we gain further insight into what Mary's life must have been like, she being more closely united to the Holy Spirit than all other creatures.

Other Passages

In addition to the four Marian references in his major works, there is also a very significant reference to Mary in John's "Prayer of a Soul Taken with Love." John always manifested a deep awareness that he belonged totally to Mary, and in this very beautiful little prayer, he gives expression to his equally deep conviction that Mary belongs totally and completely to each one of us. In this prayer, John speaks for all of us as he says to our heavenly Father:

> You will not take from me, my God, what you once gave me, in your only Son, Jesus Christ, in whom you gave me all I desire....

> Mine are the heavens and mine is the earth. Mine are the na-
> tions, the just are mine, and mine the sinners. The angels are mine,
> and the Mother of God, and all things are mine; and God Himself is
> mine and for me, because Christ is mine and all for me. (*Sayings of
> Light and Love*, 26-27)

I find this reference to Mary, in a certain sense, even more significant than all the others. Here John isn't just recounting wonderful
things *about* Mary, but is telling us she is *ours*, with us and for us, always
and everywhere. He is telling us that we must realize and appreciate that
Mary belongs totally and completely to each one of us. Our guide on
the road to union with God is no distant stranger, but our very own
Blessed Mother.

CONCLUSION

For John of the Cross, our goal in life is literally to love God as we
are loved by God. While union with God does not entail on the part of
the soul a substantial conversion into the very being of God, it does
involve a very real participation in the divine life. When united with God,
we still remain creatures, and God still remains God. Yet, our powers and
our activities are so divinized, so influenced by the Holy Spirit, that we
together with the Holy Spirit act as one. Not only are we possessed by
the Holy Spirit, but, in reality, we ourselves possess that same Holy Spirit.
It is this possession of the Holy Spirit that enables us in the very truest
sense to love God with the very Love wherewith he loves us. In the state
of union, the soul responds to God with a love worthy of and equal to
God's, and that love is his own Holy Spirit. In the state of union, the soul
loves God not just with its own ability, but with and through the very
person of the Holy Spirit, that living bond of love that unites the Father
and the Son.

All of John's writings are concerned with loving union of the soul
with God. While he mentions Mary explicitly on but few occasions, there
can be no doubt that Mary is constantly present in his thoughts. It is
axiomatic of John's teaching that we possess the Holy Spirit to the extent that we ourselves are possessed by the Holy Spirit. For John, no
human person was ever more possessed by the Holy Spirit or possessed
the Holy Spirit more fully than Mary, the Mother of Jesus and our own
Blessed Mother. She is for John and for all of us, the perfect model and

inspiration of loving intimate union with God.

For Saint John of the Cross, holiness—union with God—is much more a reality to be received than a reality to be achieved. Our efforts, our works and our prayers are necessary, but they only help us to be free to receive God's love. Even these efforts, works, and prayers are themselves God's gift to us, helping to prepare us for an even greater gift, God's own self-communication.

For John, Mary is our greatest help on our journey to union with God. Not only do we belong especially to her; John is deeply and constantly aware that she belongs especially to us. Mary helps us to see that it is with and by God's own Love that we are to love him who loves us so much.

For me, John's motto "Love is repaid only by love" gives us his entire message. According to our saint, we only truly love God when we love him as he loves us—and it is by the Holy Spirit that he loves us, and it is by that same Holy Spirit that we must love him. Our goal in life is the same as Mary's—to open ourselves to the Holy Spirit, that we, like Mary, may love God as we are loved by God, and that we, like Mary, may love God with his own Holy Spirit.

NOTES

1. See José Vicente Rodriguez, "Evangelio Mariano de San Juan de La Cruz," *Ephemerides Mariologicae* 40 (1990): 245-272.
2. See Otilio Rodriguez, "Mariologia de san Juan de la Cruz," *Estudios Marianos* 2 (1943): 359-399.
3. Ismael Bengoechea, "El Espiritu Santo y La Virgen Maria, segun San Juan de la Cruz," *Ephemerides Mariologicae* 31 (1981): 51-70.
4. Other works consulted include: Fr. Conrad, *Carmel is All Mary's* (St. Teresa's Press: Flemington, NJ, 1965); Ailbe Doolan, "Our Lady and Saint John of the Cross," *Carmelite Digest* 1 (1968): 58-60; Gabriel of St. Mary Magdalen, "Aspetti e sviluppi della grazia di Maria Santissima secondo la doctrina di San Giovanni della Croce," *Rivista di vita spirituale* 5 (1951): 52-70; Gregorio de Jesus Crucificado, "La muerte de amor de Maria," *Estudios Marianos* 9 (1950): 239-268; Ildefonso de la Inmaculada, "Nuevo principio mistico de la Mariologia: San Juan de la Cruz descubre la tecnica de la perfección de Maria," *Miriam* 15 (1963): 115-118; Christopher O'Donnell, "Our Lady of Mount Carmel," in his *At Worship With Mary* (Wilmington, DE: Michael Glazier, 1988), 107-117; Fr. Sebastian, "Our Lady in the Theology of St. John of the Cross," *Mount Carmel Magazine* 9

(1961): 44-50; and Redemptus Mary Valabek, "Mary on the Summit of Mt. Carmel: The Devotion of St. John of the Cross for Our Lady of Mt. Carmel," *Carmel in the World* 21 (1982):135-148.

JOHN OF THE CROSS:
A RADICAL REINTERPRETATION
OF DISCIPLESHIP

John M. Lozano, C.M.F.

Claretian Father John M. Lozano is professor of spirituality at the Catholic Theological Union in Chicago, IL, and the author of numerous books and articles, including Grace and Brokenness in God's Country: An Exploration of American Catholic Spirituality *(Mahwah, NJ: Paulist Press, 1991) .*

One of the many things that intrigue me in reading Saint John of the Cross is the way he interprets the demands that the following of Christ places on believers. His interpretation has drawn my attention for two main reasons: first, because the Saint's use of the Gospel sayings on discipleship shows how basic the idea was for him; and second, because his understanding of these texts constitutes an original contribution to a long and rich hermeneutic tradition.

In this essay, I will attempt to sketch the history and interpretation of these texts, to analyze the Saint's contribution to this history and to examine the role discipleship plays in his spiritual doctrine.

DISCIPLESHIP SAYINGS IN THE APOSTOLIC CHURCH

What it means to be a disciple of Jesus was one of the most pressing questions in the apostolic church. Obviously the answer to this question took on different nuances in the various traditions.

Even so, discipleship—total adherence to Jesus and communion with him—was the key concept shared by the different apostolic communities in order to describe what we would refer to today as Christian

123

identity. Of course, discipleship is a modern, abstract term not found as such in Hebrew, Aramaic or even biblical Greek; the early church instead spoke more concretely of "going after" Christ (Aramaic) or of "following" him (Greek).

The synoptic tradition of Matthew, Mark and Luke, and, in a different way, the Johannine writings, began early on to create a paradigm of discipleship. The stories of calling disciples (e.g., the first four, Levi, the rich young man) were reinterpreted through a process of growing idealization and radicalization in order to make Peter and the other disciples a pattern and source of inspiration for Christian believers.

But even before the Gospels began to take definitive written shape, oral tradition had been transmitting a series of sayings attributed to Jesus, dealing with what was to be expected of his followers. These sayings originally referred to men and women who might want to become Jesus' followers. To be a companion or disciple of Jesus meant basically to share his faith and hope in the inbreaking grace of God's reign. For those closest to Jesus, it meant forming with him a small eschatological community (a community created by hope in the coming reign of God) and sharing in his ministry of proclamation and healing.

After Jesus was crucified and raised up, those who had known him personally began repeating certain sayings that emphasized the demands discipleship placed on those who accepted the Christian call to faith and repentance. Even at this second stage, discipleship was essentially a matter of faith/hope. But the early group had now become the church, and ministry had come to mean a proclamation in the name of the glorified Jesus.

The sayings on discipleship were so important to the early Christian communities that they were carefully kept in the various traditions. One block of them was transmitted by Mark (8:34-38), followed by Matthew (16:24-26) and, in a fuller form, by Luke (9:23-26). Before Jesus' passion, the first verse of this block, "If anyone wants to be a follower of mine, let [him or her] take up the cross and follow me," may have been understood in the sense of "let him/her be ready to face the tragic destiny that hangs over everyone who is suspected of rebellion." After Jesus' death, the saying took on a deeper meaning: "let him/her be ready to share the cross of Jesus." This saying was so memorable, even shocking, that the source common to Matthew and Luke (the "Q" source) had it too (Mt 10:38, Lk 14:27), and so Matthew and Luke repeat it twice.

The group of sayings, or *logia,* underlying the source common to Matthew and Luke insisted particularly on the hardships of discipleship. Matthew and Luke have two further logia, one on the uprootedness of Jesus ("The Son of man has nowhere to lay his head"—Mt 8:20, Lk 9:58), a condition to be shared by his disciples, and the other on the need to transcend family ties ("Let the dead bury their dead"—Mt 8:21, Lk 9:60), to which Luke adds a more sweeping and general saying on the determination one must have in saying yes to the Gospel ("Whoever sets hand to the plough and looks back..."—Lk 9:62).

Finally, Luke seems to have added another saying in the form of a conclusion: "So, those who do not renounce all their possessions cannot be my disciples" (Lk 14:33). Although this formulation is probably Luke's own, its content is already found implicitly in the call stories, and more explicitly in the call of the rich young man (see Mt 19:21 and parallels).

RENUNCIATION

According to these Gospel texts, while discipleship essentially consists of following Jesus (adhering to his message, sharing in his faith), it also demands a strong renunciation as a precondition. One must be ready to lose one's life, to go beyond family bonds and to be free of any enslavement occasioned by material concerns.

The renunciation Jesus demanded was not merely material. He did not expect Peter to divorce his wife; in fact, Jesus seems to have been a visitor in their household (Mk 1:28-31 and parallels). He did not expect them materially to abandon all their possessions; after "leaving their nets and boats" (Mk 1:18-20 and parallels), the disciples returned to them later. Leaving possessions and breaking family ties meant setting one's heart so firmly on God's reign that neither wealth nor family would stop one from being faithful to it.

It was simply a new interpretation of the first and greatest commandment: to love God with one's whole heart, soul and strength (Lv 6:4-5). In its negative form, this commandment did not forbid disciples to love God's creation; rather, it forbade them to set any creature ahead of God, thus making an idol of it. In Jesus' teaching, this commandment took on an eschatological interpretation (to love the God who is definitively coming to save us) and a Christian nuance (to follow Jesus and be with Jesus). Neither the great commandment nor Jesus' invitation to follow him imposed any specifically ascetical renunciation. Jesus was talking about the spiritual freedom necessary for accepting God's reign. This may have been the original meaning of the story of the rich young man, a story that was elaborated several times, as can be seen in the different versions in each of the synoptic Gospels.

LASTING IMPACT

Christians have always been keenly aware of the importance of these Gospel passages. The stories of the call of the disciples and the sayings on the cost of discipleship have been reread constantly, with a view to adapting them to changing historical circumstances.

In the early church they were applied to the martyrs. After the first disciples, the martyrs became the prototypes of radical discipleship. Martyrs were those whose hearts were so firmly set on God's grace that they lost not only their possessions (which were confiscated) and their families (many of whom turned against them), but their very lives for its sake. Origen, in his *Exhortation to Martyrdom* (12, 14 and 37: PG 11: 557-580, 581 and 613), reverts three times to the Gospel sayings on discipleship in order to encourage Christians to die for their faith.[1] He quotes Mt 16:24-27 ("taking up the cross"; "being ready to lose one's life"; "what will it profit anyone to gain the whole world?"). He also recalls Peter's question in Mt 19:27 ("We have left everything to follow you. What can we expect?"), Lk 14:26 ("Anyone who does not hate father and mother...") and Jn 12:25 ("Anyone who loves [his or her] life will lose it, while anyone who hates [his or her] life in this world will keep it for life eternal").

With the end of the era of the martyrs, the same Gospel texts were crucial in raising up the monastic calling in the church. The stories and sayings on the call and cost of discipleship were cited by Athanasius, Jerome and others to explain the meaning of the solitary life. The Pachomian writer Theodore (in Egypt) and the author of the *Rule of the Master* (in Italy) allude to these Gospel passages in explaining the renunciation that is basic to the cenobitic life. The discipleship sayings, to which the mission charge and rule were added, enjoyed great popularity among the poverty movements of the twelfth century, forming the very core of Francis's Rule and strongly influencing the Dominicans. They reappear in the *Constitutions* of the Society of Jesus and afterward in other modern texts.[2]

Hence monks, nuns and successive groups of women and men religious have drawn their inspiration from the Gospel texts on discipleship. As martyrs exemplified discipleship by dying for Christ, religious embodied it by publicly committing their life to God's service and renouncing family and possessions. In both cases, the material renunciations to which they felt called by the Spirit are a concrete expression of setting one's heart on God's reign and thereby receiving total spiritual freedom, which is the very core of discipleship in the New Testament.

SAINT JOHN OF THE CROSS

Saint John of the Cross also considers the Gospel sayings on discipleship as basic to an understanding of the meaning of Christian existence. This is not to say that he quotes them very often, but he does allude to them several times. In his works, there are 17 references to the poor in spirit (19 if we include Mt 5:3) compared to 10 Gospel texts on discipleship (11 if Mt 5:3 is included). Hence the significance of these references lies not so much in their quantity as in their quality: Saint John of the Cross quotes these texts precisely in dealing with subjects that constitute fundamental tenets of his spiritual doctrine. In fact, discipleship is the one basic idea underlying his teaching on a person's attitude in journeying toward the goal of union with God. And for that very reason the sayings on the demands imposed on Christians by their call to follow Jesus come readily to his mind.

He expressly quotes Mk 8:34-35 on taking up one's cross and losing one's life (A, 2, 7, 10), Mt 10:36 on one's family being one's enemies (N, 2, 14, 1; 16, 12), Mt 16:24 on denying oneself (A, 3, 23, 2), Mt 16:25 and Lk 9:24 on losing one's life (A, 2, 7, 6). He twice cites the question of Mt 16:25 on what it profits to gain the whole world and lose one's soul (A, 3, 18, 3 and *Sayings of Light and Love*, 79). He cites two Matthean texts only once: Mt 19:21 on selling all and following Christ (*Sayings*, 165); and Mt 19:23 (or rather, its parallel, Lk 18:21) on how hard it will be for the rich to enter heaven (A, 3, 18, 1). In contrast, he cites one Lukan text four times: Lk 14:33 on the impossibility of becoming a disciple unless one renounces all possessions (A, 1, 5, 2; 2, 6, 4; 3, 7, 2; F, 3, 46).

The reader will have noticed that most of the quotes and allusions occur in the *Ascent of Mount Carmel* (11), followed by the *Dark Night* (3). The reason for this is clear: both the *Ascent* and the *Night* explain the need for total purification, and hence, for the denial of everything in order to be readied for union with God. The *Ascent* deals precisely with active purification, i.e., what Christians carry out actively with the help of God's grace; the *Night* describes the various levels of God's own purifying action on the soul. It is therefore only natural for the Saint to turn especially to the Gospel texts on renunciation in these two works—or rather in these two parts of one work—but with greater reason in the first part, the *Ascent.* Saint John's *Sayings of Light and Love* and his *Counsels* often move within the same perspective. In them, too, the Mystical Doctor twice recalls the Gospel texts on discipleship.

We should also point out that, among all these texts on discipleship, John of the Cross shows a special predilection for two. First, there is the radical statement of Lk 14:33 on the absolute need to give up everything if one wants to become Jesus' disciple. As we noted above, John cites this text four times. The Saint's own radical teaching on denial harmonizes perfectly with Luke's insistence on leaving everything behind. In both cases we have two witnesses to a Christian experience strongly emphasizing the need for radical discipleship. Our Saint reads the same idea in Mt 19:21 ("Go sell all you own...") and in Mt 19:21 ("How hard it is for the rich..."). Each of the latter sayings is quoted only once. In all, then, we have six passages in which Saint John focuses on three Gospel texts stressing the need to renounce all possessions.

Second, there is the saying on those who would save their life and thus lose it, as opposed to those who lose their life for Jesus' sake and thus save it. This saying is found in two Gospel traditions: in the material common to Mt 16:25 and Lk 9:24, and in the distinctive formulation found in Mk 8:35. This statement is cited a total of four times by John. In three instances (A, 2, 7, 6; N, 1, 7, 3; C, 29, 11), the Matthean/Lukan addition "for the sake of the gospel" is missing. Only in one instance A, 2, 7, 4) does John refer expressly to the Markan version. We should also note that Saint John of the Cross discovers the same basic meaning in Jn 12:25: "Those who hate their life in this world keep it for life eternal" (A, 2, 7, 6). In support of this he twice recalls the "what does it profit if one gains the whole world" of Mt 16:26/Lk 9:25 (A, 3, 18, 3; *Sayings of Light and Love,* 79).

The conclusion to be drawn from an examination of these texts is obvious. Most of them revolve around two concepts: the need for total renunciation, and the axiom that we keep our life by losing it for Christ. Saint John of the Cross has a special fondness for these two ideas.

GIVING UP ALL THAT IS NOT GOD

Let us now examine how Saint John of the Cross interprets Jesus' sayings on giving up possessions. We have seen that his favorite text on the subject is Lk 14:33, the most radical statement in the Gospels concerning the renunciation of riches, and one that Luke himself probably developed as a kind of general conclusion: "You cannot be my disciples unless you part with everything you possess."

We find this text for the first time in the first book of the *Ascent*, where John is explaining the need to mortify the appetites in order to reach union with God:

> People, indeed, are ignorant who think it is possible to reach this high state of union with God without first emptying their appetite of all the natural and supernatural things that can be a hindrance to them.... Instructing us about this way, our Lord stated according to St. Luke: *Qui non renuntiat omnibus quae possidet, non potest meus esse discipulus* (Whoever does not renounce all that the will possesses cannot be my disciple).... (A, 1, 5, 2)

In scholastic philosophy, in which John had been well educated, the "appetite" (*appetitus*) means the self as inclined toward whatever appears good and desirable to it.

"Charity, too," he writes elsewhere, "causes a void in the will regarding all things, since it obliges us to love God above everything. We have to withdraw our affection from all in order to center it wholly in God. Christ says through Saint Luke: ...Whoever does not renounce all that the will possesses cannot be my disciple..." (A, 2, 6, 4). In another text he states that a person should never strive to fix in his or her memory the images, ideas and feelings summoned up by extraordinary experiences such as visions, or dwell on them, but should remain detached from them and oriented toward God in pure hope, "for whoever does not renounce all possessions cannot be Christ's disciple" (A, 3, 7, 2). According to the last passage in which the Lukan clause appears, Saint John holds that:

> ...The soul...[must] not be tied to any particular knowledge, earthly or heavenly, or to any covetousness for some satisfaction or pleasure, or to any other apprehension; ...in such a way that it may be empty through the pure negation of every creature, and placed

in spiritual poverty. This is what the soul must do of itself, as the Son
of God counsels: *Whoever does not renounce all possessions cannot be my
disciple* [Lk 14:33]. (F, 3, 46)

Neither should one rejoice in temporal goods (wealth, status, position, family, etc.), since one may very easily "become attached to them"
and fail God.

> This is why the Lord in the Gospel calls them thorns; the one
> who willfully handle them shall be wounded with some sin [Mt 13:22,
> Lk 8:14]. In St. Luke's Gospel the exclamation—which ought to be
> greatly feared— asserts: *How difficult will it be for those who have riches
> to enter the kingdom of heaven* (those who have joy in them), and
> demonstrates clearly a person's obligation not to rejoice in riches,
> since one is thereby exposed to so much danger [Lk 18:24]. (A, 3,
> 18, 1)

RENUNCIATION

The idea of renunciation implicit in these passages and others in
the writings of Saint John of the Cross is very precise, both regarding the
objects we must renounce and the way in which we must renounce them.

Total renunciation—First, as to the objects we must renounce, John
is most explicit: we must give up everything that is not God.

He says that we must empty our appetite of all natural and supernatural things that can be a hindrance to union with God (A, 1, 5, 2).
The meaning is not that some creatures may be an impediment while
others may not; any attachment to any creature will constitute a hindrance, since we tend to become attached to any created thing that has
the appearance of good. We must therefore read him to mean that, to
the extent that anything may be an impediment to union with God, "we
must withdraw our affection" from it in order to love God above all (A,
2, 6, 4). We must be empty through the pure negation of every creature
(F, 3, 46). In the third book of the *Ascent*, from chapter 17 to the end,
John lists all the goods we must renounce by not fixing our joy in them.
They are of all kinds: temporal (riches, status, family), sensory (including artistic objects aimed at stirring our devotion, such as liturgies, sermons, paintings, churches), and even supernatural goods (such as special charisms). In earlier chapters of the same work he tells us that we
must not desire or place our joy in supernatural experiences, such as

words, visions and revelations. In fact, in book 3, chapter 2 of the *Ascent*, this general principle is applied to all concrete images, particular ideas or feelings that may have been evoked by extraordinary spiritual experiences, such as visions, voices and revelations (A, 3, 7, 2).

What is left, then, that we may rightly desire and rightly rejoice in possessing? We know the answer already: God alone.

How to renounce all things—From the passages we have quoted, it is abundantly clear how Saint John of the Cross understands the total renunciation of all creatures. We must "empty the appetite of all" (A, 5, 2). We must "withdraw our affection from all" (A, 2, 6, 4). We must "not be tied" to any spiritual experience (F, 3, 46). It is dangerous to handle riches "with our will"; in other words, to place our joy in them.

Very clearly, Saint John is not just preaching a kind of material renunciation. He does not expect people materially to renounce all riches, nor does he restrict union with God to members of religious institutes. Some of his directees were in fact well-to-do laywomen. He does not intend people to close their ears to beautiful music or their eyes to beautiful paintings or sculptures. In fact, he himself was endowed with an exquisite artistic sensibility. Today he is ranked among the greatest classic poets in Spanish literature, and he used his poems and masterly prose to raise his own heart and the hearts of others to God. He drew a famous image of the crucified Christ leaning over the world (the inspiration for Salvador Dali's well-known re-creation), and loved to carve crucifixes. John does not mean to condemn religious statues or paintings, but rather the "great attachment" that some pious people have to such objects (A, 3, 35, 4; 36, 1). Still less does he expect mystics to reject their spiritual experiences (these are, after all, God's gifts), if for no other reason than that, at least in the deepest and strongest experiences, there is nothing one can do about them.

What the Saint constantly emphasizes is detachment of the heart. As he sees it, the problem lies in the fact that we may easily stop at some created good and become attached to it. If this happens, any creature can take the place of God and become an idol. To put it in a sharper and more positive way: Saint John of the Cross insists on the need for the greatest spiritual freedom.

Spiritual freedom is precisely what he expects of someone who is having spiritual experiences in prayer. Here he is far more insistent, and for two solid reasons. First, while an attachment to material riches or social status can be easily perceived as a danger, spiritual greed can often go undetected. People may treasure their spiritual experiences to the point of fixing their hearts on them. Are they not, after all, rejoicing in God's gifts? Yes, but they may end up loving the gifts of God, instead of looking first to God, the giver. This is a very important point for spiritual direction. Many visionaries have become obsessed with their visions or inner words, constantly reverting to them, speaking or writing about them, recreating them. They succumb to an unhealthy self-centeredness. Genuine mystics, on the contrary, though grateful to God for the gifts they receive, continue their search for the invisible God. Every experience leaves them hungrier for God. They fly beyond their experiences.

Secondly, there is another, more profound reason for this greater stress on the need to be detached from spiritual experiences: all particular feelings, images and concepts of God are only finite reflections of the divinity, and if mystics remain attached to the experiences, they will close their spirit to the infinite, transcendent reality to which these experiences point. In this connection, John has some beautiful passages in which he recommends that those who would advance should abide in hope. While attachment to memories holds us anchored in the past, hope—remaining in the expectation of God—opens us to the God who is never fully attained in this life (A, 3, 2, 2; 3, 11, 1).

"LOSING ONE'S SOUL"

The second of the Gospel logia cherished by Saint John of the Cross is one of those few that were so important for the early disciples of Jesus that they have been preserved both in Mark and in the material common to Matthew and Luke (Mt 16:25 and Lk 9:24). In other words, it is one of those sayings on radical discipleship favored by the wandering preachers who seem to have been behind the material common to these two evangelists (the so-called "Q" source): "Those who would save their life will lose it and those who lose their life for my sake will save it." In the second half of this saying, Mk 8:35 has: "Those who lose their life for my sake and for the sake of the Gospel will save it."

We have seen that this Gospel text is explicitly cited four times by Saint John of the Cross, three of them in the Matthean/Lukan version (A, 2, 7, 6; N, 1, 7, 3; C, 29, 11) and one in the Markan version (A, 2, 7, 4). We also saw that the Saint discovers the same basic meaning in John

12:25, about "hating one's soul." In the passage citing the Markan version (A, 2, 7, 4), John begins with Mk 8:34 on denying oneself, taking up the cross and following Jesus (which is common to all three synoptics). An allusion to this part of the text occurs a little later (in A, 2, 7, 7).

According to these texts from the seventh chapter of the second book of the *Ascent,* "losing one's life" means denying oneself any desire for consolations or spiritual experiences in one's prayer life. Such a desire for consolations or experiences would be tantamount to seeking oneself in God, rather than searching for God alone. The interpretation offered in *Night,* 1, 7, 3 is very similar. In the preceding paragraph the Saint has warned the soul not to be looking for delights in prayer. But now he enlarges his consideration, elevating it to a level of a general principle: he finds it blameworthy to seek one's own satisfaction and not God's will. This can easily happen, especially with beginners who are not yet sufficiently strengthened by love. "They measure God by themselves and not themselves by God, which is in opposition to his teaching in the Gospel that those who lose their life for his sake will gain it, and those who desire to gain it will lose it [Mt 16:25]." John repeats the same message in *Canticle,* 29, 11, when he states that one who walks in the love of God does not seek one's own gain or reward, but only to love all things and oneself for God. But it is in the immediately preceding passage (C, 29, 10) that Saint John of the Cross gives the best definition of what he understands by "losing oneself." The soul, he says, becomes "lost to herself by paying no attention to herself in anything, by concentrating on her Beloved and surrendering herself to him freely and disinterestedly, with no desire to gain anything for herself; ... [and] lost to all creatures, paying no heed to all her own affairs, but only to those of her Beloved."

The common element in these varied but overlapping interpretations is the idea of denying self for the sake of God. In fact, Saint John of the Cross quotes Mk 8:34-35, where taking up one's cross and losing one's life (or soul) are blended (A, 2, 7, 4). In *Ascent,* 3, 23, 2, he recalls the Matthean saying on self-denial (Mt 16:24) in order to make the point that no one should rejoice in his or her natural goods, "because those who pay some attention to themselves do not deny themselves or follow Christ."[3]

There is a common core to Saint John's reading of Lk 14:33, on total poverty, and that of the sayings on self-denial. Both insist on the need to transcend self, to go out of oneself, in order to meet God in the divine uniqueness and transcendence. This is precisely the role of all authentic love. The Greek/scholastic notion of *benevolentia,* disinterested love, as opposed to that of *concupiscentia,* self-centered love, seems to have been present in the Spanish master's mind in many of these passages. Love draws us out of ourselves in order to meet the other. And in this case, the other is the Absolute Other.

What is the ultimate thrust of these sayings on "losing one's life," on "denying oneself"? It is that this is the only way to find oneself. In any kind of love, after searching for the good of the other, lovers find themselves in their beloved. But this is all the more true of love for God, since God, far from annulling creatures, gives them their very being. In stanza 29 of the *Canticle,* the soul who had become lost in such a quest for her Beloved is in fact found.

SPIRITUAL POVERTY

To this process of going beyond everything in order to be united with God, the Carmelite mystic gives the name "spiritual poverty" or "poverty of spirit." Even a cursory reading of the Saint's writings reveals how frequently this expression appears, especially when taken together with such synonyms as "emptiness" (as in *nada,* cf. A, 1, 3, 2), "nakedness," "selflessness," "spiritual purity" (*desnudez, enajenacion, pureza espiritual,* see A, 2, 7, 5; 24, 8), "dispossession" and "annihilation" or denial (*desapropiada y anihilada,* see A, 2, 7, 4). Indeed, these passages are so numerous that one would have to refer the reader to the Spanish concordance of John's complete works.[4]

For John, spiritual poverty is the attitude or state of those who give themselves utterly to the search for God alone, heedless of all that is not God. As he sees it, a person poor in spirit is one who places all his/her hope in God. Anyone familiar with the biblical tradition of the *anawim* will see that Saint John of the Cross's interpretation of spiritual poverty is not far from it. According to the Mystical Doctor, it is to this state of concentration on God above oneself and all creatures that Jesus ascribes blessedness, when he says "Blessed are the poor in spirit" (A, 3, 29, 3; F, 3, 46).

This general concept of spiritual poverty takes on various nuances in different passages. In *Flame,* 3, 46, "poverty of spirit" is all-encompassing. It is "dispossession of all, corporal, temporal and spiritual." In

Ascent, 3, 29, 3, the" poor in spirit" are those who do not rejoice in their own good works. In a few passages, "spiritual denudation and poverty," or "emptiness, darkness, nakedness regarding all things and spiritual poverty" refer to detachment from all spiritual experiences and being guided by pure faith (A, 2, 22, 17; 2, 24, 8; 3, 3, 1).

Sometimes "spiritual poverty" has a more concrete significance. In *Ascent,* 3, 39, 1, it refers to detachment from oratories and churches. In *Night,* 1, 3, 1, it is opposed to treasuring religious objects or rejoicing in spiritual conversations and books. Saint John lays such stress on detachment from religious places, objects and events because in those days it was quite fashionable for the Spanish gentry to boast about their spiritual directors, or to collect paintings, statues and relics in their private oratories, as if this meant that they were more spiritual than others. Now, although we're not so interested in collecting relics, we sometimes boast about our prayer meetings and show a certain amount of satisfaction in our own little accomplishments. We, too, may be more intent on our spirituality than on our quest for God.

Within the mystical horizons of the *Canticle,* the poor in spirit are Christians who are "stripped of all...and possess God by a very intimate and special grace." In some cases "spiritual poverty" designates a personal attitude, the attitude of those who, having been placed in passive contemplation, remain in passivity without trying to dwell on particular concepts or images. These Christians "live in pure nakedness and poverty of spirit" (A, 2, 15, 4; N, 2, 4, 1). We're dealing here with people who surrender to God's action. In still other passages, "spiritual poverty" is the state experienced by those who are passing through a purifying night, in which God deprives them of discursive meditation, of particular ideas and of consolations (A, 2, 7, 5; N, 2, 8, 5; 2, 9, 4; Letters 11 & 19 [to Juana de Pedraza]).

DISCIPLESHIP

To explain why faithful Christians must renounce everything, deny themselves or even lose their very selves (in other words, why they must live in "spiritual poverty"), Saint John of the Cross offers three reasons, two of them from the Bible, the third from a centuries-long theological tradition. We will simply summarize them here.

Beginning with the theological tradition of the *via negationis,* begun by Gregory of Nyssa and developed by Pseudo-Dionysius, Saint John insists overwhelmingly on the divine transcendence and uniqueness. This is why creatures can reach God spiritually only through darkness and emptiness. The metaphysics of divine transcendence stand out so clearly in the words of our Saint that it serves as the point of departure for a practical treatise on how to ready oneself for the encounter with God: God is a dark night for us in this life (A, 2, 2, 1); the difference between ourselves and God is infinite (A, 2, 8); and we must walk toward God in the darkness of faith (A, 2, 9).

The first scriptural reason derives from the "first and greatest commandment": we must love God with all our heart, above all else. This is one of John's grand, recurring themes. "God allows nothing else to dwell together with him" (A, 1, 5, 8). However, no one should hastily judge this teaching to be strange or one-sided. Saint John describes the bond that closely binds love of God and love of neighbor (A, 3, 23, 1; N, 1, 3, 2), showing how our defects impede us from loving one another and how mystical purification increases our love for one another (A, 3, 25, 5; N, 1, 12, 8; 13, 8). The Saint himself shows a tremendous love for all creation. He compares Christ with all that is bright and beautiful in this world: mountains, valleys, the song of the wind and even the far distant isles of the "brave new world" of America, with its exotic plants and animals (C, 14 & 15). John never condemns love for any creature, but only attachment to it—which he views as bordering on idolatry. In this we can again detect the ring of the first commandment in its primitive form: "You shall not have other gods before me" (Ex 20:2).

The third reason is Jesus Christ and our call to follow him. In the mind and heart of John of the Cross, Christ is the door, the way, the means to union with God (A, 2, 7, 11-12;), and our model par excellence (A, 1, 13, 3-4; 2, 7, 8-9).

Here again we hear the echo of the sayings on the cost of discipleship: we must deny our very selves and follow Christ (A, 3, 23, 2). Poverty of spirit is Jesus' poverty, "the pure spiritual cross and nakedness of Christ's poverty of spirit" (A, 2, 7, 5). In refusing it, we become "enemies of the cross of Christ" (Phil 3:18, cited in A, 2, 7, 5). It is in Christ that the yoke of renunciation becomes light (Mt 11:30 as cited in A, 2, 7, 7).

In the body of John's works there are two special passages fundamental for understanding the central role of Christ in his theology and spirituality. The first is found in those theologically dense paragraphs in which he proves that we must not request new revelations, since God has already been fully revealed to us in Christ (A, 2, 22, 2-8; cf. *Sayings*, 100). The second comprises the two paragraphs in which he shows us how the life of Christians is patterned on Christ's life. Here he recalls another saying on discipleship: Christ had nowhere to lay His head (Mt 8:20, cited in A, 2, 7, 10). He led an uprooted life and died abandoned: "My God, my God, why have you forsaken me?" (Mt 27:46, cited in A, 2, 7, 11). It is for this reason that our journey consists "in the living death of the cross, sensory and spiritual, exterior and interior" (A, 2, 7, 11). In a letter to Fray Luis de San Angelo, he advised his former novice never to look for Christ without the Cross (Letter 24). Elsewhere he writes: "If you desire to be perfect, sell your will..., come to Christ..., and follow him to Calvary and the sepulcher" (*Sayings*, 165). Mount Carmel and Mount Calvary are one and the same.

DISCIPLESHIP AND IMITATION

For Saint John of the Cross, Christ is certainly much more than a model. The "Son of God," as John likes to call him, is the mediator of God's revelation, the one in whom God's self-gift and self-disclosure have been offered to us in a total and definitive way, "once and for all" (Heb 1:1, cited in A, 2, 22). In the *Canticle*, Christ is the term of a passionate relationship of love and the immediate object of union.

Even so, when John speaks about following Christ, he basically means imitating him. In this he is the heir of a long tradition deriving from Saint Francis of Assisi on one hand, and Thomas à Kempis on the other: the imitation of Christ preceded by the contemplation of Christ (cf. A, 1, 13, 3; *Sayings of Light and Love*, Prologue) sums up everything we must do in order to reach union with God. "If like Moses [the soul] hides herself in the cavern of the rock (in real imitation of the perfect life of the Son of God, her Bridegroom), she will merit that, while he protects her with his right hand, God will show her his shoulders [Ex 33:22-23]" (C, 1, 10). Saint John of the Cross loves this passage from Exodus that he, following Saint Gregory of Nyssa, frequently uses in describing the mystics' vision of God (A, 2, 24, 3; F, 1, 27; 4, 12). Only in two places in the *Canticle* (1, 10 and 37, 3-5) does he give this passage a Christological interpretation. This exegesis, inspired by 1 Corinthians 10:4 ("and the rock was Christ"), appears for the first time in Saint Gregory of Nyssa,[5] from whom Saint John appears to borrow it directly.

The distinctive contribution our Saint adds in *Canticle,* 1, 10 is his introduction of the notion of imitation.[6]

The imitation of Christ is therefore essential for him. But he gives it
a very precise meaning. "A person," he writes, "makes progress only by
imitating Christ, who is the Way, the Truth, and the Life. No one goes to
the Father but through him, as he states himself in St. John [Jn 14:6].
Elsewhere He says: *I am the door; anyone who enters by me will be saved* [Jn
10:9]. Accordingly, I would not consider any spirituality worthwhile that
wants to walk in sweetness and ease and run from the imitation of Christ"
(A, 2, 7, 8). We are therefore not dealing here with the kind of moralistic and pietistic notion of imitation that was so prevalent during the past
few centuries. For the great Spanish mystic, "imitation" means sharing
in the basic attitude of Jesus: his faith/hope, and the generosity and
freedom with which he sacrifices everything to it. The imitation of Christ
that the Saint recommends is centered on embracing the denudation
and poverty of spirit necessary for union with God (cf. also A, 2, 29, 9).
To take up the cross and follow Christ is tantamount to suffering a death
"patterned on Christ's, for he is our model and light" (A, 2, 7, 9). And
the spiritual poverty that he considers a necessary condition to mystical
experience is "Christ's poverty of spirit" (A, 2, 7, 5).

JOHN'S HERMENEUTICS

Discipleship, understood basically as imitation, remains one of the
leading threads in the thought of Saint John of the Cross. To the best of
my knowledge, few other spiritual masters have so often and so wholeheartedly insisted on it. This is why he returns to the Gospel sayings on
discipleship to prove the most important points of his teaching.

In doing so, he offers a particular interpretation of these sayings.
For Origen, the martyrs followed Christ, giving up family, possessions
and life itself by dying for their faith. In the history of religious life,
beginning with the desert solitaries, one follows Christ, renouncing
family and possessions through a public profession. For Saint John of
the Cross, too, renunciation is an essential preparatory step for following Christ. He often calls it "a death," but a death that is carried out
throughout one's life. He thus brings renunciation into the whole area
of spiritual life.

In his interpretation of the Gospel sayings on discipleship, Saint
John of the Cross returns to their original meaning. He does this in

three ways. First, in his works as in the Gospels, these sayings are not addressed to a privileged minority (martyrs or religious), but to all who are ready to accept Jesus' message. Second, in his works as in the Gospels, these sayings do not demand a merely material renunciation, but a radical disposition and orientation of spirit. Third, for John as well as for Jesus and the Gospels, the demands of discipleship are based on the uniqueness of God before whom everything else disappears, and are an application of the first Commandment. In both cases, the eschatological orientation of human existence is partly visible.

The difference between the original context of the sayings (Jesus' own preaching) and the doctrinal context from which the Saint's interpretation emerges, is quite clear. For Jesus, it was a matter of an objective historical situation: since the "end" is near and God is going to intervene to save us, we must be ready to give up everything that may be an obstacle to our reception of God's definitive grace. Saint John of the Cross transfers these sayings to the horizons of a spiritual itinerary leading to union with God, horizons that would have been alien to the cultural world of Jesus. He was not the first to effect a transfer of this sort. Very close to him in time and in affection, Saint Teresa of Jesus had often recalled the story of the rich young man whom Jesus had called to follow Him (a story aimed at explaining the demand of discipleship) as a paradigm of our own indecision on our spiritual way (see *Interior Castle*, 3, 1, 6).

Saint John of the Cross's treatment of these texts is at the same time a re-reading of the Scriptures and an application of the sayings on discipleship to a particular context. But this application is far from arbitrary. In telling us not to let anything place itself between us and God's reign, Saint John of the Cross discloses a statement concerning God's uniqueness and absoluteness which is certainly at the very core of their meaning. Anything that stands below God appears in its full relativeness, and may well become an impediment if we allow ourselves to become attached to it.

NOTES

1. See *Origen: An Exhortation to Martyrdom, Prayer, First Principles: Book IV; Prologue to the Commentary on the Song of Songs, Homily XXVII on Numbers*, trans. Rowan A. Greer (New York, NY: Paulist Press, 1979), 49, 51, 68-69.

2. Cf J. M. Lozano, *Discipleship: Toward an Understanding of Religious Life* (Chicago: CCRS, 1983), 2-5.

3. It should be noted that in the passage just quoted from the *Canticle,* the Saint puts the idea of self-denial common to Mk 8:34 and Mt 16:24/Lk 9:23 together with that of divesting oneself of everything (Lk 14:33), although he does not cite the last-mentioned saying expressly. As we have seen, he does expressly cite Mt 16:24 in A, 3, 23, 3.

4. See *Concordancias de los Escritos de San Juan de la Cruz,* ed. Juan Luis Astigarraga, Agustí Borrell and F. Javier Martín de Lucas (Rome: Teresianum, 1990).

5. Gregory of Nyssa, *The Life of Moses,* nn. 245-248 (New York: Paulist, 1978), 118.

6. Saint John of the Cross also cites the Song of Songs 2:14 ("my dove in the clefts of the rock") with the same Christological interpretation, based again on 1 Corinthians 10:4 (C, 36, 2-3). Gregory of Granada (Illiberis) was the first to do so in the West. Shortly thereafter, Justus of Urgell saw in these clefts or caverns the wounds of Christ. He was followed by Saint Bede and by Saint Bernard of Clairvaux, who in turn inspired Saint Gertrude of Helfta.

EMBODIED LOVE
IN JOHN OF THE CROSS

Richard P. Hardy, Ph.D.

Richard P. Hardy is professor of spirituality at Saint Paul University in Ottawa, Ontario, Canada, and the author of numerous articles and books, including Search for Nothing: The Life of John of the Cross *(New York, NY: Crossroad, 1982).*

The demands and the apparent harshness of the path which St. John of the Cross proposes simply overwhelm most of those who try to read his *Ascent of Mount Carmel* and or his *Dark Night*. If they seek to calm their fears and overcome their hesitation by consulting studies on St. John, they find that scholars have often interpreted him in a rather ethereal, disembodied fashion. Their anxiety about his relevance to the contemporary world is increased. However, it is my contention that when we really understand St. John of the Cross's view of the Christian life , we discover a very human and indeed embodied path to God.

In the first part of this study, I wish to examine John's affirmation that in the union of love here in this life, human beings are so transformed that they become one with the will of God and actually love here and now with the love of God. In the second part, I wish to answer the question: "How does St. John of the Cross understand and present God's love for people, the world, indeed the whole of creation?" My thesis is that the fear many in the Christian churches have of body, passion and love has, in fact, led them to misinterpret St. John's view of love. They have made it something ethereal, "purely spiritual," and therefore disembodied or disincarnated. In fact, though, for St. John such a love is passionate, bodily and incarnated. I believe that seeing him in this way will enable us in the twentieth century to break through to a much more authentic Christian spirituality and indeed, a much more truthful presentation of St. John of the Cross's own teaching and hopes.

I. ONE WITH THE WILL OF GOD

THE PERSON LIVES THE LIFE OF GOD

In the Prologue of his *Living Flame of Love,* John of the Cross expresses the basic motif flowing throughout his works:

> For [God] declared that the Father, the Son, and the Holy Spirit would take up their abode in those who loved him by making them live the life of God and dwell in the Father, the Son, and the Holy Spirit [Jn 14:23], as the soul points out in these stanzas.[1]

St. John tell us that his poem speaks of the process whereby human beings come to live a new life, one that actually involves living the life of God, even within this earthly life. The interesting element here is the way this occurs. John speaks of the Trinity taking up its home in human beings by making them live the life of God here and now: seeing as God sees, loving as God loves, now in an incarnated way in the flesh and blood of those God transforms. The whole poem celebrates this, and the commentary explains it in greater detail. God's life, God's love (for the two are synonymous) are enfleshed in us as we fully *live* the life of human beings who have been transformed in this way. This transformation, John tells us, is accomplished "...through love in *this* life" (emphasis mine—see also F, 3, 5). The source of any life is love. To love makes one live in a fully human way. Furthermore, human beings live where they love, says John, and, once transformed, they love God radically and most naturally.[2] Therefore, they live in God. God's life becomes *their* life—but in the limited, historical, flesh-and-blood context of ordinary human existence.

The *whole* person is involved. According to St. John of the Cross, this is so totally an incarnated love—and hence life—in God that all the elements of human nature are brought into harmony, body and soul, sense and spirit. John sums up the entire first stanza of the *Living Flame of Love* by saying:

...Now I am so fortified in love that not only do my sense and spirit no longer faint in you, but my heart and my flesh, reinforced in you, rejoice in the living God [Ps. 84:2], with great conformity between the sensory and spiritual parts. What you desire me to ask for, I ask for; and what you do not desire, I do not desire, nor can I, nor does it even enter my mind to desire it. My petitions are now more valuable and estimable in your sight, since they come from you, and you move me to make them, and I make them in the delight and joy of the Holy Spirit, *my judgment now issuing from your countenance* [Ps 16:2], that is, when you esteem and hear my prayer. (F, 1, 36)

Before the transformation that takes place in love, one's situation is quite different. Previously, the person suffered on both the physical and spiritual (which includes the psychological) levels. The individual's desire to be one with God increased his or her impatience to the point where there was an almost frantic yearning to escape from the present situation, "the conditions of this life" (F, 1, 36). The individual experienced a disharmony between what *is* and what *is desired;* he or she constantly sought to overcome the dichotomy by getting out of this historical, flesh-and-blood existence. However, transformed now in love, the person finds himself or herself in a totally different situation. The self is no longer split, suffering, and anxious to be other than it is. The whole person is in harmony and lives in God. The will of the person and of God are one. So true is this that what God wants, the person wants, and what God does not desire, the person does not desire. Though God is the source of all, nonetheless the person is no automaton, but makes genuine acts of the will: "...You move me to make them and I make them." The conformity between the person and God is total, yet the human person is the subject of all the actions performed and all the thoughts entertained. No longer does the individual's sensory part pursue one thing while the spiritual part is pursuing something else. The anguish and impatience such division causes is brought to an end by the one incarnated divine movement flowing evenly in and through the person, in this present bodily condition of life.

According to John of the Cross the Holy Spirit accomplishes this transformation by love itself, which produces a suffering that does not destroy, but delights and divinizes, the person (see F, 2, 3). Yet John clearly reminds his readers that within this process there is an emptying that is painful despite the positive work being accomplished (see F, 3, 18 & 32).[3]

TRANSFORMATION OF THE PERSON

The positive result of what seems to be a totally negative process is a transformation of the person into someone completely focused on the living God:

> In that sweet drink of God, in which the soul is imbibed in him, she most willingly and with intense delight surrenders herself wholly to him, in the desire to be totally his and never to possess in herself anything other than him. God causes in this union the purity and perfection necessary for such a surrender. And since he transforms her in himself, he makes her entirely his own and empties her of all she possesses other than him. (C, 27, 6)

John says this as a commentary upon the verse from stanza 27 of the *Spiritual Canticle:* "And I gave myself to him, keeping nothing back." The transformation requires a surrender given most freely, for it is in accord with what the person wants : "...she most willingly and with intense delight surrenders." This surrender keeps nothing back from God, and clings to nothing other than God. It involves giving up all the securities and desires to which the person used to cling so strongly. However, to truly accomplish such a surrender requires incredible strength, and an integration of the human whole human person and personality. To want God totally and to be willing to trust God completely is the "purity and perfection" of which John speaks in this paragraph. No one can produce this total integration by his or her own unaided efforts. John clearly informs us that *God* causes this personal wholeness, so that persons can indeed give all they are unreservedly to God. Such a surrender is a graced human act. In that surrendering process, God makes us into God "by participation," so that we belong entirely to God and desire and hold nothing but God as our all. To be transformed into God means then to be centered entirely upon God and therefore to live the life of God. This is the *divinization* that God accomplishes in the human person.

However, it must be repeated that although God is the source and cause of this transformation, it is not accomplished without the personal involvement of the human being who enters the surrendering process.

In his commentary on stanza 30 of the *Spiritual Canticle,* which speaks of God and the soul "weaving garlands" and deepening their love for each other, John writes:

> And she does not say I alone shall weave the garlands, or you alone will, but we shall weave them together. The soul cannot practice or acquire the virtues without the help of God, nor does God effect them alone in the soul without her help. (C, 30, 6)

The imagery used here—of being adorned with garlands of flowers and emeralds—symbolizes being adorned, beautified and made whole by the virtues and gifts God imparts. God so loves us that over time and within each person's unique life story, God gives all those qualities that make us whole and indeed beautiful, to God and to others. These gifts have their source in God's love and flow freely to the human being, with whom God desires to become one even as we live this earthly, historical life. Yet, God respects the human person so much that in order for these gifts to be effectively interwoven—i.e., brought to completion, harmonized and fixed in us—we too must love God in return. It is the human person's love for God that enables one to receive and keep these gifts in all their harmony and beauty (C 30, 9).[4]

There is no doubt that for John of the Cross God does everything, but this does not mean that the person remains passive, merely sitting back and waiting. God challenges us to enter the process and love actively. There is no question here of a purely passive surrender that declares: "I give up. What else can I do?" Rather, we become as active as the flames of love by which the Spirit of God transforms us (see F, 3, 8-9). We learn to love and act as God loves and acts (N, 2, 4, 2).[5]

This transformation produces a definite feeling of being changed, of being taken into the divine life while yet continuing to fully live this human, historical life. St. John of the Cross expresses it poignantly:

> The soul feels its ardor strengthen and increase and its love become so refined in this ardor that seemingly there flow seas of loving fire within it, reaching to the heights and depths of the earthly and heavenly spheres, imbuing all with love. It seems to it that the entire universe is a sea of love in which it is engulfed, for, conscious of the living point or center of love within itself, it is unable to catch sight of the boundaries of this love. (F, 2, 10)

Not only is everything in created reality seen in a new perspective, but it is also *felt* in a new way. John makes no attempt to "spiritualize" this love beyond the range of human experience. He clearly states that the person *feels* the development of this love within the very core of his or her being. There is a passion and sensuality expressed in John's writings that grow stronger when he attempts to describe the experience of the person brought into this final stage of union with God. One gathers from the passage just quoted that the delight John finds in the beauty of the universe as a result of this experience is overwhelming. That delight is felt precisely because of the infinite love with which the person now relates to all that exists. The love of God is now enfleshed in this particular, historical person who has been graced by the transcendent.

BECOMING GOD

One of the most consistent themes in John's writings is the divinization of the human person through a process initiated by God. In the *Living Flame,* John tells the reader how those transformed in God actually become *God through participation.*[6] In a beautiful, ecstatic prayer that speaks of oneness with God and hence of this divinization, John underscores the profound unity between the person and God: "...that I be so transformed in your beauty that we may be alike in beauty, and both behold ourselves in your beauty, possessing then your very beauty.... Wherefore I shall be you in your beauty, and you will be me in your beauty..."(C, 36, 5). Though this particular prayer speaks only of the divine beauty in which the person participates, it can be extended to all the other attributes of God. The transformation John describes involves a total loving union of humanity and divinity through this special graced process.

In the *Spiritual Canticle* John speaks of the role of the Holy Spirit in the transformation process:

> By his divine breath-like spiration, the Holy Spirit elevates the soul sublimely and informs her and makes her capable of breathing in God the same spiration of love that the Father breathes in the Son and the Son in the Father. This spiration of love is the Holy Spirit himself.... Even what comes to pass in the communication given in this temporal transformation is unspeakable, for the soul united and transformed in God breathes out in God to God the very divine

spiration that God—she being transformed in him—breathes out in himself to her. (C, 39, 3)

Saint John of the Cross sees the person being taken into the very life and heart of the Trinity through the activity of the Holy Spirit. Yet John reminds us that this is something that can never be adequately conceived or explained, because it is so delicate and deep.

Elsewhere, John will return to this theme of transformation into divine life, with its Trinitarian dimensions: "The Blessed Trinity inhabits the soul by divinely illumining its intellect with the wisdom of the Son, delighting its will in the Holy Spirit, and absorbing it powerfully and mightily in the unfathomed embrace of the Father's sweetness" (F, 1, 15).[7] Here the human being is taken entirely into the divine life, and all the faculties are so transformed that God's infinite wisdom and the love become the wisdom and love of the finite human person to the degree possible in this earthly life. We should note especially how John combines the qualities of power and strength with the experience of delight, sweetness, absorption and embrace. God, the Trinity, is almighty; yet the divinized person experiences this union as delightful and sweet. Though such a transformation in God is beyond what can be humanly understood or expressed, this does not keep John from affirming its reality. He speaks from experience, attempting to communicate some small part of what he knows to be true.

THE HUMAN WILL TRANSFORMED INTO THE WILL OF GOD

Though at times some readers may find John of the Cross too "scholastic," especially in his detailed discussion of the intellect, will and memory as powers of the soul, we should not be misled. John is a product of his time and uses a vocabulary familiar to his original audience. But when he speaks in terms of purifying the soul's faculties, contemporary readers should remember that he is really concerned with the total person who is being changed, made into the enfleshment of God.

> This renovation illumines the human intellect with supernatural light so it becomes divine, united with the divine; informs the will with love of God so it is no longer less than divine and loves in no other way than divinely, united and made one with the divine will and love; and is also a divine conversion and changing of the memory, the affections, and the appetites according to God. And

thus this soul will be a soul of heaven, heavenly and more divine than human.

As we have gradually seen, God accomplishes all this work in the soul by illumining it and firing it divinely with urgent longings for God alone. (N, 2, 13, 11)

In this commentary on the second verse of the first stanza of the *Dark Night* poem, John of the Cross is speaking about the process of transformation, in the context of St. Paul's contrast between the "old man" and the "new man" in Ephesians 4:22-24.[8] It is God who gives the person all that is necessary to change and to focus fully on God, and who inaugurates the process of transformation. So once again, for John the process is pure gift, grace, undeserved. It is not something we can accomplish on our own, nor in an instant. Rather, the process occurs over a lifetime, within the concrete circumstances and events which make up our individual histories.

Little by little, those undergoing the process turn their attention increasingly to God. Every aspect of their human nature—faculties, affections and appetites—is directed Godward ever more intensely and completely. But there is more involved than just being turned totally to God. Souls actually find that as a result of this graced transformation, they have become divinized, loving "in no other way than divinely," with God's own love. Now they want only what God wants—a totally positive experience, in which wholeness and goodness are all that is desired. In other words, they are "wholly converted into divine love" (F, 1, 26).[9]

For John of the Cross, being wholly converted into divine love means actually living God's own life:

> ...[The soul] lives the life of God....
>
> And the will, which previously loved in a base and deadly way with only its natural affection, is now changed into the life of divine love, for it loves in a lofty way with divine affection, moved by the strength of the Holy Spirit in which it now lives the life of love. By means of this union God's will and the soul's will are now one....
>
> Finally all the movements, operations, and inclinations the soul had previously from the principle and strength of its natural life are now in this union dead to what they formerly were, changed into divine movements, and alive to God.
>
> ...Although the substance of this soul is not the substance of God, since it cannot undergo a substantial conversion into him, it

has become God through participation in God, being united to and absorbed in him, as it is in this state. (F, 2, 34)

Now that God has brought the person through purification into the state of spiritual marriage, the most complete stage of transformation possible in this life, the person lives the life of God.[10] The Holy Spirit makes the acts in and through the person, who is thus "moved by the strength of the Holy Spirit." Therefore, at this stage everything one does in love, and indeed all one's acts, can be said to be divine, because according to John the Spirit is the one who does them all, in and through the love and activities of the transformed human person (see F, 1, 4). Love flows from the will, and since "God's will and the soul's will are now one," each time the person activates the will to love, the act is truly God's act, enfleshed in the total person who now loves in this way. Though John clearly reminds the reader that the human person is not substantially transformed into God (for it is impossible to hold this without falling into monism or pantheism), he nonetheless emphasizes that the person's actions are now really God's actions in history, even though they still remain fully human.

God has established a certain equality, in which the human lover and the divine Beloved are one (see C, 12, 7; 27, 6; 38, 3-4). Before this transformation, human lovers make themselves equal to (or even lower than) limited creatures by turning their wills, their love, toward such objects in a natural and exclusive way. This happens, according to John, because love creates a certain equality between lovers and what they love. However, the same principle holds true when one loves God; an attachment to God creates a certain equality with the God we love (see A 1, 4, 3). However, we must remember that the equality spoken of here is more than just the juxtaposition of two separate but equal parties. For John, the equality created by the human person's graced love of God is so powerful that the two love in one act and through one will. And so the transformed person comes to love according to *what* and *how* God loves, and vice versa. Let us turn, then, to an examination of this *how* and *what* of God's love.

II. HOW GOD RELATES TO CREATION

We have seen that according to Saint John of the Cross, God brings human beings through a process that is both purifying and transforming. Through the process leading to spiritual marriage, we come to live the life of God, and are so united with the divine that God's will becomes in some way ours. Hence, the transformed person's love is in fact God's love. How does John of the Cross see God's love acting? This is the question we must try to answer to determine whether John is espousing the goal of an ethereal, "purely spiritual" love, or rather an embodied love replete with sensuality and delight.

GOD IS PRESENT EVERYWHERE

In relation to the created world, it is already clear that John recognizes God present everywhere, and at all times. The intimacy that the act of creation has established means that God and creatures can never be separated. John of the Cross speaks of this presence in a fascinating passage from the *Living Flame*. John first indicates how the Holy Spirit transforms persons so that they become totally concentrated on God, noting that even within the limitations of this life, such experiences of love are so intense as to be almost incredible. Yet in response to those who would claim his descriptions are exaggerated, John says:

> Yet I reply to all these persons that the Father of Lights [Jas 1:17], who is not closefisted, but diffuses himself abundantly, as the sun does its rays, without being a respecter of persons [Acts 10:34], wherever there is room—always showing himself gladly along the highways and byways—does not hesitate or consider it of little import to find his delights with the children of the earth at a common table in the world [Prv 8:31]. (F, 1, 15)

In this text John underscores the openness and infinite love of God, present to and is concerned about everyone, no matter who or where they may be. Through the image of the sun shining everywhere, John affirms God's omnipresence. He also uses the imagery of highways and byways for the same purpose. The highways are the most travelled routes, the roads others would expect a traveller to take. The byways are the short cuts that tend to be dangerous and that people avoid when they can. To say that God shows himself gladly in these places is to affirm that God is everywhere (though the phrase "wherever there is room" indicates that a certain openness is needed for that presence to be fully received).

Consequently, we can say that God welcomes and is with everyone—no matter who they may be—at every time and place. By finishing the text with the quotation from the Book of Proverbs, John underlines how utterly important this presence of God is—not only to creation, but to God. For God finds utter pleasure in being with God's own creation. To be *with* the human community is at the heart of the God in whom John of the Cross believes.

GOD RELATES TENDERLY AND GENTLY

How is God *with* the human community, then, and what are the qualities of God's presence? John of the Cross answers this question within the first stanza of the *Living Flame:* "Since this flame is a flame of divine life, it wounds the soul with the tenderness of God's life, and it wounds and stirs it so deeply as to make it dissolve in love" (F, 1, 7). This quotation implies that God's own life is tender, and that this tenderness is transmitted and incarnated within the community, through its incarnation in the person to whom God relates in this love. The flame mentioned here is the Holy Spirit, that flame of love flowing from the infinite depths of God, that is, from divine life. Although this flame may be said to afflict us and cause a painful purification as we are drawn toward wholeness, it is essentially tender despite the suffering we may concretely experience.[11] God's whole being is tenderness and gentleness, and these become key characteristics in relating to humanity and creation as a whole. The term John of the Cross uses here is "ternura," which could be translated as sensitivity or tenderness. God's way of relating to humanity is always something constructive, flowing forth from the divine tenderness, even when it is perceived as painful and destructive.

However, it is in the following paragraph that John brings out in more detail the qualities of God's relationship to humanity:

> ...since love is never idle, but in continual motion, it is always emitting flames everywhere like a blazing fire, and, since its duty is to wound in order *to cause love and delight,* and it is present in this soul as a living flame, it dispatches its wounds like *most tender flares of delicate love. Joyfully and festively* it practices the arts and games of love, as though in the palace of its nuptials, as Ahasuerus did with Esther [Est 2:16-18]. God shows his graces there, manifests his riches and the glory of his grandeur that in this soul might be fulfilled what he

asserted in Proverbs: "I was delighted every day, playing before him all the time, playing in the world. And my delights were to be with the children of the earth" [Prv 8:30-31], that is by bestowing delights on them. (F, 1, 8—emphasis mine)

Three points are particularly worth noting in this text from the *Living Flame:* 1) the flame of love is ever active, moving and causing love and delight in the person touched by the Spirit; 2) the flame is an activity of God, filled with a generosity and happiness like that of lovers who have found their beloved; 3) God simply enjoys being with humanity. Let us briefly consider each of these elements.

First, God's love toward the person is continuously active. Once God's love in the Spirit has been engaged, there is a constant deepening movement whereby the Spirit transforms the person into that very same love. Through the action of divine love within, we find ourselves being challenged to let go of selfish relationships with others and God's creation. Because previously we were altogether focused on such things, letting go (under the inspiration of the Spirit's love) is experienced as painful; it can truly be called a "wound." Yet, the aim of the divine action (i.e., love itself) that causes the wound is ultimately to bring us love and delight. God's love continues its activity within the transformed person in a framework of tender, gentle stirrings.

Second, John compares this continuing activity of divine love to the story of King Ahasuerus and Esther in the Book of Esther. The king is so delighted at having found Esther as his beloved that he prepares her for union. According to the story, Ahasuerus gives a crown to Esther and celebrates their union by hosting a great banquet and proclaiming a holiday. By this pure self-giving Ahasuerus shows how delighted he is in Esther, wanting everyone to know about it. Furthermore, the delight is mutual between Esther and the king. By describing God and the person in terms of Ahasuerus and Esther, John of the Cross wishes to affirm that God is totally taken by the loveliness of each person whom the divine Lover crowns, hosts and proclaims to the world as God's beloved, loved in and by the divine love. God and the human person delight together in the sheer gift and grace of this relationship.

Third, God enjoys humanity. Remarkably, in his quotation above from the Book of Proverbs, John seems to be saying that God even *plays* with humanity. True, John indicates that "God shows his graces" so that "*in this soul* might be fulfilled what he asserted in Proverbs" about "playing in the world." One might suppose, then, that it is only creatures who are playing, because of the delight God causes them. Yet immediately afterward, John describes the flames of divine love as *God's* "games." Thus, John maintains that God delights in human beings by giving *them* delights and by wounding them with the flames of love. A further substantiation can be found in a later paragraph of the *Living Flame* (F, 1, 15), where John once again alludes to the same passage from Proverbs (i.e., "he does not hesitate or consider it of little import to find his delights with the children of the earth at a common table in the world"). Here John of the Cross quite clearly applies the scriptural text to God, who delights to be with humanity. In fact, everywhere else that John refers to Proverbs 8:30-31, he again affirms God's delight in humanity.[12] So we may say that, for John of the Cross, God simply loves being with creation and especially with human beings. John portrays God and the human person as lovers who delight in each other and interact with real joy.

Thus, even taking into account John's often metaphorical mystical language, he clearly maintains that God is involved with humanity, that God truly enjoys human beings. Moreover, God relishes this relationship with human beings, even if John cannot adequately describe or define how we experience it. Perhaps a certain fear or hesitation of ascribing passion and delight to God has kept us from understanding and expressing the intimacy of the relationship God desires and in fact establishes with human beings. John is not afraid to celebrate it in prose and poetry, even though he lived in a time when it was sometimes dangerous to state such things under the suspicious eye of the Inquisition. Such courage is one more reason to take seriously what he says about the presence of joy, delight and pleasure in God.

GOD LOVES WITH DELIGHT IN ALL

However, John's comments on the line "O lamps of fire!" in the third stanza of the *Living Flame* give us an even clearer sense of how God relates to humanity:

> When individuals love and do good to others, they love and do good to them in the measure of their own nature and properties. Thus your Bridegroom, dwelling within you, grants you favors according to his nature. Since he is omnipotent, he omnipotently loves

and does good to you; since he is wise, you feel that he loves and does good to you with wisdom; since he is infinitely good, you feel that he loves you with goodness; since he is holy, you feel that with holiness he loves and favors you; since he is just, you feel that in justice he loves and favors you; since he is merciful, mild, and clement, you feel his mercy, mildness and clemency; since he is a strong, sublime, and delicate being, you feel that his love for you is strong, sublime, and delicate; since he is pure and undefiled, you feel that he loves you in a pure and undefiled way; since he is truth, you feel that he loves you in truthfulness; since he is liberal, you feel that he liberally loves and favors you, without any personal profit, only in order to do good to you; since he is the virtue of supreme humility, he loves you with supreme humility and esteem and makes you his equal, gladly revealing himself to you in these ways of knowledge, in this his countenance filled with graces, and telling you in this his union, not without great rejoicing: "I am yours and for you and delighted to be what I am so as to be yours and give myself to you." (F, 3, 6)[13]

In the context, John speaks of the various ways one experiences happiness and delight in this union of love; for John, the whole process follows his basic principle that love (and doing good for the beloved) is actualized according to the nature of the lover. This means that our human love flows from the limited, historical, contingent and relative creatures that we are. John attempts to answer the question "How and in what particular way does God love?" more concretely. The quotation above gives us his answer, and thus we see that, for John, God loves human persons powerfully, wisely, justly, mercifully, mildly, strongly, sublimely, delicately, freely, truly, liberally, humbly and with gladness, goodness, holiness, clemency and rejoicing. The text notes not only how God loves, but also that the person experiences the characteristics of this love. The whole description ends with the affirmation that God makes the human person God's equal, and that as a result, God greatly rejoices to be all that God is, for the sake of the one who is loved. There is an intimate relationship of harmony and self-giving established between God and the person. Hence, the love God exercises is not some kind of ethereal, abstract, non-incarnated love, but one which directly affects the historical, enfleshed being who is loved.

Furthermore, in speaking of transformed persons, who receive all kinds of new spiritual joys and delights, John notes that none is as great as what they already possess in the union of love. Consequently, the new joyful experiences, sublime as they are, simply move these persons back to the enjoyment of the greater and more substantial beauty and delight already established within. Each new transitory delight simply helps to deepen the delightful union of love. And so John continues:

> Hence, every time joyous and happy things are offered to this soul, whether they are exterior or interior and spiritual, she immediately turns to the enjoyment of the riches she already has within herself, and experiences much greater gladness and delight in them than in those new joys. She in some way resembles God who, even though he has delight in all things, does not delight in them as much as he does in himself, for he possesses within himself a good eminently above all others. (C 20 & 21, 12)

John is clearly affirming that God delights in all things. Nothing escapes that delight, for nothing escapes the creative beauty God has originally placed there. We should note that, when he speaks of the transformed person delighting more in the already possessed interior gift (i.e., union with God), and of God enjoying more self-delight than delight in creatures, John is not denying the beauty, wonder and delightfulness of created things, but is simply saying that the delight is greater in what is more fundamental. John affirms both that God loves *all* created reality and that human beings brought to union with God share God's delight in all things.

GOD LOVES IN AN ORDERED WAY

One of the John's most interesting statements on the way God deals with humanity can be found in book 2, chapter 17 of *The Ascent of Mount Carmel*. In speaking of supernatural visions, John asks why God bothers to communicate them at all when they can endanger the process of Christian growth. In his answer, he gives three principles governing God's interaction with human beings: 1) God acts in a well-ordered fashion; 2) God acts gently; 3) God acts according to the mode of the human person. This means that God deals with human beings in the way best designed (i.e., well-ordered) to accomplish what God desires to do. Furthermore, God acts gently, without forcing anything or anyone. But most important, God respects our normal human patterns of growth and learning, and deals with us according to our incarnated mode of existence. In other words, God deals with us as we are: not angels but *embodied* persons. Everything that makes us human enters into the process, and God not only respects but loves us within that context. Thus, God intends Christian growth and ultimately the transformation of the person to take place within our embodied reality.

It is important to emphasize, as John does, the *embodied* way God deals with humanity. God desires that the whole person be filled and fulfilled. Once the human person has been brought to the state of union in love, everything he or she has suffered and undergone in the purification process is more than compensated. Now, God graces the person—the total person, body and soul—with surpassing gifts.

> For God repays the interior and exterior trials very well with divine goods for the soul *and body,* so there is not a trial that does not have a corresponding and considerable reward....
>
> One day, just as with Mordecai, the soul is repaid for all its trials and services [Est. 6:10-11], and not only made to enter the palace and stand, clothed in royal garments, before the king, but also accorded the royal crown, scepter, and throne, and possession of the royal ring, so it might do anything it likes and omit anything it does not like in the kingdom of its Bridegroom [Est. 8:1-2, 15]. (F, 2, 31—emphasis mine)

Here (as my italics indicate) John speaks of how everything one undergoes on the journey to union will recompensed both in soul and body. It is not, then, merely a question receiving spiritual rewards; the *whole person* is involved and *whole person* will be gifted. But in the second part of this quotation John goes beyond our wildest expectations. He compares the person brought union with Mordecai and Esther, who received the power of the king to do anything they wished in the kingdom. The person brought to union will be like them because he or she will receive God's own authority and power of love. When we combine this teaching with what John has already said about becoming one with God's will, loving with God's love, and knowing creatures through and in God, we see that the human appetites that by their previous disorder caused enslavement and hindered the spiritual journey, now become part of the very means of living in God (see F, 2, 31). The *whole* person now lives day to day life with a redeemed sensuality and passion that is freed and freeing, rather than enslaving and enslaved. But it is our same faculties and appetites that are transformed into fully human (and "divinized") realities, for grace builds on and perfects nature. Later, in the *Living Flame of Love*, John sings ecstatically of how transformed persons become "living waters," giving life to all the world (see F, 3, 7). For John of the Cross, then, there is no such thing as a soul (in the sense of "pure spirit") being transformed and brought into complete union with God *without* the body fully entering into this process according to its capacity. God graces the *whole* human person and gives the *whole* person joy—not just a "purely spiritual" joy, but a joy that overflows into all our senses, into the very joints and marrow of our bodies. This in turn provides joy and life to the whole world in which we live.

Commenting on the verse "How gently and lovingly you wake in my heart" in the fourth stanza of the *Living Flame of Love*, John of the Cross observes how God's action in the very substance of the soul produces certain effects he calls an "awakening," which involves a profound experience of the beauty and harmony of creation (F, 4, 4-6).[14] This movement of God within makes everything take on a marvelous glow (see F, 4, 4). Since everything exists in God, and creatures are now known through God and not God through creatures, the person comes to see and experience creation as God does, through grace (see F 4, 5-6). Again, because creatures are known through God, their full value and beauty are recognized and affirmed. John does not view creatures as simply a stopping-off point or distraction on the way to union; rather, they have great importance all along the journey to the God already present within them as creator and sustainer. They are a necessary part of any relationship with God. This section of the *Living Flame* commentary is a marvelous affirmation of creation. Because of our transformation into God, everything is now perceived as a harmonious unity, and one sees and discovers for the first time the immense beauty and wonder of all that exists, because it is only in this transformed relation to God that human beings can truly see the world as God sees it.

According to John of the Cross, God made all things in creation beautiful and endowed them a variety of gifts. In speaking of Genesis 1:31 he tells us us, "To look and behold that they were very good was to make them very good in the Word, his Son" (C, 5, 4). But for John there is more: God communicates not only natural but supernatural being and beauty, through the Incarnation of the Word (ibid.) There is, therefore, nothing in the world not clothed in this marvelous beauty and wonder—both natural and supernatural. And thus everything is created

(and recreated) good. The whole world is good because of the relationship God has established with it in creation, and in the incarnation and
resurrection of the Son.

Consequently, it is only natural that God be attracted to and concerned with all that is. To love as God loves is to be creative, drawn and
attracted to all that is, concerned with it. Nothing falls outside the beauty
and wonder of God's self-communication to the the created world. So,
too, the human person is caught up in this same relation to creation.

GOD DESIRES ONLY THE EXALTATION OF THE PERSON

Although some think that the teaching of John of the Cross emphasizes only the path of suffering, this is not the case. In the *Spiritual Canticle* he clearly states that in themselves all our sufferings on the journey
are "nothing in the sight of God," since through them the human person cannot essentially give God anything, nor does God need suffering
(C, 28, 1). God desires only the exaltation of the human person in a love
through which God and the soul possess all things in common (ibid.).
God's love becomes our love; God's creation is ours; God's compassion,
power and authority are ours, exercised in and with God—without
greed, oppression, hatred or possessiveness.

According to John, then, God's search for us is more constant than
our own search for God (see F, 3, 28). Those brought into the life of
peaceful and quiet union should remember that it is *God* who is carrying them more deeply into their mutual love (see F, 3, 67). God em-
braces us so fully and yet so lightly that one is captured by nothing except God alone. At this stage, the human being no longer desires self-
ishly, but desires as God desires, in a full, freeing love (see F, 4, 14).

In the very process of being loved by God, one learns how to love in
turn. Though we know it is only in "the clear transformation of glory"
after death that we will finally learn to love God as much as God loves us
(see C, 38, 3), nonetheless a foreshadowing of that degree of love can
be found here already:

> ...in the perfect transformation of this state of spiritual mar-
> riage, which the soul reaches in this life, she superabounds with
> grace and...loves in some way through the Holy Spirit who is given
> to her [Rom. 5:5] in this transformation of love. (C, 38, 3)

Although he cannot fully explain it, John clearly maintains that something of that "equality of love," accomplished in and through the Holy Spirit, occurs already for those brought to spiritual marriage. In some way they learn even here and now to love as God loves, though less perfectly than in the total union of glory.

CONCLUSION

Only when we read John of the Cross in the light of the importance he attaches to incarnation and embodiment can we truly understand the marvelous teaching of this great Spanish mystic. There is a sensuality in the writings of this rather shy but strong little Carmelite friar that often embarrasses his readers, who sometimes prefer to accent the apparent negativity of the *Ascent of Mount Carmel* and *Dark Night*. The grim and alienating demands of detachment they seem to find there fit a spirituality owing more to the wars and plagues of the Middle Ages than to the Gospel. St. John of the Cross was familiar with the negative spirituality of his day, but wrote so that a whole new view of the world could arise like the phoenix from its ashes. He could not reject his own passionate, sensual nature. John could see the self-destructive potential of unredeemed passion, and so spoke of the need to be detached from things and attached only to God; but he also recognized that this same passion, purified, is an essential driving force toward union with God, and could be intensely experienced (as it was meant to be) within a positive framework of the exaltation of the whole human person in divine love. His life and his writing are a demonstration of this.

St. John of the Cross saw that humanity is called to live the life of God. Yet, this life, which is love, is to be lived not in some heavenly, ethereal homeland, but in our historical, bodily life here and now. In John's view that life of God rests on the foundation of the Incarnation, the final affirmation of the creative goodness of a world that belongs to God and in which God passionately delights.

Our call to be transformed into God is a call to enter into a God-loving life. But, to repeat once more, John does not see this love of God as something "purely spiritual," entirely divorced from material creation. Rather, this love is embodied in the same human nature graced in the transformation process. So true is this that in and through God, the transformed person comes to love all creation, the whole of reality, as

God does. According to John, God loves all reality with delight, passion, concern, gentleness and power. God loves to be there for (and even to play with) the children of humanity. So many of John's images of God are relational, expressive of the mutual love between the divine and human: mother-child, Bridegroom-Bride, Lover-Beloved. They are filled with the passion and sensuality arising out of the love God places within the human person.

The whole process of purification and dark nights whereby we are brought into union with God is meant to free us to be fully and perfectly sensual and passionate in relating to creation. When we let go of "creation-for-me," God brings us into a transformational union that frees and completes our human nature. Since grace does not destroy but builds on nature, this humanity and all its characteristics are perfected. Instead of being destructive as they often were before, passion and sensuality now become fully engaged in a delightfully constructive way. The love which fills the transformed person is "erotic" in the best and fullest sense, since it shares in the divine *eros*.[15]

Reading St. John of the Cross in the light of this erotic love challenges today's Christian to embrace a lifestyle that risks all for the sake of all—everything and everyone encompassed by God's unbounded love—as Christ and his disciple, St. John of the Cross, did.

NOTES

1. See also Richard P. Hardy, "Liberation Theology and Saint John of the Cross: A Meeting," *Eglise et Théologie* 20 (1989): 265-66.
2. See C, 8, 3. John develops this idea of living where you love in the context of the fear of death in C, 11, 10.
3. John also describes the very painful initial part of the process in quite poignant terms in F, 1, 19-21.
4. See also C, 37, 6 & 8; 38, 4.
5. For a basic overview of this transformation and divinization process see Eulogio Pacho, S. *Juan de la Cruz: Temas Fundamentales—1*, Colección Karmel, 16 (Burgos: Editorial Monte Carmelo, 1984), 120-22.; and John Welch, *When Gods Die: An Introduction to John of The Cross* (New York, NY: Paulist Press. 1990), 62-64.
6. F, 3, 8; see also F 3, 78. Elsewhere John of the Cross also speaks of the divinization of the human person but without using the phrase "by participation" (which may have been added in certain places to avoid difficulties with the Inquisition). See, for example, N, 6, 1; 22, 1; C, 27, 7.
7. See also F, Prologue, 2; C, 39, 4-6.

8. See David B. Perrin, "John of The Cross's Attitude Toward Creation" (unpublished research seminar paper, Saint Paul University, Ottawa, Ontario, Canada, 1991). In this fine paper of nearly 100 pages, Perrin provides an excellent presentation of St. John of the Cross's treatment of the "old man" and the "new man."

9. And indeed all the operations of the person become divine as well, as John of the Cross underscores in F, 2, 33.

10. See C, 12, 8, where St. John of the Cross tells us that the life of God lived here below is but a sketch (*dibujo*) in comparison with that life of God to be lived hereafter. Yet it is truly God's life, lived even now; indeed, God lives in us. This means that God already loves and acts in and through the person transformed into God at this stage of the journey.

11. See Constance FitzGerald, "Impasse and Dark Night," in *Women's Spirituality: Resources for Christian Development*, ed. Joann Wolski Conn (New York, NY: Paulist Press. 1986), 291: "What is important to realize is that it is *in* the very experience of darkness and joylessness, in the suffering and withdrawal of accustomed pleasure, that this transformation is taking place."

12. See C, 17, 10; 24, 3; Letter 6, to the nuns of Beas, from Malaga (November 18, 1586).

13. Compare F, 4, 12-13. See also Alain Cugno, *Saint John of the Cross: Reflections on Mystical Experience* (New York, NY: Seabury Press, 1982), 34-34; Lucien-Marie, *L'Expérience de Dieu: Actualité du message de saint Jean de la Croix* (Paris: Editions du Cerf, 1968), 138-141.

14. For further development of the notion of "awakening" see Alain Delaye, *La foi selon Jean de la Croix*, Sentiers pour l'Esprit #5 (Avrille: Editions du Carmel, 1975), 30-34.

15. For a more complete presentation of this theme, see Eugene Maio, *St. John of the Cross: The Imagery of Eros* (Madrid: Editorial Playor, 1973).

IMAGERY OF DIVINE LOVE:
THE CRUCIFIX DRAWING
OF JOHN OF THE CROSS

Graham M. Schweig

Graham M. Schweig is a doctoral candidate in the comparative study and history of religion at Harvard University in Cambridge, MA. A reproduction of the crucifix drawing discussed here may be found at the front of this volume.

The crucifix drawing of St. John of the Cross is unique in the history of Christian art. In this short study, we will analyze St. John's only surviving work of art in order to have something of his experiential, highly theistic religion revealed. Specifically, we are interested in learning what essential message is transmitted through this aesthetic imagery, and how this crucifix drawing relates to John's conjugal mysticism.

First we will be concerned with the drawing itself as an autonomous expression, not to be compared with anything outside its world. Here we are not concerned with the historical details of this work. Rather we will examine the aesthetic composition itself to see how its form gives direct expression to the religious experience of St. John. It will only be toward the end of our analysis that we will relate the drawing to his written work for further supporting our interpretation.

St. John's drawing of the crucifix was executed in pen and ink, on a grainy parchment. The drawing is in good condition, as can be seen in the reproduction of the work. Having an oval line for a border, it is quite small; the outer edges would not exceed four inches in height and three in width. Despite its small size, it is, without doubt, a powerful religious expression.

The subject matter of the work is quite simple: Christ on the cross.

162

There is no one else in the drawing looking on or praying to or glorifying him, as usually occur in works of art depicting the crucifixion. Furthermore, the background is empty, and there are no symbols accompanying the crucified Christ or the composition as a whole. There is not even a nimbus around the head of Christ. The only figures in the drawing are Christ himself and the cross. Although the work is small and lacks scenery and detail, it is complex in its composition.

The part of the composition that is perhaps its most immediately striking feature is the unusual perspective St. John provides for his viewer. The cross and the figure of Christ have a strong downward, one-point perspective from a three-quarter aerial view. One is virtually looking down from above and slightly in front of the cross, onto the left side of Christ. The effect of this unusual perspective is dramatic: it fills the composition with tension and intensity. This angle of vision of the crucified Christ immediately sets St. John's drawing apart from all other previous representations of the crucifixion in the history of Christian art.

While this angle of viewing establishes the drawing's drama, there are other elements that contribute to its intensity. The cross itself leans so far to the right of the composition that it appears to fall backwards. One struggles to keep the cross upright while viewing it. Most people, seeing the drawing for the first time, are compelled to turn the picture on its left side to compensate for this strained angle.

The strong downward force of the perspective and the weight of Christ's body are accentuated by his knees buckling under him and his head hanging parallel to the ground, and are in competition with the dramatic angle of the cross itself. Thus Christ's body falls forward to the left of the composition, pulling in the opposite direction of the backward-leaning cross.

Christ's outstretched arms add still further to the vexing tension that vibrates throughout the composition. The spikes through the palms are large, with the limits of strain in the arms portrayed by long, tendon-like lines and the drops of blood falling from them. The tension of the arms is accentuated by the swollen chest, shoulder and back muscles and the pull of the weight of Christ's body as he falls forward.

The radically different angle from which the crucifix is seen emphasizes, perhaps even more than other depictions of the crucifix, the intense suffering of Christ. The angle causes Christ's left hand, with the spike prominent, to be the part of his body that is closest to the viewer. Again, the suffering of Christ is emphasized. Finally, this angle conceals Christ's face. These features, created simply by the angle, leave the viewer with a feeling of devastation.

Aside from the influence of angle, however, there is another powerful element at work, namely, the interplay of light and shadow. The lighting is the most subtle and intriguing aspect of the composition. Light comes from above and behind the cross from the right of the viewer. While the light illuminates the sides and top of the cross, it leaves Christ's form in shadow. His head falls away from the light. This illumination gives the viewer a subtle sense of hope or relief from the utter despair portrayed in the figure of Christ.

One's vision is irresistibly drawn by the angle down toward Christ's darkened form, and is simultaneously drawn toward the light reflected on the cross. The power of this composition lies in the dialectical tension between the impact of the angle of vision and the effect of light on the subject, which produce corresponding feelings of despair and hope.

What is the significance of this vivid and dramatic portrayal of Christ's suffering? Why is the light coming from behind, and what is the source of this light? And why is the viewer placed in this position in relation to Christ?

To answer these questions of meaning, we must treat the work no longer as just an autonomous expression. The full significance of this work must be understood in light of St. John's mystical doctrine of divine love.

In his writings he intricately describes the rigorous ascetic practices of the mystical life and his experiences of divine union with God. This perfection of divine union is characterized by a marriage between the individual soul, who is always the bride, and Christ, who is the beloved Bridegroom. This "bridal mysticism" is central to St. John's teachings. Given this fact, why does St. John emphasize the crucifixion in this extraordinarily vivid drawing?

St. John wrote detailed and didactic treatises, but he also utilized aesthetic forms for expressing his religious experiences. He produced poetry that communicated divine matters in a way prose could not; indeed, all his longer treatises are commentaries on his poetry. And like his poetry, this drawing obviously was derived from inner religious experience, for its style and composition are unique. But he chose not to express this vision in poetry. Apparently, the subject of this vision was better communicated through a visual representation than through any verbal expression. In addition, this representation was not meant to be a public image or even an icon, for he had given the drawing to a holy nun in his religious order. It was the pure and simple expression of a secret vision, which was to be shared only with his spiritual associates.

If we are to complete our interpretation of this drawing, we must turn to St. John's works. In St. John's prose and poetry, the interpretation of the crucifixion drawing is powerfully aided specifically by several stanzas from the seventh of his "Romances." In the following lines, Christ is speaking to the Father:

> I will go and tell the world,
> spreading the word
> of your beauty and sweetness
> and of your sovereignty.
> I will go seek my bride
> and take upon myself
> her weariness and labors
> in which she suffers so;
> and that she may have life
> I will die for her
> and lifting her out of that deep,
> I will restore her to you.

The essential message of St. John's drawing of the crucifix is revealed by these verses. As these verses plainly express, Christ (the Bridegroom) wants to relieve the soul (the bride) of her suffering by taking it upon himself, and in doing so, restores the soul to the Father.

Thus, this small drawing reveals St. John's specific relationship with the deity. St. John, through his artistic work, powerfully conveys the experience of his relationship with God to the viewer, thus allowing the interpreter direct access to his experience: the viewer of this work is truly the bride, who is looking on from above at the tortured Bridegroom. Compelled in the direction of the light source, the viewer is restored to the Father. The drawing, even more than these revealing verses, conveys the absolute suffering and sacrifice of Christ, expressing his intensity of love for the bride. While the bride experiences feelings of grief and separation, she also possesses a sense of hope because of the element of light that conveys the presence of the Father to whom the bride is restored.

St. John's work, though small and simple, is a complete expression unto itself. And yet, as we saw, the compositional elements of form and light established a complex relationship between Christ, the viewer, and the presence of God. Indeed, certain responses are clearly evoked by the work, whether or not the viewer is familiar with St. John's writings, because it stands today as powerful imagery of divine love. The work commands our attention, as it ultimately reveals the crucifix as an expression of the intense love that the Bridegroom has for the bride as she enters the inner life of God.

THE INFLUENCE OF JOHN OF THE CROSS IN THE UNITED STATES: A PRELIMINARY STUDY

Steven Payne, O.C.D.

Steven Payne is a member of the Institute of Carmelite Studies, editorial director of ICS Publications, and editor of the journal Spiritual Life. An earlier version of this talk appeared in the international Carmelite journal Teresianum in 1991, and is revised and republished here with permission.

INTRODUCTION

First impressions might suggest that the influence of John of the Cross on North American spirituality could be easily summed up in his own words: *nada, nada, nada.*[1] After all, in the United States and Canada, John is the "unknown Carmelite"; his popularity has never approached that of St. Teresa of Avila or even of Br. Lawrence of the Resurrection, to say nothing of St. Thérèse of Lisieux (whose statue graces nearly every Catholic church on this side of the Atlantic).[2] Only a handful of American parishes are dedicated to John of the Cross, and even fewer Carmels.[3] The bulk of John's writings were not available in English translation until the 1860s, and took several more decades to be noticed in scholarly circles.[4] Even now, most serious Sanjuanist studies available in English are either directly translated from European sources or heavily dependent on them.[5] Worst of all, Americans are typically portrayed throughout the world as slaves of "inordinate attachments" to wealth and power, the virtual embodiment of everything in modern society that John of the Cross would have opposed: pragmatic materialism, consumerism, sensualism, militarism, racism and so on. The United States would seem to be inhospitable soil for John's teaching.

167

But matters are not as simple as they might at first appear. Contrary to the usual stereotypes, recent research indicates that Americans remain among the most religious people in any developed nation, at least by such measurable standards as declared belief in God and frequency of church attendance. To be sure, the same studies show that this widespread religiosity is sometimes shallow, without a solid biblical basis or sufficient awareness of the ethical implications of a life of faith.[6] Our constitutional separation of church and state has spared us the religious wars of our European ancestors, but has also led to an overly individualized, privatized and "polite" approach to religion, as if it were merely a matter of a lifestyle choice and personal preference.[7] Yet beneath the differences, American commentators have also noted certain striking affinities between our own milieu and John's, living as he did at the zenith of the Spanish empire, while suffering the effects of the social and economic tensions that would cause its decline. Whatever the reasons, contemporary Americans searching for a deeper faith are turning more and more to John of the Cross as a particularly apt guide for our times.

Actually, John has been a hidden presence in our country for a long time. In the same quiet and unassuming way he operated in life, John has left a subtle imprint on American culture and spirituality, most often indirectly. Discalced Carmelites, for example, were among the first religious to arrive in the United States, bringing with them a love of St. John of the Cross that they shared with many of the important figures in early American Catholic history. Again, the countless Americans who have read Thérèse's *Story of a Soul* could hardly have avoided exposure, however unknowingly, to the Sanjuanist themes it incorporates. Thousands of college students in the United States and Canada have encountered John in the study of T.S. Eliot's *Four Quartets*, or in the Spanish literature courses taught at virtually every major university. The expression "dark night of the soul" has become almost a cliché in American speech and journalism.

This article is no more than a preliminary report on some of the Sanjuanist traces in American culture and spirituality. Undoubtedly, with the heightened awareness created by the celebration of the fourth centenary of his death, new studies will soon begin to appear on hitherto unnoticed aspects of John's influence in the United States; thus, a more comprehensive survey will have to wait until all of these results are in. Here we must content ourselves with a few highlights.

CARMEL IN AMERICA

Certainly one of the earliest ways John came to be known in the United States is through the religious family he helped to found, and Discalced Carmelites have left signs of their presence here almost from the beginning. For example, it was three Spanish friars (Anthony of the Ascension, Thomas of Aquinas, and Andrew of the Assumption) from the same Mexican mission John was preparing to join at the time of his death who celebrated the first Mass in what is now California in 1602 at San Diego, and who gave the name "Carmelo" to the river and promontory near Monterey where Junipero Serra would later establish the Carmel Mission. Discalced Carmelite missionaries were also early arrivals in the Louisiana Territory (1720-1723).[8]

But the most important and long-lasting Carmelite influence in the U.S. came from the nuns, who in 1790 established the first community of religious women in the thirteen original states, at Port Tobacco, Maryland (later moved to Baltimore). The four Discalced Carmelite sisters who made the foundation (three Americans, one Englishwoman) came from the Carmels in the Lowlands established through the efforts of Anne of St. Bartholomew and Anne of Jesus (for whom John of the Cross wrote his commentary on *The Spiritual Canticle*).[9] Thus the new American community could easily trace its spiritual lineage back directly to Teresa and John, and brought with them many tokens of that connection, including Father Cyprien's two-volume French edition of John's *Oeuvres Spirituelles* (Paris, 1641).[10]

As the earliest community of religious women in the nation, situated in the diocese of Baltimore (the premier episcopal see of the United States), the Discalced Carmelite nuns had extensive contacts with most of the important figures in early American Catholic history, including the bishops of Baltimore and elsewhere, the Jesuits, the Visitation nuns of Georgetown, and the Sulpicians who eventually staffed most of the seminaries in the United States. Though it is hard to assess how successful they were in spreading Sanjuanist doctrine, we know, for example, that their first chaplain, Charles Neale, who had accompanied them from Europe, enjoyed translating John's poetry in to English,[11] that sisters at various times received gifts of relics or pictures of the Mystical Doctor, and that several were remembered especially for their devotion to John of the Cross, a devotion they undoubtedly made efforts to share.[12] In 1891, to mark the third centenary of John's death, the Carmel of Baltimore arranged an impressive three-day celebration, attended by Cardinal Gibbons, Charles W. Currier, and many important dignitaries.[13] From this original foundation have come over two-thirds of more than 65 currently existing American Carmels, one of the largest national groupings in the Order.[14] They continue to provide a living witness to the Teresian and Sanjuanist spirit throughout the United States today.

A NINETEENTH CENTURY EXAMPLE:
ISAAC HECKER AND THE PAULISTS

The founder of the Society of Missionary Priests of St. Paul the Apostle (CSP), commonly known as the Paulists, provides an excellent illustration of John's indirect influence on the American church in the 1800s. One of the leading figures in nineteenth century American Catholicism, Father Isaac Hecker (1819-1888) strongly defended the compatibility of American ideals with Catholic principles, at a time when American Catholics were often suspected by their Protestant counterparts of disloyalty and allegiance to a foreign power; he was likewise an ardent proponent of a truly "American piety," combining a program of social reform with spiritual regeneration.[15] In terms of his own mystical life, however, he was deeply indebted to Teresa of Avila and John of the Cross, turning to John especially when struggling to understand his own experiences of spiritual darkness. At the time of his profession as a Redemptorist in 1846, Hecker explained his own spiritual journey to his friend Orestes Brownson as follows:

> It is well known to you my friend that there are recognized in the Church two ways in which the grace of God can lead the Soul to that perfection for which He created it. The one is called passive and the other active; these have given birth to the orders contemplative and the orders active, and from which have sprung the Theology mystic and the Theology scholastic as they are termed. Neither one of these ways are entirely separated from the other, still the predominancy of one is sometimes so great as to fully warrant this distinction. ...God does not put the soul in the way passive until he has gained at the bottom of the will its full consent, and is sure of its fidelity, morally sure. God when it is his design to unite the soul to himself in this way commences by infusing into it his infinite love, the object of

which is to detach the soul from the irregular pleasures of the senses, the inordinate social attachments, and the desire of the riches, honors, and vanities of the world. Hence the chief occupation of the soul is to suffer, suffer the cruel operation of this divine love. This love of course must be stronger and greater than these passions otherwise the soul could not nor would not detach itself from the one to unite itself to another. But this love is obscure, confuse[d], & almost unperceptible to the soul, hence it is not so much the pain of being separated from its former pleasures that causes its trouble as the fact of being lead & driven by whom? Where? & How? It knows not. If it could but see the hand of God which is laid upon it, if it knew what was required of it, it would not complain.... It is this that made St John of the Cross call it the "night obscure of the Soul,".... The second night is to the first as the midnight is to the evening. God augments & throws a purer & more subtel [sic] love into the soul at this moment in order to despoil the soul of the willful use of its faculties. This love penetrates to the centre of the will, the Soul, and purges it of all that is destructible and improper. ...This second night is terrible, the Soul seems as it were held over the horrible abyss of hell by an invisible power, abandoned by God, a prey, and a subject of mockery to the demons. God seems to reject its prayers before it can utter them. All within the soul is thick darkness and without there is no reality, nothing firm, permanent, eternal. It is deprived of the use of its faculties, it can neither think, feel, or act. O great God how wonderful is the work of Thy infinite Love. ...But to be brief after the soul has been despoiled of all that is unpleasing in the sight of God, God takes up His habitation in the Soul. Already has commenced the dawn, the aurora has appeared, the full day of which is the clear vision & happiness of the blessed in the other world....

But not to detain you any longer on this matter, I would refer you my dear friend to the works of St John of the Cross which are contained in three duodecimo vols. and are complete on this subject and most estimated.[16]

Except for the association of the "active" and "passive" ways with different categories of souls and religious orders, the almost verbal dependence on Sanjuanist texts is evident. Indeed, John's writings became Hecker's constant spiritual nourishment in his later years. Thus, in a letter of 13 July 1886, Hecker's companion and fellow Paulist Walter Elliott writes to the Discalced Carmelite nuns in Baltimore that:

Every night, nearly, and during the day sometimes I read St.
John of the Cross to Fr. Hecker, who is hardly able to do much reading himself. I must say he is greedy of him, but it shows his good taste;
for what, but Scripture itself, is more ennobling than the writings of
St. John of the Cross? We are now in the second volume, having read
all the first, part of it twice over.[17]

Later, in the original 1891 edition of *The Life of Father Hecker*, Elliott
again describes Hecker's special fondness for John's works:

Next to Scripture came St. Thomas and St. John of the Cross,
the one for dogmatic and philosophical, the other for devotional
uses.... St. John of the Cross and [Louis] Lallemant, as already
stated, were his handbooks of mysticism and ascetic principles. The
former he caused to be read to him in regular course over and over
again, enjoying every syllable with fresh relish.[18]

Interestingly, it was an adapted French translation of this same
biography, published in 1897, that first raised the specter of "Americanism," later condemned in Leo XIII's apostolic letter *Testem Benevolentiae*
in 1899; Elliott's book had caused a sensation among French commentators, who alternately hailed or reviled Hecker as the representative of
a "new American asceticism," cut free of the old "passive" monastic virtues of obedience, humility, etc., and founded instead on personal re-
sponsibility and the individual inspiration of the Holy Spirit.[19] "Americanism" has sometimes been called a "phantom" heresy, since virtually
none of those involved in the controversy recognized their own views as
among those rejected in *Testem Benevolentiae*. Still, at various times
throughout the remainder of his life, Elliott was forced again to defend
Hecker and himself against the accusation of "Americanism" (at least in
the sense condemned by the apostolic letter), and often did so, in part,
by insisting on the reliable Teresian and Sanjuanist sources of their
spirituality. Thus, in a letter of December 1919 to the French Carmelite
Father Leon, responding to a renewed attack on "Americanism" in the
Messager de Ste. Thérèse, 1919-1920, Elliott writes that:

From the day I entered [the Paulists] I have been continuously
led to read and indeed to study contemplative literature. It is from
Father Hecker that I learned to love St. Teresa and to enroll myself
in her discipleship. I have read her and St. John of the Cross every

day for many years. She is a great official patron of ours. St. John of
the Cross is the same. It was by special request of Father Hecker that
our original fathers place him among our notable sponsors in
heaven. Father Hecker fixed on his feast day as the date of entering
our first house. He was always reading contemplative books and
practicing contemplative prayer. St. John of the Cross he read every
day. Other books he changed; St. John of the Cross, never.... My
dear Father, what you and your brother Carmelites detest and abhor—"Americanism"—that do I and all other Paulists detest and
abhor. What you love we love, namely, the contemplative spirit as the
inspiring force of all Catholic activity.[20]

Clearly, then, St. John of the Cross exerted a powerful influence on
the spirituality of Father Hecker and the early Paulists. It remains to be
seen whether future research may also reveal a Sanjuanist thread in
Hecker's more strictly theological views. For our purposes, what is interesting is that such a dynamic and quintessentially American figure and
religious community should have had such strong initial ties to the
Mystical Doctor. A similar pattern could be found in the history of many
other American congregations, suggesting that John's doctrine, though
from a foreign land and culture, has never been totally foreign to the
American spirit.

SANJUANIST TEXTS IN ENGLISH

Until fairly recently, the United States has been almost totally dependent on Britain for works by and about John of the Cross in English.
As noted above, despite early editions in other languages, the "complete" writings of John of the Cross did not appear in English until 1864
(in David Lewis's two volume edition), a year after the publication of
Canon Dalton's brief anthology, *The Spirit of St. John of the Cross*.[21] Lewis's
translation also circulated in the United States, and was frequently reprinted, eventually with corrections and introductions by Benedict
Zimmerman, O.C.D.[22] Subsequent translations of individual works
gradually appeared, including an edition of the "Precautions" by the
Discalced Carmelite nuns of Wheeling, West Virginia in 1918.[23] But all
of these were superseded in 1934-1935 with the appearance of E. Allison Peers's famous translation of John's *Complete Works*, based on the so-
called "critical edition" of Padre Silverio.[24] The three volume Peers edition contained both the A and B redactions of the *Spiritual Canticle* and

Living Flame of Love, as well as other valuable documents, including the 1622 defense of John's orthodoxy by Fray Basilio Ponce de León. This three volume translation was later published in an American edition by the Newman Bookshop (Westminster, MD) in 1946, and subsequently revised and reprinted many times; individual volumes of the *Ascent, Dark Night, Spiritual Canticle* and *Living Flame* also circulated widely here in inexpensive paperback "Image Book" editions.

The Peers translation is fairly literal, and very British in tone and choice of vocabulary, but for many years has served American readers well. More recently, however, Kieran Kavanaugh and Otilio Rodriguez have produced the first truly American translation of *The Collected Works of St. John of the Cross* (Garden City, NY: Doubleday & Co., 1964). ICS Publications rereleased this single volume edition in 1973, and without aggressive promotion has already sold over 100,000 copies in the United States alone (without counting editions of the same translation available in India and the Philippines), a small sign of John's growing popularity.[25] While both the Peers and Kavanaugh/Rodriguez translations are highly regarded, American researchers seem increasingly to be using the latter for everything except the A redactions of the *Canticle* and *Flame* (not included in Kavanaugh/Rodriguez) and John's poetry, a trend likely to accelerate with the release of a newly revised centenary edition of the Kavanaugh/Rodriguez translation in 1991. John's poetry, meanwhile, is available in several English versions, though (perhaps not surprisingly) none are considered altogether satisfactory by literary experts.[26]

EARLY STUDIES ON JOHN OF THE CROSS IN ENGLISH

Serious study of Sanjuanist doctrine began slowly in North America. Some of the first English-speaking authors to make significant use of St. John of the Cross came from beyond the boundaries of the United States or the Roman Catholic tradition. In 1856, for example, Robert A. Vaughan's popular *Hours With the Mystics* introduced John to a wider range of the British reading public, though casting him in a negative light.

> Unfortunately, Vaughan's evaluation of St. John, like that of so many commentators, was deeply colored by his distaste for "Romanism." He describes John's mysticism as "unnatural" and quietistic, and at-

tributes to him the promotion of a "doctrine of blind obedience to ecclesiastical superiors" by means of which Rome was attempting to enslave the world. Yet Vaughan admits to a certain "melancholy admiration" for John, whom he considers a "consummate ascetic" and a "genuine," though "miserably mistaken," mystic.[27]

Dean Inge repeated many of these same charges in the Bampton Lectures of 1899, published the same year under the title *Christian Mysticism,* accusing John of "nihilism and acosmism," as well as "a terrible view of life and duty."[28]

The following year, Canadian psychologist R. M. Bucke published an intriguing, idiosyncratic work entitled *Cosmic Consciousness,* in which he lists "Juan de Yepes" among those who had almost certainly attained this state; his extended discussion of John, though somewhat overly hagiographical, is far more positive in tone than Inge's or Vaughan's. Bucke had become interested in mysticism after an ecstatic experience of his own, and the thesis of his book, after analyzing a number of ostensible mystics (including Old Testament prophets, Jesus, the Buddha, Walt Whitman, and John), is that "cosmic consciousness" has occurred with increasing frequency down through history, and will gradually "become more and more universal and appear earlier in the individual life until the race at large will possess this faculty."[29] Not many have been convinced by Bucke's evidence, but the book is still widely read, and often regarded as a forerunner of various "transpersonal" and "consciousness" psychologies as well as certain "New Age" themes.

One enthusiastic early reader of *Cosmic Consciousness* was the American psychologist William James, whose own Gifford Lectures of 1901-1902, published under the title *The Varieties of Religious Experience,* quickly became a classic in the psychology and philosophy of religion. James also discusses John of the Cross, though not always favorably, describing him as "a Spanish mystic who flourished—or rather who existed, for there was little that suggested flourishing about him—in the sixteenth century."[30] James himself remained fascinated with mysticism, and though reluctant to draw any larger metaphysical conclusions, maintained nonetheless that "the existence of mystical states absolutely overthrows the pretension of non-mystical states to be the sole and ultimate dictators of what we may believe."[31]

Another important work in this period is Evelyn Underhill's *Mysticism: A Study in the Nature and Development of Man's Spiritual Consciousness,* which was "immediately recognized as a remarkable book" upon its publication in 1911.[32]

> Within the year of issue it was reprinted, then re-edited and re-printed again. Two years later it reached its fifth edition. Its popularity stemmed from the fact that it carved out a new subject, made it intelligible, and interpreted it with convincing power. Although Underhill appealed to psychology, philosophy, and theology, her contribution does not rest principally on her analysis of her subject. Above all her book is a personal defense of the achievement of the mystics that she was able to understand because she lived intimately with the texts.[33]

Underhill made particularly effective use of John's works in a chapter on "The Dark Night of the Soul," where many English-speaking readers discovered their first detailed introduction to this theme. It would be safe to say that authors such as R. M. Bucke, William James and Evelyn Underhill have played an important role in gaining for John, if not a place of honor, at least a serious hearing among American psychologists and philosophers of religion.[34]

TWENTIETH CENTURY EXAMPLES:
DOROTHY DAY AND THOMAS MERTON

John's name and doctrine were invoked again in a curious episode of the 1930s and 1940s, involving a popular retreat movement developed by a Canadian Jesuit and avid reader of St. John of the Cross, Onesimus Lacouture, SJ. Evidently Lacouture's retreat form was "characterized by its rigor," and emphasized overcoming our natural "pagan" existence by acting always according to supernatural motives.[35] Lacouture attracted many followers in Canada, and later in the United States, after he gave a retreat in Baltimore in 1938. Among the movement's early adherents were the Josephite priest Pacifique Roy, SSJ, and also Father John J. Hugo of the Pittsburgh diocese, who made two retreats under Lacouture and soon amplified and published his notes under the title *Applied Christianity*, bearing the imprimatur of Cardinal Spellman, and replete with quotations from the Mystical Doctor.[36] Following Lacouture's model, Hugo himself became a highly successful retreat master in the United States, drawing many clergy, religious and laity to the movement. But the initial successes began to create conflict and opposition. "The controversial character of the [Lacouture] retreat" claims one author, "obviously arose from its emphasis on the spirituality of St. John of the Cross, his insistence on 'detachment' from those impulses for power and possessions to which the person was subject."[37] Lacouture and Hugo were both accused of propagating a "new Jansenism," and of misconstruing the proper relation between nature and grace in the spiritual life.[38] Hugo defended himself at length against the charges in *A Sign of Contradiction,* once more by appealing to the doctrine of John of the Cross, among others.[39] Ultimately, however, Lacouture was banished to an Indian reservation in upstate New York, while Hugo was told to discontinue his retreats. The "movement," as such, effectively died out, and has been all but forgotten.[40]

But it left a lasting impact on at least one person. Dorothy Day, co-founder of the Catholic Worker Movement, a major figure in twentieth century American Catholicism and perhaps the symbol the Church's social conscience in the United States, came into contact with "the retreat" at a particularly important moment in her life. She was not much impressed by a first reading of Lacouture's retreat notes, but an initial visit to the Catholic Worker community by Father Roy, subsequent days of recollection under his guidance, and his retreat for the Catholic Worker group at Easton farm in 1940 won her over. Diffident about his own skills as a retreat master, Roy referred her to Father Hugo, who gave the Catholic Worker retreat the following year, and became Day's confessor during the last 40 years of her life. For Dorothy Day, these retreats marked a turning point in her spiritual journey, as she later acknowledges. She did not involve herself in the ongoing theological disputes over nature and grace, and could appreciate both sides of the argument. What interested her was the challenge from the Lacouture-style retreat to a life of heroic sanctity, embracing "the folly of the Cross."

> To us the retreat was the good news. We made it as often as we could, and refreshed ourselves with days of recollection.
> ...If people did not go away from the retreat examining their consciences as to the work they did in the world, then it was a failure. Such a retreat should be like a shock treatment, we thought, putting the "old man" to death, bringing us to new life.[41]

In other words, Dorothy Day was brought to a more intense level of

Christian dedication through a retreat program and spiritual formation drawn largely from the principles of St. John of the Cross. And while her favorite Carmelite saint seems to have been Thérèse of Lisieux, she continued to read John of the Cross throughout her life, frequently echoing Father Hugo's favorite Sanjuanist maxim: "In the evening [of life], you will be judged on love."

Despite his atypical career, and whatever his personal limitations, perhaps no one better represents and speaks to the restless spiritual search of contemporary Americans than Thomas Merton, who has been called "symbol of a century."[42] Merton, too, was deeply influenced by John of the Cross, whom he called "the most accessible of the saints."[43] Merton first began a serious reading of John of the Cross in 1939 and 1940 while he was still living in Greenwich Village. As he writes in *The Seven Storey Mountain:*

> So at great cost I bought the first volume of the Works of St. John of the Cross and sat in the room on Perry Street and turned over the first pages, underlining places here and there with a pencil. But it turned out that it would take more than that to make me a saint: because these words I underlined, although they amazed and dazzled me with their import, were all too simple for me to understand. They were too naked, too stripped of all duplicity and compromise for my complexity, perverted by my appetites. However, I am glad that I was at least able to recognize them, obscurely, as worthy of the greatest respect.[44]

Later, in 1950, after becoming a monk of Gethsemani, he explained to Abbot Fox in his retreat notes:

> I had been hoping to meditate a little on the Cautions of St. John of the Cross. I have at least glanced through them. I took them as the standard of my religious life at solemn profession and have never really lived up to them. I know they contain the secret of success. Using them I know that I can make good use of the opportunities God has given me here. I *can* lead a contemplative life here. It takes some doing, but if I do not insist on having everything exactly my own way, Our Lord will do most of the work.[45]

And elsewhere he writes, to Dom Jean-Baptist Porion, O.Cart.:

For me to be a Cistercian is to be a man who loves God in a Cistercian monastery—in sympathy with St. John of the Cross and Ruysbroeck and a few other people who are *not* Cistercians, and also with a few others who are. It does not seem to be to be a reserved or even a mortal sin to live in a Cistercian monastery with more actual sympathy for St. John of the Cross that St. Bernard of Clairvaux.... I am happy with St. John of the Cross among the rocks.[46]

During his early years as a Trappist, then, Merton avidly studied the Mystical Doctor, and produced a number of writings on John of the Cross, most notably *The Ascent to Truth;* the article on John in *Saints for Now;* and the essay on John's ascetical doctrine which first appeared as an introduction to John's *Counsels of Light and Love* (Wheeling, WV: Discalced Carmelite Nuns, 1953), and was later included in *Disputed Questions.*[47] His works of this period show a remarkable enthusiasm for the Spanish Carmelite, and introduced many American readers to the study of John of the Cross. After 1953, however, his explicit work on John seems to have stopped. Perhaps Merton felt frustrated with the overly scholastic approach to Sanjuanist themes that had marred *Ascent to Truth.*[48] In any case, during his early years as a Trappist, Merton did as much as anyone in this century to arouse American interest in John of the Cross. It is only unfortunate that he never seemed to have appreciated the full power of Sanjuanist mysticism to incorporate the very social justice and inter-religious concerns which Merton himself later helped raise, and which have been more deeply explored by those who have followed in his footsteps (e.g., Daniel Berrigan, William Johnston and others).

AMERICAN USE (AND MISUSE)
OF "DARK NIGHT" LANGUAGE AND IMAGERY

We have already noted that the expression "dark night of the soul" has now entered popular American discourse, often without any awareness of its Sanjuanist origins. One obvious example of this phenomenon is F. Scott Fitzgerald's famous reference in "The Crack Up" to "the real dark night of the soul," where "it is always three o'clock in the morning, day after day."[49] More recently, *People* magazine has referred to the Stuart

murder scandal in Massachusetts as "A Dark Night of the Soul in Boston," while Tom Wolfe describes the astronauts' "post-orbital remorse"
as a "dark night of the ego."[50] Such examples abound in American journalism and everyday speech, and have been discussed elsewhere.[51]

In her Prologue to *The Long Dark Night of the Soul,* a study of opposition to the Vietnam War among American intellectuals in the late 1960s
and early 1970s, author Sandy Vogelgesang argues that her title is especially apt for capturing:

> ...the mood of the U.S. Intellectual Left during the [President]
> Johnson period. More than coincidence made such contrasting fig-
> ures as Daniel Berrigan and Norman Mailer choose that image to
> characterize their opposition to the Vietnam War. Father Berrigan
> compared his antiwar experience to the original line from St. John
> of the Cross in *The Dark Night of Resistance.* Mailer borrowed the
> phrase for his coverage of the March on the Pentagon in 1967.[52]

Indeed, as Vogelgesang notes, Daniel Berrigan found John's life
and "dark night" imagery well suited for reflecting on his own situation
in 1970, while hunted by the FBI for his anti-war activities.

> I should like to use, as a general guide, master text, source of
> imagery, the book of John of the Cross, *The Dark Night of the Soul.*
> The choice is deliberate. It implies in the first place that my
> present situation is primarily an experience in and of the spirit, that
> its only coherence and meaning are to be sought on those terms.
> Otherwise, one is playing cat-and-mouse with the hunters, and the
> chase becomes frivolous, thoughtless or pathetic.... I claim for my-
> self the dignity of a Christian and a man, present to his tradition....
> ...[John] was neglected, cast down from the places his talents
> would justly claim, maligned, broken. Yet in the dark socket of exis-
> tence into which he had been flung to be ground to powder, a most
> stunning event occurred.... In a dungeon, the light broke upon him.
> John was granted something due no mortal man: access to the mys-
> tery of love....
> ...He suffered greatly, as a condition of life and a condition of
> faith. He suffered because his convictions were unacceptable to
> power, ran counter to the grain. He never submitted obediently to
> Byzantine men, even though their power was announced in awe-
> some rhetoric, and wielded the keys of the divine will. John was
> seeking a simple human good (we would say today). He wanted a

community in which men would choose how they would live and where, within the freedom granted them by the truth of a tradition. He was willing to negotiate with opponents; he traveled unwearyingly in service to rational solutions. But when power breathed close and threatened hard, his adversaries came up against something harder than Spanish bone. The struck flint; and flint, in the nature of things, awakened fire. John burned with a fire which human conflict ignited, sustained elsewhere, burning on behalf of men.

...I want to be faithful to his method, which is rational and coherent, but whose content is also, and from another point of view, surreal, nightmarish. A classicist, an ecstatic, a good fighter, a faithful man, a hound nervous as lightning in the traces, a merciless surgeon of the soul, a Jesus prayer.[53]

Berrigan goes on to ponder the significance, in his own situation, of the imagery of night, of leaving the house, of going out unseen.

The symbol: a going forth, from a house at rest, at night.

The house: in many senses; the *alma domus*, the structured universe, womb, rest, tomb; premature age, reward after effort, retirement plan....

Leaving the house. It has to do with the beginnings, the first stirrings of conscience, the first serious step as a consequence, the first march, the first legal jeopardy, the first trial attended.[54]

He likewise challenges mystics and contemplatives to "cut loose from their good order and country discipline" and begin to share with the political activists "all those good things [they] purportedly hold in escrow," guiding them "into their unexplored inner spaces."[55] Successive chapters are a kind of free-form meditation on the political spirituality he finds suggested by Sanjuanist texts.

To be sure, the immediate crisis of the Vietnam War has long since passed; ironically, in his 1968 convention acceptance speech, Richard Nixon had already declared that "a long, dark night for America is about to end" (well before the national "dark night" of the Watergate scandal!).[56] *The Dark Night of Resistance* is a product of its time; written on the run, it conveys an enormous sense of urgency but lacks the polish of some of the author's other works. Yet, whether one agrees with Berrigan's political stance or not, this book forcefully raises important issues about the social implications of mysticism in general, and Sanjuanist spirituality in particular, and the potential danger of interpreting John in an overly privatized and individualistic way that divorces spiritual from social transformation. These same concerns, obviously, reappear later in the more recent works of liberation spirituality. In short, *The Dark Night of Resistance* is a prophetic book, in more than one sense.

The expression "dark night of the soul," then, continues to be used widely and often carelessly in American discourse (and not just in our spiritual and devotional literature), but there is at least a growing recognition that the experience it evokes can have, as the recent Apostolic Letter suggests, "a kind of collective character."[57] Americans as a whole, and not just as individuals, have been undergoing successive periods of national "soul-searching" in recent decades, chastened by the failure of many of our plans and aspirations. John's teaching on the educative role of "passive purification" has proved extremely helpful in understanding the positive value of such experiences.

AMERICAN CARMELS IN THE TWENTIETH CENTURY

Lest there be any doubt, it should be noted that throughout this century Carmel in the United States has continued to promote Saint John of the Cross, though usually in quiet and less dramatic ways. We already noted the many communities of Discalced Carmelite nuns scattered throughout the country, which together with over 20 communities of friars and hundreds of Secular Carmelites continue to impart Sanjuanist doctrine through newsletters, public liturgies and celebrations, classes, preaching, retreat work, and simple fidelity to the Carmelite way of life. For example, though the monastery of the Discalced Carmelite friars in Washington, DC was only founded in 1916, by 1919-1920 they had already published a full-length biography of John of the Cross and a translation of *Holiness in the Cloister* by Father Lucas of St. Joseph.[58] Some U.S. Carmelite periodicals of the past, such as *Mount Carmel* (Washington, DC), *Little Flower Magazine* (Oklahoma Province) and *Revista Carmelitana* (Tucson, AZ), helped foster interest in Carmel and St. John of the Cross in their time; others, such as *Spiritual Life* (Washington Province), *Carmelite Digest* (California-Arizona Province), *Living Prayer* (Carmel of Barre, VT) and *Apostolate of the Little Flower* (Oklahoma Province) continue to thrive. The Spiritual Life Institute, founded by Father William McNamara, O.C.D., has offered for many years a distinctive and powerful American presentation of Sanjuanist themes, through the publication of *Desert Call* and the teaching of its members. Individual American Carmelite friars, nuns and seculars have written numerous books and articles on John. Various Carmels continue to produce material by and about the Mystical Doctor, and ICS Publications hopes soon to expand its Sanjuanist offerings. Carmelites of the Ancient Observance have shown increasing interest in the Mystical Doctor, and many are leading American experts on his teaching. The Carmelite Forum, composed of American Carmelites of both the Ancient and Primitive Observances, has offered popular two-week programs in Carmelite and Sanjuanist spirituality for the past several summers.

These are but a few expressions of Carmelite devotion to John of the Cross in the United States. Though the Order remains small in this country, it has played an important role in spreading his message.

JOHN OF THE CROSS IN AMERICAN ARTS AND LITERATURE

John's influence on American arts and literature is modest but growing. For example, though Anglo-American poet and Nobel laureate T. S. Eliot was already a British citizen by the time he published *Four Quartets,* his masterpiece made an enormous impact on both sides of the Atlantic. One cannot read selections like the following without noting the almost literal borrowing from John of the Cross:

> To arrive where you are, to get from where you are not,
> You must go by a way in which there is no ecstasy.
> In order to arrive at what you do not know
> You must go by a way which is the way of ignorance.
> In order to possess what you do not possess
> You must go by the way of dispossession.
> In order to arrive at what you are not
> You must go through the way in which you are not.[59]

Yet Eliot's debt to John goes beyond such paraphrases.

> Since Eliot first discovered John's works while at Harvard, was still interested enough to cite them as a "devotional monument" in "Lancelot Andrewes" (1926) and to quote them ironically in an epigraph to *Sweeney Agonistes* (1926-7), as well as to review an abridged

version of John's works in 1934, it is more than probable that he continued reading John in depth and with understanding. Dame Helen Gardner tells us that when Eliot was writing "East Coker" (1940) he used E. Allison Peers's translation of John's works. Eliot's preoccupation with Christian mysticism is evident throughout the corpus of his religious works. *Murder in the Cathedral*, for example, presents the inward journey of the protagonist, as he picks his way among ever more subtle and dangerous temptations towards his goal in "the night of God."[60]

In fact, as the author of this comment shows, throughout *Four Quartets* Eliot "uses John of the Cross, not as a theologian, but as an eclectic poet familiar with mysticism," borrowing "the scheme, concepts, images, and symbols derived from John."[61]

Nor was Eliot the last to borrow from John of the Cross, who reappears at odd moments in the work of such contemporary American poets as Paul Mariani and Charles Simic.

> ...In abject submission, I offer
> The simplicity of this instant,
> The Divine Office of the empty plate,
>
> Mating season
> Of the hand and the glass,
> Respectful homage
> Of the wine to the light,
> Clarity
> That I talk to, that I quarrel with...
>
> They say of St. John of the Cross
> That he would sit,
> Just the way I'm sitting now
> In a small dark place,
> And through a window
> Gaze at a distant landscape.[62]

It goes without saying, of course, that Jessica Powers, herself a Carmelite nun (Sr. Miriam of the Holy Spirit, O.C.D.), was deeply influenced by John of the Cross, and many of her best poems are directly inspired by Sanjuanist texts.[63]

Among visual artists, interest in John of the Cross has not been confined merely to the analysis of his famous drawing of Christ on the Cross. In 1985, for example, Bill Viola's multimedia "Room for St. John of the Cross" received the first Polaroid International Video Art Award from Boston's Institute of Contemporary Art, out of 200 entries.

> On entering an unlit gallery, viewers are confronted with a large video image of mountains projected on a screen and a roaring soundtrack of wind and earthquake-like rumbling. The mountain image was shot with a hand-held camera in a moving car, making it jagged and disorienting. In the center of the gallery is a cell the size of the one in which the saint was confined. Unlike the prototype, however, this cell has a window, which reveals an earthen floor, spartan furniture and, on a table, a small color television with a fixed image of the same mountainscape as that on the large screen. As a visitor leans through the window to examine the interior of the cell, the booming sound recedes. In its place is a second soundtrack: the muted cadence of the poems being read quietly in the original Spanish.[64]

Recently, John Michael Talbot, one of the more successful practitioners of Christian popular music, released an album entitled *The Lover and the Beloved*, devoted almost entirely to songs based on the poems of John of the Cross.[65] Meanwhile, actor Leonardo Defilippis toured the United States during the centenary year in "The Living Flame of Love," his one-man-show on John's life, and Gian Carlo Menotti premiered a new John of the Cross Cantata in April, 1991 at the Kennedy Center in Washington, DC. In short, Americans are coming to appreciate John not only as a mystic and spiritual theologian, but as an artist as well.

RECENT TRENDS

In this final section we will briefly review a few contemporary currents in American spirituality where John's doctrine seems to have special relevance or hold special promise.

In the first place, and surprisingly, despite his past reputation as a writer only for the mystical elite, in this country John has proved a remarkably effective resource for popular works on prayer and spirituality. One of the most successful introductions to the spiritual life, for example, is a series by Thomas H. Green, an American Jesuit working in the Philippines. His teaching, though put into practical terms, is drawn almost entirely from Teresa, John of the Cross, and Ignatius Loyola.[66] Again, Susan Muto uses texts from John of the Cross to introduce Americans to the "art and discipline of spiritual reading."[67] Evidently, John is not as inaccessible to the average Christian as has often been assumed in the past!

Second, one of the most significant developments in North America today has been the explosion of "recovery" literature, programs and support groups, most based on the famous "Twelve Steps" of Alcoholics Anonymous. The United States has been called an "addictive society," with men and women now joining together to overcome their dependence on everything from drugs and alcohol to food, gambling, and sex. In such a context, some authors are beginning to uncover a fresh meaning in the Sanjuanist analysis of "inordinate attachments."[68]

Third, while the charismatic movement is perhaps not as influential in the United States as it once was, it has continued to mature. Many groups are now turning to John of the Cross for guidance toward a more contemplative style of praying.[69] John's discussion in Book III of *The Ascent* would also appear to have much to contribute to the modern interest in the "healing of memories."[70]

Fourth, Catholic Americans, many of them from the charismatic movement, seem to be particularly active in Medjugorje pilgrimages and in the activities surrounding other contemporary visionaries and apparitions. Those concerned about possible excesses in these developments often cite John's sober assessment of private visions and revelations as a useful corrective.

In the fifth place, and perhaps paradoxically, the same Sanjuanist lessons are also useful in responding to certain aspects of popular "occultist" and "New Age" phenomena. Without more thorough study it is difficult to say whether John is generally respected as a spiritual teacher in such circles (though it is intriguing, for example, that a "pre-New-Age" author such as Carlos Casteneda cites John in his phenomenally successful series of books, and that Werner Erhard, founder of EST, gives lectures of "Juan de la Cruz").[71] Still, John offers those involved in such movements a useful reminder that one comes to realize an authentic identification with God, not through channeling, workshops with Shirley MacLaine or reading *A Course in Miracles,* but only through a loving *surrender* to God "in the living, sensory and spiritual, exterior and interior death of the cross" (A, 2, 7, 11).

Sixth, John of the Cross has been hailed as a proponent of "creation-centered spirituality" by Matthew Fox and others.[72] While this may well represent an anachronistic and simplistic judgment, it has at least opened up from many American readers the positive side of John's teaching on creation, so often neglected in the past.[73]

Seventh, John provides guidance and encouragement today for many American Catholic feminists experiencing frustration and impasse in the face of apparent institutional intransigence,[74] while at the same time reminding those on the other end of the spectrum, disturbed by *rapidity* of changes in the Church, to lean only on the secure insecurity of "dark faith." To those on both sides of current ecclesiastical controversies in the American Church he continually points out that we can never afford to become fixated on anything less than God, since the infinite divine reality always ultimately surpasses even our most revered images, preconceptions and programs.

Finally, John of the Cross is a major contributor to the dialogue now occurring at various levels between Catholicism and other traditions. Protestants who might otherwise be suspicious of a Roman Catholic Counter-Reformation mystic have found hope in John's stress on the primacy of faith and his discussion of the "dark night" experience.[75] John's *nada* doctrine and emphasis on detachment has offered a point of departure in Buddhist-Christian conversations, and in dialogues with other faiths.[76] He has even proved an important figure in the modern encounter with Marxism and atheism.[77]

CONCLUSION

In this article we have touched upon some of the ways in which John of the Cross has influenced important spiritual writers and movements in the United States. Obviously, much more remains to be said. Just within the last few years, many new American publications on John have appeared, and the numbers will continue to grow.[78] Certainly, not all points mentioned here are uniquely American. Much of the Sanjuanist scholarship now being conducted in the United States deals with universally recognizable themes, and would be equally at home in almost any nation, easily entering into the emerging global dialogue on spiritual issues. But I have tried in some way to show how the United States, with its "First World" concerns, has nonetheless learned to welcome John of the Cross as teacher and friend. And the process continues. It will only accelerate, I suspect, with the growing "Hispanicization" of the United States, which is rapidly changing the face of religion and culture in this country. As we enter the twenty-first century, this development could turn out to be one of the most decisive factors for our future appreciation of John in North America.

NOTES

1. Though this article deals specifically with the influence of John of the Cross in the United States, much of what is said applies also (with appropriate qualifications) to English-speaking Canada. At the same time, I recognize that Canada (especially the French-speaking region) has its own unique spiritual traditions.
2. Many founders and foundresses of American religious congregations had a special devotion to St. Teresa, which still marks their communities. Br. Lawrence's *The Practice of the Presence of God* is widely read by American Protestants, and available in many editions. And, as elsewhere in the world, devotion to St. Thérèse of Lisieux dominated American Catholic spirituality earlier in this century, and remains strong.
3. As far as I can determine, the only currently existing American Carmel that has John of the Cross as its official patron is the friars' monastery in Oakville, CA; the Carmels of nuns in the United States are generally dedicated to Mary, Joseph, St. Teresa or St. Thérèse. The Washington province's novitiate in Waverly, NY was dedicated to John of the Cross, but has since been closed; the Carmel of Wheeling, WV was under the patronage of Saints Teresa and John, but has been joined to the community of Elysburg, PA. Interestingly, though, in the United States not all places of worship with images of John of the Cross are necessarily Roman Catholic; in the Boston area, for example, John is shown in one of sixteen clerestory windows dedicated to founders of religious orders in the monastery chapel of the Society of St. John the Evangelist (commonly known as the Cowley Fathers, the oldest Anglican religious order for men) in Cambridge, MA, and his representation is also appears in the parish church of St. John the Evangelist on Beacon Hill, run for many years by this same Anglican community.
4. See Steven Payne, *John of the Cross and the Cognitive Value of Mysticism: An Analysis of Sanjuanist Teaching and its Philosophical Implications for Contemporary Discussions of Mystical Experience* (Dordrecht: Kluwer Academic Publishers, 1990), 1-3, 13 and below.
5. For older and more recent works on John originating in Britain, or translated from other European languages, see, for example, Bruno de Jésus-Marie, *Saint John of the Cross,* ed. Benedict Zimmerman (New York, NY: Sheed & Ward, 1932); Crisógono de Jesús Sacramentado, *The Life of Saint John of the Cross,* trans. Kath-

leen Pond (Longmans, Green & Co., 1958); E. W. Trueman Dicken, *The Crucible of Love: A Study of the Mysticism of St. Teresa of Avila and St. John of the Cross* (New York, NY: Sheed & Ward, 1963); Reginald Garrigou-Lagrange, *Christian Perfection and Contemplation according to St. Thomas Aquinas and St. John of the Cross,* trans. by M. Timothea Doyle (St. Louis, MO: B Herder Book Co., 1937); Jacques Maritain, *Distinguish to Unite, or The Degrees of Knowledge,* newly trans. from the 4th French edition under direction of Gerald B. Phelan (New York, NY: Charles Scribner's Sons, 1959); Colin Thompson, *The Poet and the Mystic: A Study of the Cántico Espiritual of San Juan de la Cruz* (Oxford: Oxford University Press, 1977); Karol Wojtyla, *Faith According to Saint John of the Cross,* trans. Jordan Aumann (San Francisco, CA: Ignatius Press, 1981).

6. See George Gallup, Jr. and Jim Castelli, *The People's Religion: American Faith in the 90's* (New York, NY: Macmillan, 1989), 20-21 and passim.

7. See Robert N. Bellah et al., *Habits of the Heart: Individualism and Commitment in American Life* (Berkeley, CA: University of California Press, 1985).

8. See Peter-Thomas Rohrbach, *Journey to Carith: The Story of the Carmelite Order* (Garden City, NY: Doubleday & Co., 1966), 327-329; Franz-Bernard Lickteig, "The Propaganda Fides Archives and Carmel in the United States," *Sword* 36 (February, 1976): 21-43; John P. O'Brien, "California Missions, Part II: Spanish Voyages from Mexico North to California: The Carmelites," *Arms of the Cross* 4 (Fall, 1985): 1-12; Stephen Watson, "The First Carmelite Friars in California," *Carmelite Digest* 1 (Winter, 1986): 42-49; C. Douglas Kroll, "Unknown and Uncelebrated: California's First Mass," *Carmelite Digest* 4 (Spring, 1989): 3-9.

9. See *The Carmelite Adventure: Clare Joseph Dickinson's Journal of a Trip to America and Other Documents,* ed. Constance FitzGerald (Baltimore, MD: Carmelite Sisters of Baltimore, 1990); Charles Warren Currier, *Carmel in America: A Centennial History of the Discalced Carmelites in the United States,* 200th anniversary edition (Darien, IL: Carmelite Press, 1989); *Journey to Carith,* 331-334; *Who Remember Long: A History of Port Tobacco Carmel* (Port Tobacco, MD: Carmel of Port Tobacco, 1984).

10. I am grateful to Sr. Constance FitzGerald, O.C.D., and the Baltimore Carmel for this and other information from their archives.

11. The Baltimore Carmel has a copy of at least one of his translations in their archives.

12. See, e.g., *Carmel in America,* 233, 243, 257.

13. See the detailed descriptions of the event in *The Baltimore American* (25 November 1891): 8; and *The [Baltimore] Catholic Mirror* (18 November 1891). By that date, the Carmels of St. Louis (1863), New Orleans (1877) and Boston (1890) had also been founded, and presumably marked the occasion with celebrations of their own.

14. See *Carmel in the United States of America, 1790-1990* (Eugene, OR: Queen's

Press, 1990), which contains brief histories of all the U.S. Carmels.

15. See Joseph P. Chinnici, *Living Stones: The History and Structure of Catholic Spiritual Life in the United States* (New York, NY: Macmillan, 1989), 100-112.

16. *The Brownson-Hecker Correspondence,* ed. and introduced by Joseph F. Gower and Richard M. Leliaert (Notre Dame, IN: University of Notre Dame Press, 1979), Letter #45 (1 November 1846), 138-140.

17. Archives of Baltimore Carmel.

18. Walter Elliott, *The Life of Father Hecker* (New York, NY: Arno Press, 1972 [reprint of 1891 ed.]), 409.

19. See Chinnici, *Living Stones,* 121ff.

20. This letter is included among the "Americanism" papers in the Archives of the Paulist Fathers, New York, NY. A copy can be found in the Archives of the Baltimore Carmel.

21. See *The Complete Works of St. John of the Cross,* trans. from the original Spanish by David Lewis, ed. by the Oblate Fathers of S. Charles, with a preface by Cardinal Wiseman, 2 vols. (London: Thomas Baker, 1864); and *The Spirit of St. John of the Cross, consisting of his maxims, sayings and spiritual advice on various subjects,* trans. Canon Dalton (London, 1863).

22. See, for example, the four volume edition of the Lewis translation published in London by Thomas Baker in 1906-1912, and again in 1918-1922.

23. See *Instruction and Precautions of St. John of the Cross, preceded by a short sketch of his life, and followed by some spiritual letters to the nuns of his Order—a Novena and prayers in honor of the Saint* (Wheeling, WV: Monastery of the Discalced Carmelites, 1918).

24. *The Complete Works of Saint John of the Cross, Doctor of the Church,* trans. from the critical edition of P. Silverio de Santa Teresa, C.D. and edited by E. Allison Peers (London: Burns Oates & Washbourne, 1934-1935). Peers includes an extensive bibliography of previous studies and translations of John of the Cross, in the "Select Bibliography" of vol. 3, as does Pier Paolo Ottonello in *Bibliografia di S. Juan de la Cruz* (Rome: Teresianum, 1967).

25. *The Collected Works of St. John of the Cross,* trans. Kieran Kavanaugh and Otilio Rodriguez, with introductions by Kieran Kavanaugh (Washington, DC: ICS Publications, 1973). A second edition was published in 1979, and a newly revised and updated edition in 1991, for John's centenary.

26. Besides the Kavanaugh/Rodriguez translations in *Collected Works,* 711-737, see, for example, *The Poems of St. John of the Cross,* Spanish text with a translation into English verse by E. Allison Peers (London: Burns Oates, 1947); *The Poems of St. John of the Cross,* Spanish text with a translation by Roy Campbell (London: Harvill Press, 1951); *The Poems of St. John of the Cross,* original Spanish texts and new English versions by John Frederick Nims (New York, NY: Grove Press, 1959); *The Poems of St. John of the Cross,* English versions and introduction by Willis Barnstone (Bloomington, IN: Indiana University Press, 1968); Gerald Brenan, *St. John*

of the Cross: His Life and Poetry, with a translation of the poetry by Lynda Nicholson (Cambridge: Cambridge University Press, 1973); and Antonio T. de Nicolás, *St. John of the Cross: Alchemist of the Soul* (New York, NY: Paragon House, 1989), 75-151.

27. Payne, *John of the Cross and the Cognitive Value of Mysticism*, 2. With the original edition of *Hours With the Mystics* unavailable, the Vaughan quotations are taken from a later American edition, i.e., Robert A. Vaughan, *Hours With the Mystics: A Contribution to the History of Religious Opinion*, 6th ed., 2 vols. in one (New York, NY: Charles Scribner's Sons, 1893), vol. 2, 149-152, 183-197.

28. See William Ralph Inge, *Christian Mysticism* (New York, NY: Meridian Books, Living Age Books, 1956), 228-230.

29. R. M. Bucke, *Cosmic Consciousness: A Study in the Evolution of the Human Mind* (New York, NY: Causeway Books, 1974 [facsimile of original 1900 edition]), 317-318.

30. William James, *The Varieties of Religious Experience: A Study in Human Nature, Being the Gifford Lectures in Natural Religion Delivered at Edinburgh in 1901-1902* (New York, NY: Modern Library, 1936), 299. See also Kevin G. Culligan, "William James and *The Varieties of Religious Experience:* The Birthday of a Classic," *Spiritual Life* 18 (1972): 15-23.

31. James, *Varieties*, 418.

32. Evelyn Underhill, *Mysticism: A Study in the Nature and Development of Man's Spiritual Consciousness*, 12 ed. (New York, NY: Meridian Book, Noonday Press, 1955); Dana Greene, *Evelyn Underhill: Artist of the Infinite Love* (New York, NY: Crossroad, 1990), 53.

33. Greene, *Evelyn Underhill*, 54.

34. See, for example, several of the articles in *The Highest State of Consciousness*, ed. John White (Garden City, NY: Doubleday Anchor Books, 1972); and *Understanding Mysticism*, ed. Richard Woods (Garden City, NY: Image Books, Doubleday & Co., 1980). This is not to deny that other authors, such as Ernest Hocking, Baron von Hügel and, later, R. C. Zachner and W. T. Stace, also played an important role in introducing John to a larger American audience.

35. See William D. Miller, *Dorothy Day: A Biography* (San Francisco, CA: Harper & Row, 1982), 335ff.

36. John J. Hugo, *Applied Christianity* (Bronx, NY: D. J. Fiorentino, 1944).

37. William D. Miller, *All Is Grace: The Spirituality of Dorothy Day* (Garden City, NY: Doubleday & Co., 1987), 46.

38. See Francis J. Connell, "Review of *Applied Christianity,*" *American Ecclesiastical Review* 113 (July, 1945): 69-72; and Joseph Clifford Fenton, "Nature and the Supernatural Life," *American Ecclesiastical Review* 114 (January, 1946): 54-68.

39. John J. Hugo, *A Sign of Contradiction: As the Master so the Disciple*, 2 vols. (n.p.[privately printed], 1947).

40. From time to time, however, vestiges of the old controversy resurfaced, as in

arguments in the later 1940s over an anonymous pamphlet entitled "Brother Nathaniel's Brainstorm," in which an unnamed Carmelite prior is portrayed as opposed to smoking, on the basis of Sanjuanist principles regarding "attachments." See Joseph P. Donovan, "A Bit of Puritanical Catholicity," *Homiletic and Pastoral Review* 48 (August, 1948): 807-814; Louis A. Farina, "Is Detachment Puritanical?" *Homiletic and Pastoral Review* 49 (February, 1949): 356-367. Farina was associated with Father Hugo and the Lacouture retreats.

41. Dorothy Day, *The Long Loneliness: An Autobiography* (Garden City, NY: Image Books, Doubleday & Co., 1959), 254. For Day's description of the retreat movement itself and the persons involved, see 240ff. Compare Chinnici, *Living Stones*, 191-193; also Miller, *Dorothy Day*, 335-341 and *passim* for her relationship to Father Hugo.

42. See Anthony Padovano, *The Human Journey: Thomas Merton, Symbol of a Century* (Garden City, NY: Doubleday & Co., 1982).

43. Thomas Merton, "St. John of the Cross," in *Saints for Now*, ed. Clare Boothe Luce (New York, NY: Sheed & Ward, 1952), 258. In the same place, Merton also lists John of the Cross as his "favorite saint," along with Benedict, Bernard and Francis of Assisi.

44. Thomas Merton, *The Seven Storey Mountain* (Garden City, NY: Image Books, Doubleday & Co., 1970), 290.

45. Letter to Abbot James Fox (Retreat Notes 1950), in Thomas Merton, *The School of Charity: The Letters of Thomas Merton on Religious Renewal and Spiritual Direction*, selected and edited by Patrick Hart (New York, NY: Farrar, Straus, Giroux, 1990), 19.

46. Letter to Dom Jean-Baptiste Porion, in Merton, *The School of Charity*, 33.

47. Thomas Merton, *The Ascent to Truth* (New York, NY: Harcourt, Brace and Co., 1951); Thomas Merton, "St. John of the Cross," in *Saints for Now*, ed. Luce, 250-260; and "Light in Darkness: The Ascetical Doctrine of St. John of the Cross," in Thomas Merton, *Disputed Questions* (New York, NY: Farrar, Straus and Cudahy, 1960). For other writings on John of the Cross from this period, see "Thomas Merton's Practical Norms of Sanctity in St. John of the the Cross," ed. and introduced by Robert E. Daggy, *Spiritual Life* 36 (Winter, 1990): 195-197.

48. Mott notes Merton's uneasiness in 1964 upon learning that *The Ascent to Truth* was "popular among Zen scholars and monks"; see Michael Mott, *The Seven Mountains of Thomas Merton* (Boston, MA: Houghton Mifflin Co., 1984), 399. See also chapter 3, "The Ascent to Truth," in William H. Shannon, *Thomas Merton's Dark Path: The Inner Experience of a Contemplative* (New York, NY: Farrar, Straus Giroux, 1981).

49. F. Scott Fitzgerald, *The Crack-Up, with Other Uncollected Pieces, Notebooks and Unpublished Letters*, ed. Edmund Wilson (New York, NY: New Directions, 1956).

50. "A Dark Night of the Soul in Boston," *People* 32 (November 13, 1989): 52-55; Tom Wolfe, "Post-Orbital Remorse, Part III: The Dark Night of the Ego," *Rolling*

Stone (15 February 1973).

51. See Steven Payne, *"The Dark Night* of St. John of the Cross: Four Centuries Later," *Review for Religious* 49 (November/December, 1990), 891-900.

52. Sandy Vogelgesang, *The Long Dark Night of the Soul: The American Intellectual Left and the Vietnam War* (San Francisco, CA: Harper & Row, 1974), 9-10.

53. Daniel Berrigan, *The Dark Night of Resistance* (Garden City, NY: Doubleday & Co., 1971), 7-14.

54. Ibid., 20-27.

55. Ibid., 11-12.

56. See Jay Matthews, "The Nixon Time Capsule: In California, the Public Browses Through History," *Washington Post* (21 July 1990), section C, 2.

57. John Paul II, "Master in the Faith: Apostolic Letter of His Holiness John Paul II for the Fourth Centenary of the Death of Saint John of the Cross," *L'Osservatore Romano* 52 (24 December 1990), #14.

58. See Paschasius Heriz, *Saint John of the Cross* (Washington, DC: n.p., 1919); and *Holiness in the Cloister*, adapted from the Spanish of Lucas of St. Joseph by Paschasius Heriz (Chicago, IL: M. A. Donohue & Co., 1920). The latter was later revised and republished as Lucas of St. Joseph, *The Secret of Sanctity of St. John of the Cross*, trans. Mary Alberto (Milwaukee, WI: Bruce, 1962).

59. T. S. Eliot, "East Coker," III, in *Four Quartets* (London: Faber & Faber, 1944), 20.

60. Corona Sharp, "'The Unheard Music': T. S. Eliot's *Four Quartets* and John of the Cross, *University of Toronto Quarterly* 51 (Spring, 1982): 264.

61. Ibid., 276.

62. From "The Cure," in Charles Simic, *Charon's Cosmology* (New York, NY: George Brazillier, 1977), 38. See also Paul Mariani, "The Intensest Rendezvous, *Spiritual Life* 37 (Fall, 1991): 131-138.

63. See, for example, "The Mystical Sparrow of St. John of the Cross," "The House at Rest," and "The Books of St. John of the Cross," in *Selected Poetry of Jessica Powers*, ed. Regina Siegfried and Robert Morneau (Kansas City, MO: Sheed & Ward, 1989); Kieran Kavanaugh, "Jessica Powers in the Tradition of St. John of the Cross: Carmelite and Poet," *Spiritual Life* 36 (Fall, 1990): 161-176.

64. Charles Giuliano, "Visionary Video," *Art News* (May, 1985): 11; see also Thomas Frick, "Boston," *Art in America* (June, 1985): 145-146; Barbara London, ed., *Bill Viola: Installations and Videotapes* (New York, NY: Museum of Modern Art, 1987).

65. John Michael Talbot, "The Lover and the Beloved" (Chatsworth, CA: Sparrow Music, 1989). This album includes songs adapted from "The Dark Night," "The Spiritual Canticle," "The Living Flame of Love," "For I know well the spring that flows and runs," and "I went out seeking love." Elsewhere Talbot has recorded a version of the "Pastorcico."

66. See Thomas H. Green, *Opening to God: A Guide to Prayer* (Notre Dame, IN:

Ave Maria Press, 1977); Idem, *When the Well Runs Dry: Prayer Beyond the Beginnings* (Notre Dame, IN: Ave Maria Press, 1979); Idem, "The First Blind Guide: John of the Cross and Spiritual Direction," *Spiritual Life* 37 (Summer, 1991): 67-76.

67. See Susan Muto, *Approaching the Sacred: The Art of Spiritual Reading* (Denville, NJ: Dimension Books, 1973); Idem, "The Counsels of John of the Cross: Wisdom For Today," *Spiritual Life* 37 (Winter, 1991): 212-224.

68. See Gerald May, *Addiction and Grace* (San Francisco, CA: Harper & Row, 1988); idem, "Lightness of Soul: From Addiction Toward Love in John of the Cross," *Spiritual Life* 37 (Fall, 1991): 139-147.

69. Unfortunately, little has been written so far on John and the charismatic movement. One useful anthology, though not directly on Sanjuanist themes, is Paul Hinnebusch, ed., *Contemplation and the Charismatic Renewal* (Mahwah, NJ: Paulist Press, 1986).

70. See, for example, Dennis Linn and Matthew Linn, *Healing Life's Hurts: Healing Memories Through the Five Stages of Forgiveness* (Mahwah, NJ: Paulist Press, 1978); Idem, *Healing of Memories: Prayers and Confession—Steps to Inner Healing* (Mahwah, NJ: Paulist Press, 1974); Matthew Linn, Sheila Fabricant and Dennis Linn, *Healing the Eight Stages of Life* (Mahwah, NJ: Paulist Press, 1988).

71. See, for example, the adaptation of John's metaphor of the solitary bird on the opening page of Carlos Castenada, *Tales of Power* (New York, NY: Simon & Schuster, 1974); and chapter 9 of Richard de Mille, *Casteneda's Journey* (Santa Barbara, CA: Capra Press, 1977), where he notes intriguing parallels and differences between John and Casteneda (including the role of female figures named "Catalina" in both their lives). Basil Pennington reports that "A few years ago Werner Erhard sponsored a day at Madison Square Garden. The immense center was completely full for the eight-hour program. Erhard spent most of the day reading and commenting on Juan de la Cruz, better known as St. John of the Cross. These thousands of people had paid $65 for the day"; see M. Basil Pennington, "Mastery in Ministry: Centering Prayer," *Priest* (June, 1988): 7.

72. See, for example, Matthew Fox, *Original Blessing: A Primer in Creation Spirituality* (Santa Fe, NM: Bear & Co., 1983), 312; and Camille Campbell, *Meditations With John of the Cross: A Centering Book* (Santa Fe, NM: Bear & Co., 1989).

73. See Ross Collings, *St. John of the Cross* (Collegeville, MN: Liturgical Press, 1990), 26-60, for a fine discussion of this point. Collings is a Discalced Carmelite of Australia, but his book has recently been published in the United States, where it now widely available. See also Richard P. Hardy, "John of the Cross: Loving the World in Christ," *Spiritual Life* 37 (Fall, 1991): 161-172.

74. See Constance FitzGerald, "Impasse and Dark Night," in *Living With Apocalypse: Spiritual Resources for Social Compassion*, ed. Tilden Edwards (San Francisco, CA: Harper & Row, 1984), 93-116 (reprinted in Joann Wolski Conn, ed., *Women's Spirituality: Resources for Christian Development* [Mahwah, NJ: Paulist Press, 1986]); Idem, "A Discipleship of Equals: Voices from the Tradition—Teresa of Avila and

John of the Cross," in *A Discipleship of Equals: Towards a Christian Feminist Spirituality*, ed. Francis A. Eigo (Villanova, PA: Villanova University Press, 1988), 63-97.

75. See Georgia Harkness, *The Dark Night of the Soul: From Spiritual Depression to Inner Renewal* (Nashville, TN: Abingdon Press, 1945). Compare Catherine Marshall, *Light in My Darkest Night* (Old Tappan, NJ: Fleming H. Revell, 1989), 168ff.

76. See especially the important series of works by William Johnston, including *The Still Point: Reflections on Zen and Christian Mysticism* (New York, NY: Fordham University Press, 1970); Idem, *Silent Music: The Science of Meditation* (San Francisco, CA: Harper & Row, 1974); Idem, *The Inner Eye of Love: Mysticism and Religion* (San Francisco, CA: Harper & Row, 1978): Idem, *The Mirror Mind: Spirituality and Transformation* (San Francisco, CA: Harper & Row, 1981); Idem, *Christian Mysticism Today* (San Francisco, CA: Harper & Row, 1984). Johnston is an Irish Jesuit working in Tokyo, but he has lived and taught in the United States and his writings are widely read here. See also Mary Jo Meadow and Kevin Culligan, "Congruent Spiritual Paths: Christian Carmelite and Theravadan Buddhist Vipassana," *Journal of Transpersonal Psychology* 19 (1987), 181-196.

77. See Michael Buckley, "Atheism and Contemplation," *Theological Studies* 40 (1979), 680-699.

78. See, for example, Leonard Doohan, *The Contemporary Challenge of John of the Cross: An Introduction to His Life and Teaching* (Washington, DC: ICS Publications, forthcoming); Thomas Dubay, *Fire Within: St. Teresa of Avila, St. John of the Cross and the Gospel—On Prayer* (San Francisco, CA: Ignatius Press, 1989); Susan Muto, *St. John of the Cross for Today: The Ascent* (Notre Dame, IN: Ave Maria Press, 1991); George Tavard, *Poetry and Contemplation in St. John of the Cross* (Athens, OH: Ohio University Press, 1988); and John Welch, *When Gods Die: An Introduction to John of the Cross* (Mahwah, NJ: Paulist Press, 1990).